BRIGHT LIGHTS IN THE DESERT

Bright Lights
in the Desert

THE LATTER-DAY SAINTS OF LAS VEGAS

FRED E. WOODS

with a Foreword by Michael S. Green

UNIVERSITY OF NEVADA PRESS | *Reno & Las Vegas*

University of Nevada Press | Reno, Nevada 89557 USA
www.unpress.nevada.edu
Copyright © 2023 by University of Nevada Press
All rights reserved
Cover photographs © Martin Anderson; © Getty Images Shawn Jones / EyeEm

Manufactured in the United States of America

FIRST PRINTING

Library of Congress Cataloging-in-Publication Data available at https://lccn.loc.gov/2022031535

The paper used in this book meets the requirements of American National Standard for
Information Sciences—Permanence of Paper for Printed Library Materials, ANSI/NISO
Z39.48-1992 (R2002).

This book is dedicated to
the Las Vegas Latter-day Saints
who have helped their desert region
"blossom as the rose," inspiring many of
its inhabitants and visitors
to contribute continued service to
their neighborhoods
and communities.

Contents

Foreword

by Michael S. Green

If you thought of the terms *Mormons* and *Las Vegas*, you would probably be inclined to think of them separately. Las Vegas has changed and grown, but in many minds it remains an adult playground, "sin city" and "the green felt jungle," where if it happens there, it stays there. The Church of Jesus Christ of Latter-day Saints (LDS) would seem to be the polar opposite of Las Vegas—yes, controversial in its own way, both in the past and in the present, but more likely to be associated with temples, almost squeaky cleanliness, and an aversion to caffeine, much less the stronger stuff available on the Las Vegas Strip.

As with so many things in history and life, the image and reality differ. Las Vegas and the LDS Church have a long association, going back to when Mormon missionaries became the first Anglo people to settle in what is now a community of nearly three million residents, many of whom live lives similar to those of any other Americans (and, lest we forget, tens of millions of annual visitors who come to play, dine, shop, gamble, and generally be entertained). The fort they built in 1855 is the oldest standing structure in the state of Nevada and became the hub from which Las Vegas ultimately developed into a ranching area, a railroad town, and then a tourism mecca. The Saints played a role in each of these, in ways both surprising and unsurprising.

That is the story Fred Woods set out to tell, and he has told it superbly. He begins at the beginning of LDS influence with the fort-mission that was the subject of his first book on Las Vegas, *Gamble in the Desert*. From there he delves into the Saints' departure from Las Vegas and eventual return, followed by its mushrooming role in the community. Indeed, one of the ironies of this history is that Mormons have been one of the most powerful groups or influences in shaping Las Vegas, along with, for example, Jewish mobsters.

But the connections between the LDS Church and Las Vegas are less ironic than they might appear, as Woods shows and as history also tells us. The church originated in the Second Great Awakening, the series of revivals that helped breed reform movements, utopian communities, and new religious groups—all of which describe important patterns in the Mormon Church's history. The Second Great Awakening also contributed to the rise of the abolitionist movement, which affected—in ways politically beneficial and otherwise—the birth and success of the Republican Party. When that party held its first national convention in 1856, its platform attacked "the twin relics of barbarism": slavery and polygamy.

By that time, Las Vegas also had a reputation. It had been part of the northern route of the Old Spanish Trail and known for its oasis of springs bubbling up amid grass and cottonwood trees. That made it attractive to travelers, but also to horse thieves. In the Great Horse Raid of 1840, led by onetime fur trapper Bill Williams and Ute chief Walkara, hundreds of horses galloped through the Las Vegas Valley. As it turned out, Las Vegas was already developing an image as an outpost for dubious activities, and Mormons were known more for plural marriage than for their communitarianism and subsistence lifestyle, among other qualities that most people would have been likely to find admirable.

Both the church and the town would evolve different images while retaining vestiges of their earlier reputations. The history and habits of the Saints still prompt commentary and satire (as recently as 2002, at the Salt Lake Olympics, NBC News correspondent Tom Brokaw discussed his ability to find beer in town; also, there is the Book of Mormon, and then there is *The Book of Mormon*). As for Las Vegas, well, where to begin? I grew up in Las Vegas, my parents worked in casinos, and tourists used to think that the employees must have lived in the casinos because no one actually lived in Las Vegas. Today the urban and suburban area receives much more attention, but the megaresorts on the Strip are in some ways their own world, and many tourists learn little of the universe of Las Vegas beyond it.

Woods tells that story and much more in the pages that follow. In addition to a general history of the LDS Church in Las Vegas, he delves into specific areas, including construction of the temple in eastern Las Vegas and an eye-opening account of how Mormons helped African Americans rebuild a church in the historically segregated West Las Vegas area and what it meant to everybody involved. He examines the church's broader role in the community, from the first banker who would regularly loan money to casino operators to how its members have shaped public and private education.

He also tells the story of Harry Reid, and thereby hangs a tale. Decades ago, powerful US senator Pat McCarran told a young aide completing law school that he had a political future, but that no Nevadan could ever hope to be on the national ticket because of the state's reputation. A few decades later, Reid supplanted McCarran as the most powerful Nevadan ever to hold office in Washington, leading his party in the Senate for his final two terms. When Reid died, his main eulogist was a former president of the United States, with remarks as well by the current president. As he lay dying, Reid learned that Clark County officials had renamed the local airport in his honor—and that his name had replaced that of McCarran.

The story of the LDS Church in and of Las Vegas comes full circle, both evolving from having outlaw reputations to becoming part of the mainstream. The story long has needed to be told. Turn the page. Woods tells it beautifully.

Preface

I spent the first two decades of my life enjoying the sunny climate and cosmopolitan culture of Southern California. Following my conversion to the Church of Jesus Christ of Latter-day Saints as a young adult, I moved to Idaho and then to Utah to attend school but returned to the Golden State annually to visit my family. On those drives home, I often stopped and spent the night with some good Latter-day Saint friends living in Las Vegas. Intrigued and connected with Vegas since my youth, I later began researching the early years of Las Vegas Latter-day Saint history, an effort that culminated in *A Gamble in the Desert: The Mormon Mission in Las Vegas (1855–1857)*. This publication coincided with the sesquicentennial commemoration of the Old Las Vegas Mormon Fort[1] and the centennial anniversary of the city that never sleeps.

Fifteen years after *A Gamble in the Desert* was published, I determined to highlight the history and influence Latter-day Saints have had in the Las Vegas region up to the present time. To date, the only published book in the marketplace dealing with this topic was authored by journalist Kenric Ward and is titled *Saints in Babylon: Mormons and Las Vegas*. Although well written, *Saints in Babylon* unfortunately lacks documentation and includes only a short, general bibliography of secondary sources; more complete documentation would have helped substantiate the author's claims. Since Ward's contribution, nearly two decades have passed without any academic treatment of Las Vegas Latter-day Saint history, further necessitating this current work.

Bright Lights in the Desert: The Latter-day Saints of Las Vegas illuminates the tremendous influence the Las Vegas Saints have wielded in politics, education, business, entertainment, cultural refinement, and family stability in their community. Chapters 1 and 2 outline general Las Vegas Latter-day Saint history, commencing with the erection of the Old Mormon Fort settlement (1855) and moving through the establishment of early Las Vegas stakes (1960) to provide a historical base for the remainder of the book.[2] By this point the church had formed solid roots in Vegas soil. Chapters 3–7 highlight subjects topically to demonstrate how the Saints have borne fruit through a look at various branches of their influence in society; the chapters still provide adequate historical background from the latter half of the twentieth century to the present. The city of Las Vegas and its neighboring cities of North Las Vegas, Henderson, and Boulder City, constituting the greater desert metropolis, are considered. I have utilized numerous primary sources coupled with scores of interviews. This book demonstrates the Latter-day Saint contribution to the beauty, stability, and spirit of the Las Vegas region. Along with other like-minded local citizens of varied faiths and cultures, the Latter-day Saints have made a concerted effort to enhance education, strengthen families, and energize communities throughout the Vegas locality.

Positioned at the base of Sunrise Mountain, the stunning Latter-day Saint temple erected in 1989 stands as a beacon to this desert oasis and is a source of light and spiritual nourishment for church members, who now number more than 105,000 in this metropolitan region. Though representing only about 6 percent of the region's population, members of the Church of Jesus Christ of Latter-day Saints in the Las Vegas area are among the most influential body of citizens in an expanding community that now numbers more than 2 million people. In addition, the influence of the Saints is sprinkled throughout the entire state. They worship north to south and east to west in 345 congregations scattered statewide. Currently, two Latter-day Saint temples, three missions, and thirty-four family history centers serve communities throughout the great state of Nevada.[3] This book tells the inspiring story of the Saints' impressive contributions to and influence in the Las Vegas region. Finally, this book is a companion to a documentary film with the same name produced by Martin L. Andersen and Fred E. Woods, which is augmented with scores of interviews in addition to the main film. It can be viewed online at http://truth-and-reason.com/A-E_LasVegas.html.

Acknowledgments

The author wishes to thank the following institutions and individuals who have assisted him with his research at Brigham Young University: the John Topham and Susan Redd Butler BYU Faculty Research Award from the Charles Redd Center to aid in this study; the College of Religious Education and the Department of Church History and Doctrine for financial support; the Harold B. Lee Library Interlibrary Loan staff; Jennifer Schill, Harold B. Lee Library director of faculty services; Cindy Brightenburg, reference librarian, and Ryan Lee, curator of Nineteenth-Century Mormon and Western Manuscripts for the L. Tom Perry Special Collections. I am particularly grateful to the Religious Education Faculty Support Center staff for their transcription work for scores of interviews and especially Beverly Yellowhorse, their supervisor, for her careful review of the entire manuscript.

I am grateful to Su Kim Chung, head of public services for the University Libraries Special Collections and Archives, University of Nevada, Las Vegas, and her team for their support. A special thanks is extended to UNLV history professor Michael S. Green, who has been most helpful in answering questions, arranging interviews, and writing the foreword to this work. Gratitude is expressed to all those whom I interviewed and to Martin Andersen, David and Jana Dixon, S. Mahlon Edwards, Carson Fehner, Michael S. Green, Joyce Haldeman, Bruce W. Hansen, Wendell Waite, and Senator Harry Reid, who reviewed part or all of my draft manuscripts. Martin also joined with me in conducting most of the interviews, and we coproduced a companion documentary film to supplement this work. Finally, I thank the University of Nevada Press for their editorial contributions and particularly my wife, JoAnna, for the many hours she spent editing this manuscript and for her continual support and encouragement of all my projects the past forty years.

BRIGHT LIGHTS IN THE DESERT

1

The Latter-day Saint Corridor and the Old Las Vegas Mormon Fort

Called "to take a mission to Las Vegas
to make a settlement and cultivate the Indians."
—"Diary of John Steele," spring 1855

Not long after Brigham Young led the pioneer Saints into the Salt Lake Valley in 1847, he soon ingeniously positioned strategic forts along a specific route that stretched from Salt Lake City to Southern California, including what was then known as the Las Vegas Mormon Fort.[1] Using these way stations, migrating Latter-day Saints, passing travelers, and mail carriers could find nourishment and rest in a secure environment to help them complete their journeys. This chain of settlements became known as the Mormon Corridor.[2]

Church leaders made members aware of plans for a California settlement, "passable during the winter months," that would serve as a receiving station for Latter-day Saint immigrants and a southern gateway to the Mormon Corridor. Indicated in a communiqué was information that church apostles Amasa M. Lyman and Charles C. Rich had left Salt Lake City with a company of Saints and 150 wagons "for the purpose of establishing a settlement in the southern part of California, at no great distance from San Diego, and near the Williams' ranch and the cajone pass, between which...we design to establish settlements as speedily as possible...to have a continued line of stations and places of refreshment between this point and the Pacific."[3]

After reviewing regional reports drawn up earlier by the Mormon Battalion[4] and from data collected by Latter-day Saint explorer Jefferson Hunt on his southern explorations that took him through the Vegas region[5] to California, Lyman and Rich purchased the Rancho de San Bernardino for $77,500. Although short-lived (1851–57), this church settlement of thirty-five thousand acres played a key transitional role in migration by serving "as a port of entry for converts coming from the Pacific missions; as a gathering place for California Mormons generally; and as a rest and supply station for church missionaries going to and from California and Pacific missions." If this colony could have endured, it would have also been a gathering spot for Pacific Islander converts.[6]

Most Pacific Islander converts passing through San Bernardino were from Australia. Several voyages carrying these Australian Saints between 1854 and 1856 disembarked at San Pedro and temporarily gathered in San Bernardino before making their way to the Salt Lake Valley.[7] The San Bernardino colony secured a station for the mail and served as an out-post for goods intended for Salt Lake City from Los Angeles. This route shaved off mileage and time that shipping needed goods via the Missouri River required.

In December 1851, Lyman and Rich wrote the following letter to Franklin D. Richards, who oversaw the British Mission, including emigration matters:

> We are situated about one hundred miles from San Diego, seventy miles from the seaport of San Pedro, and fifty miles from Pueblo de los Angelos. Our location here is made in view of forwarding the gathering of the Saints from abroad and from Europe in particular, by this route, should we be enabled to settle in this country as we wish…and we wish to learn from you, at your earliest convenience, what you may know, or can learn, in relation to the practicability and probable expense of transporting the Saints from Liverpool to San Diego, by any of the present routes across the Isthmus.[8]

Unfortunately, this change in travel routes did not materialize at that time. The following month, another general epistle explained the obstacles: "By recent communication of President F. D. Richards of England, we learn that the prospect of immediate emigration of the European brethren to San Diego, as we had anticipated, is in no wise flattering, there being no regular shipping from England to that port; therefore Elder Richards will continue to ship the Saints by way of New Orleans to Kanesville [Iowa], as hitherto."[9]

There simply was no established shipping route to America's western borders from England. Although disappointed, Brigham Young was satisfied that by 1855, twenty-seven settlements dotted the southern route between Salt Lake City and the Pacific, aiding transportation and securing the mail dispatch along the Mormon Corridor.[10]

Brigham Young, 1855. Courtesy of
Church History Library, Salt Lake City.

THE CALL TO LAS VEGAS

For many converts, an appointment (or "call," as the Saints refer to it) to erect these new settlements was a leap of faith. Historian Leonard J. Arrington explained the process: "Calls to participate in the founding of new colonies…were usually issued from the pulpit in a session of the general conference. In most cases, the names of the leaders and all other colonizers were specified. Each company was carefully selected to include men with the skills and equipment needed to subdue the wilderness."[11]

Historian Elbert Edwards explained the requirements of colonization in the southern Nevada desert region of which the Las Vegas settlement was the first: "The early development of Southern Nevada is largely the history of the Mormon colonies called by the central authorities of the Church to establish settlements wherever conditions would warrant, and where national resources would support its expanding population.… Other influences are found in the hope of developing possible trade and travel routes to aid rerouted immigrants seeking to reach the west from Europe and the Eastern Seaboard, and the desire to convert the Indians in their religion."[12]

The Las Vegas Mission assignment represents a typical example of men called to colonize. On April 6, 1855, during a church general conference held in Salt Lake City, thirty men were appointed "to take a mission to Las Vegas to make a settlement and cultivate the Indians."[13]

Besides the proselytizing ambitions of the mission, it operated as a crucial strategic aid station to give relief and respite to weary travelers and emigrants when crossing the barren and perilous desert, "one of the driest and hottest locations in continental North America."[14] Two weeks later, on April 22, 1855, most of the missionaries gathered at the Seventies Hall in Salt Lake City to be set apart (blessed by the laying on of hands) for their missions. The Record of the Las Vegas Mission notes, "Remarks were made by Prest B [Brigham] Young.... Instructions also Elder [Orson] Hyde [which] gave us very good counsel and instructed us to prepare to move on without delay, to go prepared to sustain ourselves by raising a crop this season."[15]

THE MISSIONARIES

Who were these brave souls willing to leave family and farm for an undetermined period of time to fulfill the call from their prophet leader? According to John Steele, a shoemaker from Ireland who had traveled to America following his conversion,[16] the men called were "mostly young men and many of them I had been before associated with both in the Mormon Battalion and elsewhere. A first-rate set of boys."[17] These hardy souls were each given a blessing when set apart for their missions. Called to the Las Vegas Mission on April 6, 1855, John Steele was given this charge and blessing in his home by Apostles George A. Smith and Wilford Woodruff on May 23, 1855, as they laid their hands on his head: "Brother John Steele...thou has been appointed of the Lord to be a missionary unto the Lamanites a savour [sic] unto the house of Israel to lift thy voice even unto the wild men of the wilderness and reclaim many of them Back to the knowledge of the Lord,...thou shalt be a father unto the children of the forest they shall Look unto thee and call thee father and hundreds of them shall rejoice in thy mission."[18]

William Bringhurst, a native of Philadelphia who emigrated to Utah in 1847,[19] was designated by Brigham Young to serve as president of the mission.[20] Bringhurst subsequently chose William S. Covert, a cabinetmaker

John Steele. Courtesy of Church
History Library, Salt Lake City.

from New York who had joined the church in 1838,[21] as his first counselor,
and Ira S. Miles, a native of Vermont who had emigrated to Utah in 1847,[22]
as his second counselor.[23]

One indispensable man called to the Las Vegas Mission because of his
knowledge of Native American languages was George W. Bean, a native
of Illinois who had converted in 1841, at only ten years old.[24] Bean had
been prepared for his assignment as interpreter and clerk of the Las Vegas
Mission by an accident that provided unanticipated experience. While
the teenage Bean was loading a six-pound cannon, it misfired, and as a
result his left arm was amputated just below the elbow. The local Native
Americans whom Bean had previously befriended began to pay young
George visits and taught him their language. Because of this unanticipated benefit, Bean viewed the accident as "a blessing in disguise." In addition, because of his disabled condition, he was given responsibilities such

William Bringhurst. Courtesy   George W. Bean. Courtesy of Church
of Frank Esshom, *Pioneers and*   History Library, Salt Lake City.
Prominent Men of Utah (1913).

as city and court recorder in Provo, Utah, as well as clerk of the Provo
Ward, which more than qualified him for his assignment as clerk of the
Las Vegas Mission.[25]

Bean recalled being "stunned to learn [his] name had been listed and
voted upon to go on a mission." He had previously received an offer to
assist Colonel Edward J. Steptoe, an officer in the US Army, as an interpreter for five dollars per day, plus supplies. Instead, he chose to work as
an interpreter for free and pay all of his own expenses. After recovering
from the initial shock of the assignment, Bean met with President Young
to learn for himself that the news was true concerning his call as interpreter to the Las Vegas Mission. Bean reported, "President Young knowing of those other offers, asked me how I liked the call as Missionary.
I told him that I loved my religion above all else and that I was ready to
go where ever I could serve the Kingdom best. He was pleased with the
answer and blessed me."[26]

A SACRIFICE FOR ALL

Because the missionaries were asked "to prepare to move on without
delay," George W. Bean quickly made preparations for his wife and young
daughter, who would be left behind. He wrote, "Having some money I
bought up a bin full of wheat [and] some land.... We had several cows,
etc., and some cash, leaving behind the wife and child, my most concern,

well provided for, so my thoughts were at ease." He added, "My wife...was comforted with my visit to President Young and his blessing.... She assured me she would take good care of things in my absence and had faith all would be well with us."[27]

DIAMOND OF THE DESERT

As Brigham Young had done with his vanguard company in 1847, the men again used John C. Frémont's 1844 report to help navigate this Las Vegas desert oasis, which included a description of the springs.[28] After a difficult journey of more than four hundred miles south from Salt Lake City, the missionaries at last reached the Vegas region in mid-June. A couple of days after the first group arrived, President Bringhurst, George W. Bean, and a few others began exploring, searching for the most suitable site for settlement. Just four miles west of their camp, they happily discovered the Las Vegas Springs.

Exhilaration rejuvenated these fatigued and dehydrated missionaries when they discovered the liquid salvation that, in 1853, one traveler named Heaps referred to as "the Diamond of the desert, so beautiful and bright does it appear in the centre of the dreary waste that surrounds it."[29] These delightful and refreshing twin springs bubbling up from the middle of the desert were a welcomed reprieve from the searing conditions of the inhospitable terrain. Dry blowing dirt encrusted the ears and noses of these overland travelers and ensured that grit between their teeth was a constant companion. The blistering sun baked and cracked their skin and lips and leathered their squinting eyes. That their arduous trek ended with more than fifty miles of waterless desert caused even the cheeriest of temperaments to evaporate.

Bean described these curious springs and the surrounding area to the editor of the *Deseret News,* noting there was "a nice patch of grass about half a mile wide and two or three miles long, situated at the foot of a bench 40 or 50 feet high"; the springs were "from 20 to 30 feet in diameter and at the depth of two feet the white sand bubbles all over as tho it was the bottom, but upon wading in, there is no foundation there, and it has been sounded to the depth of 60 feet, without finding bottom; and a person cannot sink to the armpits, on account of the strong upward rush of the water."[30]

After surveying the area and visiting the springs, the group concurred that the location where they had initially encamped was the best spot for establishing the fort and farmlands.[31] This site was just west of a large mesquite grove that may have been the largest one on Las Vegas Creek. Although the men utilized the mesquite in erecting fences around their farmlands, the removal of these sustenance plants eliminated a major source of food for the local Paiutes.[32]

GRUBBING, PLOWING, AND PLANTING

On Monday, June 18, 1855, the laborious work commenced in earnest. The men began by marking off the dimensions for the fort and farmlands. They placed the fort, which measured 150 square feet, on a slope of a bench a few rods from the creek. Thirty garden lots were sectioned out just at the bottom of the bench at one-fourth an acre apiece. Farmland was sectioned into fifteen five-acre lots, and the company immediately went to work clearing the lands and planting their gardens.[33] By drawing names, two men were assigned to each five-acre lot, giving each man the responsibility of two and a half acres. They spent the rest of June "grubbing, plowing and planting."[34]

John Steele explained that most of the thirty men initially favored having stewardship over five acres of land apiece, but when they realized how difficult the task of grubbing the prickly mesquite bushes was, they contented themselves with just two and a half acres. With division of labor and keen cooperation, the company members worked at their arduous tasks like a colony of ants: "Captain Bringhurst and Brother Snider laid out a corral 8 rods wide by 150 feet.... James Bears [Bean]

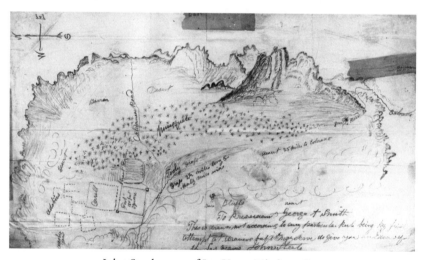

John Steele map of Las Vegas Mission, 1855.
Courtesy of Church History Library, Salt Lake City.

plowed his garden lot yesterday 20th, the first soil was turned over.... All hands busy making water ditches, roads, plowing and planting. The crops planted in the gardens is mostly up through the ground.... I plowed on my 2 1/2 acres. The ground is very dry and dusty. The weather still is very hot, although it has been blowing this three days."[35]

BEAN'S MISSION HISTORY

Several early Las Vegas missionaries provide a credible sketch of daily life at the fort, but we are especially indebted to George Washington Bean, who compiled the bulk of the "Record of the Los [*sic*] Vegas Mission." Therein is described the weekly events of the nearly two-year history of the mission. Bean left Salt Lake City with the understanding that he would serve as interpreter for communications with the Native Americans in this desert region, but before he had even arrived in the Vegas area, he was selected as the mission clerk.[36] The Native Americans Bean interacted with were Paiutes and Mojaves who had already been in this area for many years. They were nomadic, and the Latter-day Saint settlers presented a possible threat to natural resources.[37]

In addition to authoring the official mission record, Bean also diligently composed a personal journal rife with delicious details omitted from the formal one. With these two records and his talent for the native tongue, Bean opened a window for us to glimpse this intriguing history. His background provides insights into his unique contributions.

DAILY ROUTINES

Bean was spared many of the labor-intensive activities of settlement because he had but one arm for his demanding clerical assignments. He noted, "At the suggestion of Bro Bringhurst the brethren agreed to do my portion of the fort, carrell [corral] & other public works."[38] But Bean contributed by working hard nonetheless, writing, interacting with the Native Americans, and studying.

For most of the men, daily life at the fort meant engaging the help of the local Paiutes, exploring for timber, planting, tending to crops, and erecting fences or laboring on the fort itself. The missionaries utilized whatever materials were available. Building a corral made of mud for animals required the efforts of every missionary. A fence made of mesquite branches protected the farms from the cattle. The men often employed the aid of a Native American guide to lead a small party on the three-day trip to secure lumber.

Although the men were assigned to diverse tasks, they shared one common denominator throughout the life span of the mission—the great anticipation of receiving mail. Buoying their spirits and providing respite from the physical backbreaking labor, the monthly arrival of mail from family and friends was like a cool, refreshing drink to these parched missionaries.

GARDENING

Along with building the fort, planting and nurturing crops was necessary for long-term subsistence. Harsh climate conditions made planting and harvesting vexatious at times. Thomas E. Ricks lamented in a letter to his wife, "I shall not have much garden stuff, the ground being so dry the seeds did not come up. I soaked the peas in water and then set them out in the sun. In two hours, they were scalded and that spoiled them."[39]

That first summer, they sowed just a little wheat; the season was too advanced for that type of grain, but what was planted grew well. Some of the corn suffered because it was planted in salty soil. But for the most part, the corn, potatoes, green peas, and various vine plants did well. The settlers, taking note of how the Paiutes raised corn, believed they could harvest two crops a year.[40]

RECREATION AND EDUCATION

Hundreds of miles away from their families, these men wisely balanced their service days with appropriate recreation and education. On July 27, 1855, James T. S. Allred wrote in his diary that they were all so happy to finish the corral that they held a dance at night in celebration.[41] On their first Christmas Eve at the fort (December 1855), the missionaries enjoyed playing a game of ball and then danced the night away. About a dozen of the men mounted their horses and commenced a wolf hunt on Christmas Day. That afternoon they played "ball" again, and at last "all were tired and satisfied with the days sport."[42]

The days following Christmas were particularly cold and windy, so some elected to stay indoors and read. But by late in the day, a game of ball proved irresistible.[43] By New Year's, the missionaries again made the effort to recognize the holiday properly and to promote good cheer and sociality among one another. On New Year's Eve, Bean stood guard during the late night and called upon some of the men to fire an eight-gun salute to usher in the new year. The following morning, Bean described the festive day:

This being the commencement of the New Year, I begun [sic] the service of the day by drinking the healths of our families & friends & wishing success in all our undertakings the liquor used was wine of our own making from the juice of the wild grape. the morsel was sweet and the only complaint was not enough of it. Immediately after breakfast the boys assembled & we had a game of townball until all were tired then got our mules up & took a ride up to the springs and had a good bath. The water was worm [sic] & buoyant as ever.[44]

Along with the much-needed recreation, the missionaries spent time educating one another in the evenings. Bean logged in his journal on November 11, 1855, that the men voted to begin a formal method of education and to hold a lyceum on Saturday nights, of which Bean was appointed secretary. In this lyceum, the men posed and debated many philosophical questions, including the formation of man's character, the treatment of Native Americans and African Americans by the US government, and problems of intemperance.[45]

FAMILIES AT THE MISSION

Even with the occasional recreation and regular educational stimulation, the pangs of familial longings were not appeased. By mid-September 1855, President Bringhurst received correspondence from Brigham Young granting permission for the missionaries to return home for visits and for their families to return with them to the Las Vegas Mission if they wished. Of course, these procedures were to be carried out with order and prudence. The fort was not to be left with too few men to protect it, and families could come only if there were enough provisions to provide for their needs.[46] Young also stipulated that families could join the mission only when adequate defenses were in place to ensure their security.[47]

By the first week of November, Bringhurst determined that the mission was progressing so well that a few of the brethren could be allowed to make visits home. Eleven missionaries expressed their desire to bring their families back with them to the mission. They were instructed to leave on Thursday, November 8, and were to return by March 10. The mission history recorded their names as follows: "Bro Covert, Snyder, Milam, Steel [Steele], Perry, Hulse, Burston, Allred, Turner, Cuthbert, and James A. Bean."[48] Their short months at home were filled with making arrangements and preparations to integrate and provide for their families at the Las Vegas Mission.

ADDITIONAL MISSIONARIES CALLED

In February 1856, Brigham Young deemed it prudent to call nearly thirty more missionaries to the Las Vegas Mission. As usual, during a meeting in the Salt Lake Tabernacle, twenty-nine men were called from the pulpit to serve in this desert region. Unlike the first batch of missionaries called, these men were extended the invitation to bring their families with them from the outset. Their names were listed in the *Deseret News* as follows:

> From Great Salt Lake County—Williams Camp, John S. Fullmer, Lewis Robins, Lorenzo Brown, Andrew Cahoon, Almon L. Fullmer, Thomas Hall, Hyrum Kimball, George Mayer, Samuel Thompson, Aaron Farr, Alexander A. Lemon, Justin Merrill, Samuel Turnbow, Ute Perkins, Daniel Shearer, Allen Stout, John Snider, William Moss, Francis Boggs, Jacob L. Workman, Elijah K. Fuller. From Provo— Edson Barney, Philander Colton. From Parowan Miles Anderson,[49] John Lowder. From Beaver County—Beeson Lewis. From Palmyra— William W. Riley, John H. Redd.[50]

THE SECOND EXODUS

Travel for this second wave of missionaries to the Las Vegas fort was more formidable than for the first group because the second group had women and children with them. However, these women travelers may have worked to the company's advantage, for as the group passed through populated areas, they were offered considerably more aid than had been given to the company the previous year. Martha Burston Wheeler noted when arriving with her husband, William, in the spring of 1856, "We found they had built a small fort and some houses. We had a house of one room without a roof on it. It was built of adobes but they had to go twenty or thirty miles to get timber for rafters and had to saw them with an old fashioned rip saw worked by two men. The work was slow but the houses had joists for upstairs so they put covers of anything they could get over the top to keep out the hot sun."[51]

CONTACT AND ACTIVITIES WITH NATIVE AMERICANS

As the interpreter at the Las Vegas fort, George W. Bean had more contact with the Native Americans than any other person. Less than a month after he arrived at the fort, Bean actively engaged in public relations with the local tribes. On July 11, 1855, he wrote in his journal, "Wrote a letter & sent to the Chief of the Iats [Mojaves] also 1 to the Piede Chief in that

Paiutes in front of adobe house. Courtesy of the Library of Congress.

country, but sent no presents as they wished xcept some tobacco." This gesture to the Iats chief was apparently needed to keep the peace with this tribe because, as Bean had written in his journal three days earlier, "Some Indians came in this evening & reported that the Iats were unfriendly towards us & intended to kill and steal from us."[52] Although local Native Americans stole from the Vegas Saints throughout the fort's existence, remarkably, not a single life was lost. This was largely due to Bean's interpretive skills and diplomatic efforts.

Bean's interpretive services were in constant demand because of the continual flow of Native Americans visiting the Mormon fort. Just three weeks after the missionaries arrived at their new location, John Steele wrote that he was busy "planting, guarding, herding, washing, cooking, mending, etc." Their camp was "constantly occupied by several of the Piute Indians [and] from a distance some from beyond the Colorado from the Iates [sic]."[53]

Although the Iates (Iats) made visits, the most prominent tribe in the area during the Latter-day Saint mission was the Paiutes, also referred to as the Piedes. In addition, the Quoeech (known also by the derogatory term "Diggers") made calls on the new white settlement. Bean's mission record notes that "some other Indians have come down from the Mountain lately very hungry & sick.... We have adopted our former habit of sending them away from the fort to sleep."[54] Furthermore, when some of the Latter-day

Saint wives joined their husbands at the mission, a new dimension of challenges and opportunities arose between the missionaries, their families, and the Natives.

The missionaries, eager to share their religious beliefs with the Native Americans, began inviting them to their Sunday services within a month after arriving in the Vegas area. Some of the meetings were more successful than others. Bean observed in his journal that during one Sunday in the summer of 1855, the missionaries "had a little trouble in making [the Native Americans] keep still during meeting."[55] Most of the time, however, the local Native visitors behaved well and were eager to learn the ways of the white man. The official mission record for September 2, 1855, offers an example of a typical Sabbath: "A good many Indians were at meeting today very well behaved & appeared interested and anxious to understand the nature of our proceedings in the meeting."[56]

It was an exciting and momentous day indeed when the first public prayer was offered by a local Paiute leader at worship services: "Chief Joshua [Patsearump] met with us today & prayed in public congregation it is the first Indian of this tribe who ever done the like & his spirit of supplication was excellent & well adapted to the degree of knowledge which they at present enjoy."[57]

Sunday, November 4, 1855, was another noteworthy day, when "at the appointed hour for meeting the Indians came together to the number of 70, including Patsearump. After Prest Bringhurst had addressed the congregation he called upon Bro Geo Bean to talk to the Lamanites assembled and explain to them as well as he could the nature of the obligation they were about to take upon themselves by going into the waters of baptism." The Natives "listened with great attention and promised to lay aside as much as possible their evil practices. After a short intermission in which time they were washing their bodies. They were called together at the water and the ordinance of baptism administered to fifty six persons male and female they were also confirmed at the same place & time, and a record made of the same."[58] After that joyous occasion, corn and a few squashes were given to the Native Americans, and all were satisfied with the day's events.[59]

Less than a month later, John Steele, in a letter to George A. Smith, noted these fifty-six baptisms: "I helped to baptize and confirm many of them, and as a general thing, both Indians and white men seemed to feel first rate and especially the missionaries." He also explained that the food at the fort was all the lure they needed to bring the local Natives in: "The brethren do not need to go out much among the natives, for all there are will come to them as soon as it is known that there is corn in Egypt."[60]

PRIVILEGES FOR THE NATIVE AMERICANS

The Native Americans in the region enjoyed the advantages, privileges, and authority of membership in the Latter-day Saint faith. Baptized Natives considered worthy of the trust were ordained to offices in the priesthood and were taught the accompanying duties to officiate and administer within their stewardships.[61]

The Latter-day Saints' relationship with these Native desert people required careful skill and attention. An excerpt from a letter sent by Brigham Young to the Paiutes shows the respectful equality and sensitivity with which he tried to communicate: "We think a great deal of you all, and consider you as our brothers and our friends; and we shall always be your friends any how; we do not want you to get angry, but to ask the Great Spirit about us.... We want you to help build houses to live in, and raise cattle and horses and wheat and every thing good that you can, so you can be like us, & talk to us as we talk to one another."[62]

The missionaries found it advantageous to commission some of the local Native Americans to serve missions to their own tribes.[63] Delegating such responsibilities provided the Native Americans with additional native-speaking teachers who understood their own cultural idiosyncrasies and proved a safety measure for the Saints. A case in point was the generally hostile Iat tribe. The local Iat chief and two others arrived at the fort in a friendly manner and desired baptism. They were obliged and given the assignment to return to their people to instruct them in the principles they had been taught. These three men were the only Iats ever to be baptized during the tenure of the mission. President Bringhurst had prayed concerning having some of his men visit this tribe, but "he did not think the time had Com for So few men to viset Such a hostile tribe as they are."[64]

With time, the missionaries grew to love the local Native Americans they served. By the fall of 1856, a school had been provided for both the white and the Native children. Some houses were also erected on the Native American farm about two miles from the fort.[65] The local Natives were learning to appreciate and depend on their new peculiar neighbors.

Tragically, by the early winter of 1857, this delicately balanced relationship would come to an end with the mission closure, which the local tribes lamented.

Typical of Brigham Young, he consistently kept many irons in the fire. He desired one of these irons be made of lead. Ore specimens brought to the church officials from the Vegas district encouraged Young to persevere in his explorations. By the middle of February 1856, he assigned Nathaniel V. Jones of Salt Lake City to go to the Vegas vicinity in search of lead. After preparing, Jones departed from Salt Lake City on April 14 to fulfill this obligation.[66]

Young penned a letter to Bringhurst on March 3, revealing his manifold ambitions for the mission:

> We have appointed a goodly number to rejoin your place this spring and hearing that a specimen of ore which Br William. D. Huntington has found near that point which we understand exists in large quantities and which upon trial proves to be a rich lead ore we have appointed an additional number with a view of working the Mines, who however will not go until after harvest you will see the names of the Missionaries in the Deseret News. We expect that you will be enabled to raise cotton in considerable quantities this year as well as an ample supply of food.[67]

When this letter reached Vegas, John Steele was temporarily serving as president of the mission, in the absence of Bringhurst and his two counselors.[68] Steele embarked on a lead exploration with a Native American guide in the spring of 1856.[69] On April 22, he recorded that he had found an abundance of lead and packed 180 pounds of it back to the mission.[70] The next day he sent a letter to President Young, accompanied with an ore sample of his recent discovery: "Found the lead oar mountain of which you have had a specimen I believe I might say that there is plenty of or I should rather say silver, it there I think from the best evidences that I could find that it extends for miles I send you a small Chunk 3 1/2 lbs also some of the Rock that it grows in." Steele requested that Brigham "be so good as to send us word what proportion is silver & what is Lead it would satisfy many enquiries and oblidge your obedient servant."[71]

Young encouraged Steele to continue his mining intentions, notwith-standing the lack of silver found in the sample: "The lead ore you were so considerate as to forward me lately has been examined by Bro. Carring-ton with considerable care, but no trace of Silver was detected by the dry method, as it is termed.... [Yet] I am pleased with the diligence exercised by yourself and associates at reasonable opportunities, in searching out the resources of the regions around your locality, and am always gratified with descriptions of your travels, and with the Mineralogical specimens you forward."[72]

Steele's enthusiasm for his findings are captured in a letter he sent to his wife, Catherine, along with a sample of his precious metal: "[I] found the best Lead oar and it exists in great abundance." He added, "I think if wer prospered this lead will be a source of great welth for us."[73]

Obviously, the lead sample and letter that Steele sent to Young aroused interest, because two weeks later three men, Nathaniel Jones, P. K. Smith, and Ira Hatch, were dispatched to the region with instructions to explore the lead possibilities.[74] Jones possessed a letter from Young authorizing him to "call on men and animals or anything he might want for the furtherance of his mission."[75]

Steele enthusiastically led Jones to the ore; however, upon closer inspection, Jones believed there was not enough quality lead to justify opening mining activities. But Steele was persistent. He hired another Native American, who maintained that he knew of another far more plenteous lead site. Steele returned with another positive report, describ-ing the find as "the Silver Mountain" that presented "a very flattering pros-pect." Jones immediately sent an outfit and several men to explore, but the extreme heat hampered their efforts.[76] Although they did not survey the prospects personally, they were encouraged when they left for home on May 22, 1856, determined to return in September.[77]

DISHARMONY AND POWER STRUGGLES AT THE MISSION

On July 7, 1856, William Bringhurst returned to Las Vegas and resumed the responsibilities of mission president.[78] Just one week later, he informed Brigham Young by letter of his ambitious plans to organize a mining company and to commence operations as soon as possible. Young's reac-tion to this letter hints at his suspicion that perhaps Bringhurst had a personal interest in the lead-mining business. Young absolved William of any stewardship and authority over the mining and warned against self-interest in the endeavor. Instead, he appointed Nathaniel V. Jones to direct the lead-mining operation and asked that Bringhurst "render him all the assistance in team work and manual labor" that he possibly could. Young concluded his terse remarks requesting that Bringhurst and his fellow missionaries would "feel an interest in this matter, and look to the benefit of Israel and the prosperity of Zion, more than self-interest."[79]

Nathaniel V. Jones and four others arrived at the fort on August 8, bearing instructions from President Young that stated, "Jones is hereby empowered to call to his aid in the said manufacture and transportation of lead building of furnaces mining the ore &c. such persons as his judgement and necessities may dictate, not only southern missionaries, but others of the brethren in the southern settlements if need be."[80]

Jones further clarified that the object of his mission was to pull the most recently called missionaries from the Las Vegas Mission and reenlist them in his lead-mining mission, which was "a separate & distinct concern." Jones also flexed his authority to proceed by indicating that "those brethren who came this season & engaged with him would be discharged by him & allowed to return home as soon as the required amount of lead was obtained[;] this authority was given him by Prest. Young according to his statement."[81]

This bold declaration must have heated up the proceedings considerably. But Jones did not stop there. He publicly criticized the mission leaders for not rendering appropriate support when he first arrived and presented them with Young's letter. Furthermore, he intended to claim the necessary assistance and proceed at once with his assignment. The mission record documents the remainder of the meeting: "Prest. Bringhurst then arose & said...he could not feel clear in giving liberty for those brethren to leave this mission & go with Bro Jones. they were placed under his charge & until the proper documents were produced by Bro Jones."[82]

After this apparent deadlock, Jones requested permission to speak to the missionaries, and permission was granted. Jones then indicated that whereas Bringhurst had refused to support his orders authorized by President Young, "[Jones] consequently would be under the necessity of calling upon the brethren as individuals to go with him to the mines according to the spirit of the instructions from Prest Young. He said he knew his duty & would be responsible for all his acts & stand between the brethren & all blame in the matter."[83]

The following day, as Jones tried to gather the men to commence the mining endeavors, another confrontation ensued between him and Bringhurst. Both men seemed convinced that Brigham Young would support their respective positions and that the only way to settle their differences was to write to President Young for clarification. When it was agreed that Bringhurst should petition Young on the matter, Jones forthwith departed with six men for the lead mines.[84]

The letter Bringhurst penned, in part, reads as follows: "Nathaniel V Jones and company arrived here on the 8th inst all well and had a safe journey. immediately upon his arrival he asked for the exclusive control separate and apart from this Mission of all the Missionaries who were sent here last spring. I have objected to this but at the same time stand ready to assist and cooperate in the accomplishment of his Mission as much as is in my power. We still differ upon this point and I would be happy to receive a word of enlightenment from you upon the subject."[85]

In a timely reply, Young made it clear that petty differences paled in comparison with the task at hand: "In regard to the subject of difference between you and brother Jones. I wish to say there is no occasion for the least feeling for it is our desire to have all the brethren, whither appointed to that mission last spring, or at any other time, render brother Jones all the assistance which they can, and he shall require, and let us have out one or two hundred tons of that lead without delay or stopping to settle the differences—we will settle the differences afterwards."[86]

The letter also demoralized Bringhurst by suggesting that the Las Vegas fort was better suited as merely a post than as a productive settlement. That being the case, Young believed that too many men were stationed there to be gainfully employed and therefore encouraged Bringhurst to make plans to make a settlement on the Muddy or perhaps on the Colorado. A defiant Bringhurst shot back a reply to President Young, essentially driving the nail in his own ecclesiastical coffin, insinuating that he was not willing to give Jones the full authority to take the men he needed to mine lead and to release them to return home when they had completed their work.[87]

RELEASE OF WILLIAM BRINGHURST

Bringhurst accelerated tension by getting on top of a wagon and demanding that the men declare themselves either for Jones or for himself. Any man who possessed loyalties to Jones and who had assisted him without the consent of Bringhurst was immediately expelled from the Las Vegas Mission.[88] Obviously, this tug-of-war for power eroded the missionaries' support for their president. Finally, Young felt he had borne enough of Bringhurst's stubbornness in refusing to fully acknowledge Jones's authority and in withholding full support of the lead operations under Jones's direction. President Young was resigned to relieving Bringhurst of his presiding office and temporarily disfellowshipping him from the church.[89]

A NEW PRESIDENT

To fill the vacancy, Samuel Thompson, a former Mormon Battalion member from New York, was appointed to preside over the Las Vegas Mission, with these instructions from Brigham Young: "You will take charge of all papers, records, and other Property, and business pertaining to the mission, and render Bro N. V. Jones, such assistance as he may require to carry on the lead business, so far as it may be in your power, without infringing upon the design, and objects of the mission, Keeping in view our relations with the Indians."[90]

As the new year dawned, Young commended Thompson for his efforts with the Native Americans and reiterated his wishes for the lead business: "We like the idea of your holding meetings with the Indians at their wick.e.ups [and] trust that it will have a salutary influence over them. We also wish that you would aid by your influence and by furnishing such assistance as can be spared to Bro Jones in the lead business, also endeavoring to conciliate the Indians and protect the stock."[91]

Despite commendable efforts with the local tribes, within a week of receiving this letter from Young, Thompson regrettably reported the grim realities of problems with the Native Americans who resorted to stealing food in their state of acute hunger as well as the continual bickering among the missionaries. Thompson noted, "There seems to be almost an entire lack of energy & determination on the part of the Brethren who are now here, every thing seems to be dull and forbidding. Men generally seem to be nearly discouraged, not knowing whether they will be called on to remain here or not."[92]

THE LAS VEGAS AND LEAD MISSIONS CLOSE

In light of Thompson's report, President Young informed Thompson one month later that the mission needed to close: "I regret to learn the uneasy feelings that exist among the Indians towards your settlement: and the division existing among yourselves: We now give you liberty to leave the Los Vegas Fort to Solitude and the Indians. It would appear you cannot sustain yourselves. and consequently this station becomes an expence to the kingdom, and at prisent seems, not to add any honey to the hive." Young also encouraged Thompson to give the Native Americans presents and to leave them with good feelings toward the missionaries.[93]

The demise of both missions unfolded nearly simultaneously. Jones informed Brigham Young as follows: "Dear Sir—Since my communications of last month, circumstances have changed very much with us. For about one month & a half the Indians have manifested a hostile Spirit towards us, they are determined to Steal & Kill all of our animels." In addition, he reported that most of the ore was in an impure state. Furthermore, water needed for sluicing was eleven miles away, which made the work most difficult. He concluded that the lead mining "certainly will neaver pay."[94]

Before Jones's letter had even reached Young, Brigham had already made this decision: "We have come to this conclusion. That as soon as you have used up the cattle sent you from Iron Coy [County] And completed the working up of all the ore you have got out or can get out, during the time these provisions last, pick up and come away, bringing all with you, that is valuable: and if at any future time we require more lead, we can send out 50 men for a winter and procure what we may need."[95]

By this time, Jones and his men had become discouraged that their mining aspirations were coming to naught, and they contemplated shutting down.[96] They all seemed to be on the same page, because within three weeks, Young sent official notice to the men of the "Los Vegas Lead Mines" to withdraw from their assignment: "We wish you now to consider your mission at an end, and would be glad to have you come home, at your earliest convenience."[97]

THE END OF A SHORT ERA

Upon his return to Salt Lake City, Jones rendered a personal debriefing to President Young regarding the mission difficulties. Among diverse challenges, obtaining fuel for the furnace required a twelve-mile trek from the Potosi mine site.[98] Jones also explained, "The difficulties attending the working of the mines are very great. All the provisions and forage for animals have to be hauled 230 miles over a very hard, difficult road."[99] Another predicament involved laboring with such a small group of men[100] who were isolated from the protection and security of the Mormon fort, which lay thirty miles away. Jones noted, "The difficulties attending the working of the mines, together with the hostile feelings of the Indians, I did not consider it wisdom to remain longer."[101]

With the close of the desert mine, some who had been called to assist in the lead-mining operation, as well as at the Las Vegas Mission, never made it to their fields of labor. John Woodhouse explained that en route to commence labor, "We met an express who told us that on account of Indian troubles it was decided to abandon the mission and for us to send a part of our company with cattle to assist the people to move, and the rest of us to return, also telling us of the Indian troubles."[102]

Although there were many reports of Native American trouble, apparently some of the local tribes continued to visit the Las Vegas fort and desired that the men stay. When news reached them that the Latter-day Saint missionaries were leaving the region, they were disappointed. President Thompson advised Brigham Young of the situation with the local tribes: "The Indians seem to be verry friendly and verry sorry to have us leave. They seem to be sorry that their conduct has had an influence to cause us to leave. They are verry anxious that either we or some other good Marmons [sic] should be sent on soon to remain amongst them." Thompson also noted their plans to close the mission: "I received your last [letter dated February 4] liberating us from the Los vegas we are now expected to start on Monday next the 23rd ult. We should have left sooner but the Brethren had not returnd from California.... We are rather weak to move with ease we shall be under the necessity of leaving some of our considerable stuff in the care of the Indians."[103]

Three days later, Alexander A. Lemon wrote of their March departure, "23 Monday We Started on our Journey."[104] George Mayer also wrote of leaving: "Being called away from the Los Vegas by President Brigham Young, we left on the 22nd of March for our several homes.... We were instructed by Samuel Thompson that we must all leave. Some would liked to remain till word could have been sent to President Young."[105] Mayer also indicated, "The Indians were very friendly, requested some of us to stay with them, and desired that the mission should be kept up. We travelled through the different tribes of Indians without any trouble. The Los Vegas Indians sent some men with us to the Muddy Indians. They received us kindly and herded our cattle."[106]

Just two months after the Las Vegas Mission closed, one of the church leaders presiding over the San Bernardino settlement passed the deserted fort and recorded his regret for how this mission had come to an end: "Saturday, May 9, 1857 Left camp at 7½ oclock reached Los Vegas at

7 oclock ev found the fort a Desolation a sad moment of the foly of poor short sighted selfish man who can sacrifice the intrests of a Kingdom and people on the alter of personal selfishness."[107]

Thus concluded the short-lived era of the Las Vegas Mission and mining enterprise, which involved lessons learned, repeated history, and human nature at its best and worst—all under the unyielding, relentless desert sun. Erected from faith and the sweat of the men's brows, it was a place where both character and commitment were forged in the vast expanse of a brutal desert.

Notwithstanding the obstacles, perhaps the undertaking may have been worth the gamble. Although the Las Vegas Mormon Fort mission lasted less than two years, from the perspective of more than a century, this gloomy sketch takes on a brighter hue. Admittedly, the mission ended with bickering and selfishness among some of the missionaries, but the Las Vegas Saints rendered many acts of service to the Native Americans. Moreover, Bringhurst not only returned to full fellowship in the church, but also later served as a bishop[108] in Springville, Utah, where he died a faithful Latter-day Saint in 1872. It also appears that most of the men who launched this desert mission endured in faith to the end.[109]

In addition, several accomplishments should not go unrecognized. The Las Vegas Mormon Fort was the birthplace of the first white child born in what is now known as southern Nevada,[110] and it was the location of the first US post office in the region, named Bringhurst.[111] It was also the first time white settlers had settled among local Native Americans in this area, and some members of local tribes joined the church. In addition, the fort served as an important stopping place for mail carriers and for passing migrants and freighters during the mid-nineteenth century, helping to launch commerce between California and Utah. Last, but not least, the Las Vegas Mormon Fort is believed to be the oldest non–Native American building in southern Nevada. Although Latter-day Saint mining efforts had failed in this region, others successfully mined the area a short time later. And while the house of worship hastily erected at the old Mormon fort was not completed, its foundation represents what was to follow as the Saints continued to pour into the Vegas region, helping to form thriving communities and establishing permanent roots for their families.[112]

2

Post–Old Mormon Fort
Early Settlement to
Las Vegas Stakes (1857–1960)

The wilderness and the solitary place shall be glad for them;
and the desert shall rejoice, and blossom as the rose.
—Isaiah 35:1

After Brigham Young released the missionaries from their assignments at
the old Las Vegas Mormon Fort, one settler from the first group, Albert
Knapp, a former Mormon Battalion member, returned to the fort in 1861
and set up a store intending to sell goods to the local miners. His brother
William joined him three years later, providing wagon repair to passing
travelers.[1] One team of authors wrote:

> Cabins and stockades built by the Mormons and their Indian work-
> ers remained at the deserted fort, welcome shelter for carriers of the
> Overland Mail and other travelers to and from California. During
> the Civil War, several California newspapers reported that the old
> Mormon fort was to be renamed Fort Baker, a new military post for
> four companies of Union soldiers. As it turned out, the story had
> been deliberately and falsely planted by Colonel James H. Carlson,
> Commander of the First California Volunteers, to deceive Confed-
> erate spies.[2]

When the war ended, in 1865, Octavius Decatur Gass purchased the
old fort and began using it as a ranch. Unfortunately, he lost it in 1881
due to his failure to repay a loan to a fellow rancher named Archibald
Stewart. Two years later, Stewart moved his wife, Helen, and their children from Pioche, Nevada, 175 miles south to this Las Vegas acreage. The
following year, Archibald Stewart was killed by a neighbor on an adja-
cent property known as the Kiel Ranch. To her credit, Helen continued
to run the ranch successfully for another two decades until she sold the
property in 1902 to Montana senator William Clark for $55,000. Clark
wanted the land for a rail line that eventually became known as the San

Albert Knapp.
Courtesy of Mary Bryant.

Pedro, Los Angeles & Salt Lake Railroad, which ran through this terri-tory.[3] About three decades after the Latter-day Saint pioneer settlers left the fort, and prior to the Clark purchase, additional Saints were hired to survey the land for a future railroad between Los Angeles and southern Nevada. During their inspection, they discovered gold, which resulted in the formation of a new mining company that brought goods into the region and made the forthcoming railroad more fruitful.[4]

About this same time, T. S. Kenderine, not of the Latter-day Saint faith, passed by the ruins of the old Las Vegas Mormon Fort. Through his lens, Kenderine provided an account of the desolate condition of the dilapidated settlement and included a drawing of the fort's remains: "We came upon the remains of a Mormon settlement. Some years ago a colony was planted here by Saints.… The enterprising colonists were in high expectation of reaping a rich reward for their labor, when the Vegas Indians, who were in considerable numbers in this valley, began to give them serious trouble by their thieving propensities, and at last it was as much as the isolated settlers could do to preserve their lives." Kenderine further noted, "Sad were the thoughts which the sight of

T. S. Kenderdine drawing of Las Vegas Mormon
Fort, 1858, Nevada State Museum Las Vegas.
Courtesy of the Library of Congress.

this lone and dismantled fortress raised, as in silent isolation it stood on this once blooming oasis of the desert. Prowling coyotes, venomous reptiles, and those wretched imitations of humanity, the Diggers, now lay claim to those walls which once formed an abiding place for civilized people. Thorns and dry, withered weeds now covered the once verdant fields, which, for want of irrigation, were now returning to their original sterility, and the whole valley presented a scene dismal and desolate in the extreme."[5]

But a new Latter-day settlement was not far on the heels of these bleak remnants. The coming of the railroad encouraged rapid settlement in the Las Vegas region. Former church assistant historian Andrew Jenson noted, "Among the railroad employees were a number of Latter-day Saints (some with families)."[6] Another author also confirmed that some of the eager buyers at the railway sales of Vegas town-site lots held in 1905 were Latter-day Saints.[7] Soon the population swelled to two thousand.[8] Ed Von Tobel was an eyewitness to the sales that catalytic year and remembered that the town of Las Vegas "appeared pretty dreary, but the bidding was good on downtown lots," which he took advantage of.[9]

ASSEMBLING THE SCATTERED SAINTS

One of the Latter-day Saints who moved to this desert locality during this early period was Charles C. Ronnow, a business partner to Ed Clark. Southern Nevada historian Elbert B. Edwards observed, "The two formed

Clark Forwarding Company, Las Vegas, ca. 1905.
Special Collections & Archives, University
Libraries, University of Nevada, Las Vegas.

a very interesting partnership. They were partners throughout their lives, although Ed was a very devout Catholic and E. E. [C. C.] was an equally devout Mormon of Danish ancestry. Not only were they partners in business, but Ed lived in the Ronnow household throughout this life."[10] In 1905, Ronnow moved with his family to Vegas less than two months after the first lots were sold in what was then "a town full of tents."[11]

Clark and Ronnow, cofounders of the Clark Forwarding Company, launched their business with public advertisements soon after the town of Las Vegas was laid out.[12] Ronnow and his family lived right next to the Clark Forwarding workplace. Born in 1865, Ronnow had previously served as a bishop in Panaca, Nevada (1894–99), and as a Latter-day Saint missionary to Scandinavia from 1899 to 1901. Ronnow would also play an early leadership role for church members in Las Vegas.[13]

By the end of the nineteenth century, the Church of Jesus Christ of Latter-day Saints had already established roots across southern Nevada. The St. George Stake, established in 1877, comprised the southeastern Nevada towns of Bunkerville, Mesquite, Overton, St. Thomas, and Alamo.[14] These Nevada towns later became part of the Moapa Stake, created in 1912.[15] From these towns, many Latter-day Saints migrated to Las Vegas when employment prospects opened up on the railroad, at Hoover Dam, and in the Clark County School District.

Several factors led to the increase in the southern Nevada Latter-day Saint population in the early twentieth century. By the time World War I came to an end, economic opportunities were limited, and good land for cultivation was scarce. Arrington explained, "Utah suffered immensely from the post–World War I depression that began in 1921. The consequence was that thousands of Utahans began a migration out of state seeking opportunities to earn a livelihood. The great bulk of these migrated to California, but a considerable number moved to Nevada, particularly the Las Vegas area."[16]

Nevada natives also came to Las Vegas seeking employment during this period. One southern Nevada Latter-day Saint who migrated to Las Vegas before the Utah influx was a young man named Newel K. Leavitt. Leavitt, an employee of the Clark Forwarding Company, was a store clerk and distributed groceries, grain, and hay as well as ice and beer to the local saloons via a delivery wagon.[17] Leavitt had recently returned home to Bunkerville from a mission to the Southwestern States Mission (1910–12).[18] He saved his ninety-dollar monthly salary from the Forwarding Company, and in 1913 Leavitt married his Latter-day Saint childhood sweetheart, Nettie Earl.

Lisa Leavitt Messenger, a great-granddaughter of Leavitt, provided additional details about Newel and Nettie's background in the small community of Bunkerville, where they were born and raised. She explained, "It was rustic, it was tough. People built from scratch in the middle of nowhere; they fought for everything they had. The children were very close. It was a small, close-knit, Mormon community." Messenger added, "Newel Leavitt was a few years older than Nettie. They grew up to be friends through their teenage years, they communicated a little bit during his mission, and when he came back, Nettie had it in her mind that if he asked her to marry him she was going to say yes."[19] True to her intentions, Nettie accepted Newel's proposal, and the married couple moved to a two-room house in Las Vegas located on the corner of Sixth and Bridger Streets.[20]

Leavitt continued his missionary efforts after his marriage and during his employment was actively engaged in trying to establish the church in Las Vegas. Nettie Earl wrote, "Newell was a hard worker, a mover, and a doer.... He took it upon himself to find out how many Mormons there were.... In the store and on his delivery route he asked his customers if they knew of any Mormons in Las Vegas. He wrote down their names and addresses." In addition, Leavitt held Sunday-school classes in his own home and led the singing. Initially, there were only two classes: one for

Newel K. Leavitt and Nettie Earl home, 1914.
Courtesy of Lisa Leavitt Messenger.

the adults, which he taught, and the other for the children, which Clarice Craner provided instruction for.[21]

Lisa Leavitt Messenger explained the need for her great-grandfather to start his own church meetings:

> Newel Leavitt wanted to attend regular church services, but there weren't any here of his faith. He made friends with a Methodist man who said, "Come to my church." And so, for a while he did, and he was eventually asked to teach a bible study class there. He was so versed in the scriptures from his mission time. He also shared his musical talents.... Newel played the Mandolin,...the piano too, [and] he sang. He was later part of a quartet in Las Vegas, and he was able to share a lot of his religious faith to people of all sorts of faiths through his musical talents.[22]

Leavitt's perseverance and dedication paid off, and church meetings in his private home eventually moved to other locations advertised to the public. For example, in mid-July 1913, the *Las Vegas Age* provided this notice under the headline "L.D.S. Meeting," stating, "The members of the Church of the Latter Day Saints are notified that services will be held in the auditorium of the school house Sunday evening, July 6th at eight o'clock. John M. Bunker of the Moapa stake will preach. All are invited."[23]

The following spring, another advertisement, titled "Latter Day Saints," appeared in the *Age,* noting, "The members of the Church of Latter Day Saints will hold services in the Botkin building Sunday morning at 10 o'clock and Sunday evening at 7:30. All are invited."[24]

ESTABLISHING BRANCHES AND WARDS

Leavitt "sent a list of all the members to the president of the Moapa Stake, Willard L. Jones, in Overton, Nevada."[25] This action led to the creation of a dependent church branch in 1915 wherein C. C. Ronnow was the first elder to preside.[26]

The official Moapa Stake Historical Record notes the following in chronological order regarding the official organization of the church in Las Vegas:

> March 21, 1914: Letter from Newel K. Leavitt was read in which it was asked if it were possible to get some kind of an organization of the Church started in Las Vegas. It was decided to have a meeting called at Las Vegas, April 5, for the purpose of effecting an organization.
>
> April 26, 1914: President Jones reported that he had arranged with Brother John M. Bunker and I. J. Earl to meet with the people of Las Vegas on May 3d and organize a Sunday School and perhaps arranged for a presiding elder.
>
> May 29, 1915: Brother Wells reported the visit of himself and Stake Clerk Flowers to Las Vegas. Said they were in a disorganized condition thru Bishop Whitehead having released officers. Said he thought it advisable to be Charley Ronnow in [as] Presiding Elder of the branch.[27]

This same year, in 1915, local newspapers continued to publish service times and the names of local church leaders. W. A. Whitehead was listed as the bishop, probably because although Ronnow was a presiding elder of the branch, the Las Vegas Branch was dependent on the Overton Ward (Moapa Stake), of which William A. Whitehead was the bishop.[28]

Members of this small Las Vegas branch not only supported each other but also had the opportunity to bless their brothers and sisters from afar. The front page of the *Age* highlighted this story at a time when worldwide conflict was ever present. The church presidency announced a day set aside "for receiving donations for the assistance of members…who reside in foreign countries and are suffering from the effects of the European war." The announcement further explained, "Donations made

Beckley's Store, Las Vegas. *Left to right*: Jake Beckley, Bryan Bunker,
and Will Beckley, 1930. Special Collections & Archives,
University Libraries, University of Nevada, Las Vegas.

through the local branch of the church will be forwarded with others
and applied to that purpose."[29]

The following year, "on January 1, 1916, the Las Vegas Branch was
attached to the Bunkerville Ward as a dependent branch. In 1920,
Charles C. Ronnow was released and Ira J. [Joseph] Earl was sustained as
Presiding Elder."[30] Two years later, on April 30, 1922, the Las Vegas Branch
became an independent branch. Church leaders periodically visited the
branch because it fell under the direct supervision of the Moapa Stake.[31]
On June 1, 1924, the first Las Vegas ward was formed, with Ira J. Earl
as bishop.[32]

Marion B. Earl remembered the challenges church members faced
when renting facilities for Sunday worship during this early period:
"When the branch was first organized, they met in the Odd Fellows Hall.
When I moved to Las Vegas in 1923, we held Sunday School and Sacrament meeting in a dance hall above Beckley's Clothing store,[33] located at
First and Fremont Streets, where the Pioneer Club now stands. There was
always a Saturday night dance[34] there so on Sunday morning we would
have to go early and sweep up the cigarette butts and cigar stubs and the
beer cans, mop up the beer stains from the floor and air the place out so
we could hold our meetings." Earl further noted, "In 1924 and '25, we built
the first L.D.S. chapel in Las Vegas, on the northwest corner of Sixth and

Carson, a small frame building. It had a small stage and a small room on each side of the stage and a main hall which would seat about 175 people. To create classrooms for Sunday School, we stretched a wire from the front door to the stage and another wire from one side of the chapel to the other. With curtains on these wires we made four class rooms."[35]

ECUMENICAL COMMUNITY EVENTS

Throughout this era, Latter-day Saints enjoyed a robust social life and community unity, as evidenced in the *Las Vegas Age:* "Churches Unite in Service of Thanks," to be held on Thanksgiving Day, 1927, at the local Episcopal church. The Baptist, Methodist, Latter-day Saint, and Episcopal congregations joined together in a spirit of gratitude and worship that commenced with Latter-day Saint bishop Ira J. Earl offering the opening prayer. Music for the joyful event was provided "by the combined choirs of the four churches."[36] Several years later, the Grace Community Church and the Latter-day Saints enjoyed an outdoor service in which a combined choir performed for the Boulder City citizens.[37]

Even more impressive and unique is the participation of Latter-day Saint children in a daily Vacation Bible School sponsored by the Methodist Church in Las Vegas. The *Age* explained, "The school is made up mainly of Methodist children, but there are also Baptists, Latter Day Saints, Christian Scientists, Presbyterians and Catholics. The school is conducted on a non-[s]ectarian basis and is open to all children of the town."[38]

This kind of interaction reveals the ecumenical nature of Las Vegas in the early twentieth century. Latter-day Saints were more involved in the Las Vegas community than was the norm for those of the same faith residing in other cities during this era.

ACTIVITIES OF SAINTS ADVERTISED IN THE PRESS

The local newspaper reported on a Latter-day Saint "Pioneer Day Celebration" held when Ira J. Earl presided as bishop over the congregation: "Members of the Church of Jesus Christ of Latter-day Saints held their annual Pioneer Day Celebration, Friday evening, July 24th on the green just west of W. J. Stewart's residence. Sandwiches, ice cream and root beer were served. Speeches were made on the early settlers.... Games were played and the city band after their concert on the court house lawn came down and favored the crowd with a few selections.... Everybody had a good time."[39]

After serving for five years as the Las Vegas Ward bishop, Earl was replaced by Bryan L. Bunker in a ward conference held February 17, 1929.[40] The following month, another Latter-day Saint conference in southern Nevada was postponed due to an outbreak of smallpox.[41] However, missionary work continued beyond the Vegas boundaries in 1929 with young people sent from the desert city on full-time missions.[42] By the end of December 1930, Bunker's congregation had swelled to 410 members, making up nearly 8 percent of the population of the city of Las Vegas.[43] Such growth and leadership eventually caught the attention of the *Las Vegas Age*, which published the headline "L.D.S. Officers Hold Meeting," noting that local church leaders were convening in the home of Judge Wm. E. Orr under the direction of Bishop Bunker and listing the names of the officers and their spouses.[44] By this time, auxiliary officers were serving in the ward, including Annie Dotson, who directed women's activities as the local Relief Society president.[45] The year 1930 marked the centennial anniversary of the Church of Jesus Christ of Latter-day Saints. Many local leaders and members traveling to Utah for the spring and fall church general conferences were given round-trip rail discounts if they used Union Pacific trains to travel to Salt Lake City and back to their Nevada homes.[46]

During the early 1930s public presentations by church members were advertised. For example, the *Las Vegas Review-Journal* announced that Lewis E. Rowe would be giving an address by radio.[47] Another article advertised "an illustrated lecture on American Archaeology in connection with the Book of Mormon."[48] Other adverts informed the public of "Mormon" dances held at the Boulder City Legion Hall.[49] Additional local ads warmly informed the community of church meetings held at the chapel located at "Sixth and Carson Streets. Sunday School: 10:00A.M. Preaching Service: 7:30PM. PUBLIC CORDIALLY INVITED."[50] Occasionally, more details described upcoming church events. For example, one article, titled "Latter Day Saints Services," reported, "Today is Fast Day in conjunction with Sunday school.... Tonight a very fine program [has] been arranged. Marion Earl, who has just returned from Washington, D.C. will be the speaker. Mrs. Earl, who has been studying voice in Washington, will sing.... The Relief Society will meet Tuesday at 2:30 at the church and enjoy an old-fashioned 'Quilting Bee.'"[51]

After Bishop Bunker took office, vibrant weekly activities and church growth continued, and Bunker determined that the ward needed a bigger building for church meetings. The *Las Vegas Age*, in a piece titled "L,D,S, [*sic*] Work on Church Plans," reported the following: "A building committee of the L.D.S. Church is working on the problem of providing a new and adequate church building to take the place of the one now in use. 'The present church is far too small for our needs,' said Bishop Bryan Bunker yesterday, 'and we will probably either build a new one on the present site at Carson and Sixth or at some other location[,] the site to be chosen later.'"[52] Another local paper also observed, "The Latter Day Saints have completed negotiations for a new site, and will soon start in actual construction of an edifice that will be a distinct credit to the city."[53]

However, three years later, with church membership swelling to five hundred, the Vegas Saints were still meeting in the same building, and a new place of worship became a critical necessity. The "History of the Las Vegas First Ward" recounts the members' mixed reactions to the announcement of the new building's location and some who strongly opposed the change:

> What! Build a chapel way out there in the *mesquites and salt grass?* Some of the dissenters felt that a delegation of the more sensible members of the ward should go to Salt Lake and persuade the general authorities of the folly of the location. There were even hints that a movement should be started to remove the Bishopric. When it became clear that the 9th and Clark site was final, there were strong comments that people would not walk thru the ankle deep dust in fair weather and ankle deep mud in wet weather, way out there to church.[54]

Yet plans for the construction of the new building moved forward, and in March 1932 a quarterly conference was held near the building site at the local grammar school's gymnasium. By this time, average church attendance was 550. The visiting general authorities for this conference were church president Heber J. Grant and Elder David O. McKay of the Quorum of the Twelve Apostles.[55]

This Moapa Stake conference captured front-page attention. President Grant's visit brought much excitement and joy to local members. Although the *Age* announced that it was the first time a church president had visited their city,[56] in reality President Grant had made his first visit to Vegas two years earlier.[57] During the conference, the Caliente Ward was created, making it the twelfth ward in the Moapa Stake. There were 552 people who attended the weekend conference, making it the largest number of members ever gathered in a Moapa Stake conference since the stake's creation in 1912.

Elaborate arrangements were made for guest speaker President Grant, and it was reported that he gave "one of the most stirring speeches ever heard in Las Vegas." Grant "laid great stress on the young people of the church and the need for them to adhere to the teachings of the church. Most heavily did he strike at gambling and easy divorce laws of the state, as being detrimental to the welfare of the people of the church." This criticism came just one year after the legalization of gaming and softer divorce laws were passed in the state of Nevada.[58] Grant's remarks were published in the *Las Vegas Age* and appeared in print again less than three months later at the Moapa Stake's twentieth anniversary. Willard L. Jones continued to preside over the stake, as he had since its inception. The *Las Vegas Age* inclusively noted, "Not only the people of the l.d.s. church, but all…are invited to attend the celebration."[59]

The much-needed new church building was completed in October 1932, but the dedication of the building was deferred until three years later when it was completely paid for, in adherence to church policy.[60] In December 1935, the dedication of the new Latter-day Saint building on Ninth and Clark Streets was a front-page headline: "Mormon Church Is Dedicated." The article reported that this sacred edifice was 125 by 140 feet, with a seating capacity, including balcony space, of up to 600. This news piece revealed that substantial monetary contributions were made by local church members, including $1,599.91 through labor donations. It is noteworthy that $3,645.50 of the total investment ($46,337.28) was donated by those who were not members of the church.[61]

A small portion of the funds collected from those not of the Latter-day Saint faith came via a modest admission charge for a church program that the community was invited to attend at the Latter-day Saint meetinghouse. The *Age* announced, "l.d.s. Church Presents Program" and mentioned that this "pleasing program" would consist of seven different performances: comedy, music, and "vaudeville features." The article promised that the event would "be one of the finest entertainments presented this winter," adding, "a small admission fee, 15c and 25c, will be charged, the proceeds to go towards the new church fund."[62] Charging admission was an exception to the rule, as most Latter-day Saint events were free of charge. Raising funds for the first Latter-day Saint building constructed in Las Vegas was deemed a worthy exception.

At the building's dedication, Elder Rudger Clawson, president of the Quorum of the Twelve Apostles, gave the dedicatory prayer, and Bryan L. Bunker was replaced as bishop by J. Harold Brinley, whom a former ward

member remembered as the bright high school principal who "gave wonderful talks."[63]

In the same issue announcing the dedication of the Latter-day Saint
building, another front-page article read "Plan Dance at Mormon Church,"
which took place at the new building a week later. This piece revealed, "A
delightful feature of the occasion will be the famous 'Dixie Players,' from
St. George, Utah, which are said to produce the most beautiful dance
music heard in this section. The public is welcome to attend and enjoy
the fine dance floor and inspiring music."[64] The monetary contributions
by nonchurch members for the new Latter-day Saint edifice and the fact
that the community at large enjoyed participating at various events in
the church building suggest that the Saints were intermingling with their
neighbors and assimilating into the larger society, which was growing
because of dam construction.

THE TABERNACLE CHOIR VISITS LAS VEGAS AND BOULDER CITY

The same year that the new Latter-day Saint chapel was dedicated (1935),
the Mormon Tabernacle Choir[65] held a brief unofficial concert at the old
Las Vegas courthouse. The local press reported, "LDS Choir is a decided
hit," noting that "more than 1000 people enthusiastically received the program of the music presented by the l.d.s. tabernacle choir on the courthouse lawn,"[66] an opportunity that arose incident to the choir returning
to Salt Lake after performing in San Diego at the California Pacific International Exposition.[67]

The Las Vegas Chamber of Commerce also sought help from the community to transport choir members to Boulder City for a performance.[68]
Two days later, the Tabernacle Choir gave a short performance at the
Hoover Dam, on July 29, 1935.[69] The dam was completed in 1936 after
five years of steady construction. During this period, twenty-one thousand men worked on this monumental project, including Latter-day Saint
employees.[70]

SOCIAL ACTIVITIES, FRUGALITY, GIFTS, AND FUNDS

The completion of the Hoover Dam in March 1936 was met with exhilaration. This same month, local Saints likewise exulted when Latter-day
Saint Fred S. Alward "presented the Las Vegas First Ward with an electric
organ at a cost of $1250.00." Also in 1936, Bishop J. Harold Brinley initiated
a ward-budget plan to raise funds necessary for ward-maintenance costs.
Each family was assessed the minimum cost of $2.50 for each quarter of

the year. Those families meeting this obligation were rewarded with the privilege of attending all of the ward functions free of charge. Marion B. Earl reflected, "That was a pretty good bargain in those days because we had a dance every Saturday night. They were Gold and Green balls, costume dances, and ward banquets." The year 1936 proved prosperous, as the ward membership grew from 772 to 825, and consequently church donations increased.[71] This balanced, conscientious behavior was exemplary. This same year the press announced that Latter-day Saint "home missionaries" were being called in the Vegas area as well as in southern Nevada, which undoubtedly contributed to church growth in the region.[72]

In 1937, unemployment was still a serious problem in America. The Latter-day Saint principles of frugality and self-reliance were held up as a worthy standard to the general public. "Mormons Care for Their Own" was printed in the *Age*, along with the statement "A fundamental doctrine of the Mormon faith is that every member is self-sustaining.... Thus, at the depth of the depression, [church president] Heber Grant...devised the ecclesiastical public works plan.... Mormon stores from coast to coast where workers are paid, not in cash, but with all the food, medicines and fuel needed by their families; church workshops where Mormon women repair old clothing and make thousands of new garments...to create more jobs."[73]

SENATOR BERKELEY L. BUNKER APPOINTMENT
BRINGS MORE MEDIA ATTENTION

Two years later, in 1939, Bishop Harold Brinley was released, and in the fall Berkeley L. Bunker was called as the new bishop. His brother Bryan L. Bunker replaced Willard L. Jones as president of the Moapa Stake after Jones had presided over the stake for twenty-seven years.[74] At the time of Bryan L. Bunker's calling as stake president, the local press published an article titled "A Splendid Choice," noting, "Las Vegas and all of southern Nevada are genuinely interested in the L.D.S. church because it has always been a powerful factor for good ever since the first pioneers colonized this area.... The church plays an important part in the life and activities of the people here and is a strong influence in [the] upbuilding of the spiritual thought of all, whether members of the faith or not." The press further noted, "The appointment of Bryan L. Bunker to the Stake Presidency, then, is a matter of interest not only to members of the church itself, but to all those concerned with the advancement of religious thought in this area."[75]

Senator Berkeley Bunker. Special Collections & Archives,
University Libraries, University of Nevada, Las Vegas.

While Bryan Bunker was well known in southern Nevada, where he
served as stake president for thirteen years, his brother Berkeley Bunker
served just over a year as a local Latter-day Saint bishop. His ecclesiastical service came to a screeching halt when he was appointed as a US
senator from Nevada, replacing Senator Key Pittman, who passed away
shortly after he was elected. Though his term as Las Vegas Ward bishop
was short, Bishop Bunker presided over the local Saints with diligence
and compassion. During his brief service, he generously rendered welfare
aid to his congregation, including providing food to one destitute family
and overseeing the construction of a house for them made possible from
church funds.[76] What is even more noteworthy is that Bunker's senatorial
appointment helped bring the Church of Jesus Christ of Latter-day Saints
out of obscurity in both southern Nevada and the nation.[77]

SORROW AND STAMINA AMONG THE SAINTS

About the time the church began receiving more media prominence and making even deeper connections with the community, a second Las Vegas ward was created in North Las Vegas on March 3, 1940, due to substantial growth in the area.[78] The general dividing line for the two wards was Fremont Street, with the Las Vegas Ward comprising what was south of Fremont Street and the North Las Vegas Ward what was north of Fremont Street.[79] The division was announced to the public, noting that Johnson E. White would serve as the new bishop of the North Las Vegas Ward.[80] Later, scheduled meeting times for the two wards were printed in the local news.[81]

Several months later, a tragic event affected Saints in both wards. Faithful members of the North Las Vegas Ward, Thomas H. Myers, his wife, and four of their children perished in a propane gas explosion that obliterated their house. Local official ward records document this tragedy: "A veritable 'explosion of the atmosphere' supercharged with butane gas, which was being transferred from large tanks to small ones sent (15) fifteen persons to the hospital. Of the fifteen injured, eight (8) were members of the Thomas Myers family. The other nine were children who were children playing in the neighborhood. Seven persons lost their life." The official ward record further notes, "The blast occurred shortly at 11 o'clock, August 7, 1940, in the rear of the home of Thomas Myers.… The flames swept both ways from the gas tank like a monstrous flash, and then settled down to burn in the large tank, in the Myers home."[82]

The local *Las Vegas Age* press announced, "Terrible Tragedy Takes Seven," reporting that sixteen people were seriously burned in the explosion. The tragedy occurred "while Thomas H. Myers, distributor of Petrolane gas[,]…was transferring the liquified gas from the large tank in which it was transported into smaller tanks in an effort to salvage the fluid which was escaping through a defective valve."[83] Several days later the funeral was held, and Marion B. Earl remembered, "That was one of the saddest funerals I have ever attended. That funeral was the last joint meeting of the two wards. The Las Vegas Ward conducted the funeral service, and the North Las Vegas Ward the gravesite service."[84] The *Review-Journal* printed the headline "1,000 Pay Last Honor to Victims of Gas Explosion," noting the large crowd and that "floral wreaths and baskets were banked high at the altar."[85] The remaining Myers children and the local Saints moved forward as best they could.

By January 1941, Reed Whipple replaced Berkeley Bunker as bishop of the Las Vegas Ward and provided the same stable leadership Bunker had. The *Age* announced to the Vegas community, "Reed Whipple New Church Bishop," reporting that Whipple, a respectable citizen, was an employee of the local First National Bank.[86] During Whipple's years of service as bishop, the ward chapel was repaired and the kitchen remodeled.[87]

WORLD WAR II YEARS

Months before the bombing of Pearl Harbor, local Latter-day Saint Clyde Bunker entered military service. The North Las Vegas Ward bishopric discussed hosting a farewell party for Bunker and Glen Anderson, who had just joined the National Guard.[88] Other Saints soon followed as the war escalated. At this time Bishop White received a letter from the church presiding bishopric requesting reports of all men who had been drafted in the North Las Vegas Ward. White kindly encouraged local members to write letters to the servicemen, "so they may keep informed as to just what was going on in their ward at home."[89]

The following month, in a subsequent meeting, the bishopric discussed the challenge of contacting "all the Mormon Boys" in the local army camps. Bishop White suggested this task be turned over to the local stake missionaries, which was unanimously approved.[90] Three weeks later, "a committee was formed to contact l.d.s. boys now in army camps here to welcome them to our church services and entertainments."[91] Months later, the North Las Vegas Ward bishopric minutes note, "Discussed the soldiers that have come into our ward and ways of making them feel at home."[92] These same minutes record, "We talked about the boys from North Las Vegas Ward in the armed forces, in regard to keeping in touch with them."[93]

Latter-day Saint servicemen no doubt invited their military friends of varied faiths and cultures to local church social activities. This necessitated Bishop White requesting that friends of members who visited the church building refrain from smoking.[94] But activities and fellowship paid off, as the North Las Vegas Ward swelled to 520 members by November 1941.[95] Two weeks later, Pearl Harbor was bombed, and the two Las Vegas wards met to decide whether to hold church meetings in the afternoons instead of the evenings because of the possibility of required blackouts, due to wartime conditions.[96] The following year, in 1942, evidence demonstrates that Bishop White continued to welcome visitors to church meetings and "advised all young men entering the armed forces to attend church regardless of denomination."[97]

In 1941, the Army Air Corps Gunnery School, later known as Nellis Air Force Base (1950), was established just a dozen miles north of the Strip. Its location was selected for the same reason the trail, mail, and rail selected it: it was near the midway point between Los Angeles and Salt Lake City.[98] During the war years of 1941 to 1945, thousands of military personnel were enrolled in courses at the gunnery school.[99] The population continued to increase during this time, and residential construction soared in Las Vegas, North Las Vegas, and an area called Basic, which later became known as Henderson. Basic was home to Basic Magnesium, Inc. (BMI), a plant erected to support war efforts.[100] This was also an era when Latter-day Saints from the Las Vegas region and the state of Nevada joined other Americans in defending their country during World War II.[101] Other young church members from the Vegas locality made plans to study in Provo, Utah, at Brigham Young University.[102]

During this period of world conflict, Las Vegas grew rapidly and underwent many changes, while the church also expanded but retained its stable foundation. Latter-day Saint growth and activity in southern Nevada continued to flourish, as evidenced in the *Las Vegas Age*.[103] Additional ecclesiastical units were organized, including the Basic Branch, which was formed to serve the people working for BMI, supplier of much-needed magnesia. In this emerging industrial town, Moapa Stake president Bryan L. Bunker formed a church branch at the local Basic schoolhouse. The *Age* announced, "More than sixty members live in the vicinity and many families in Basic are interested [in the church]."[104]

During the war period and beyond, the local Saints worshiped at the St. George Temple, located about 120 miles north of Las Vegas. As early as 1940, mention is made of monthly temple excursions. Many church members traveled by bus as a group, and by the end of the 1950s, they were paying $3.50 for bus fare to the temple.[105] In addition, church members and families were assessed funds to pay for temple cottages made available to members needing accommodations when they visited the St. George Temple.[106] Las Vegas Latter-day Saint Mahlon Edwards remembered his parents staying in the cottages,[107] and Wendell Waite recalled that there were five to ten cottages for the Las Vegas Temple visitors located just south of the St. George Temple.[108]

Throughout this period, the press continually mentioned the Latter-day Saints' connection to the local community. For example, in 1941, a public event was held at the local church building, in which "Las Vegas enjoyed a delightful concert…by the 'Nevada Serenaders'" and "the Singing Mothers of the L.D.S. church under the direction of Mrs. Marion

Earl."[109] The general church minutes of the North Las Vegas Ward also noted that the Singing Mothers performed in their local sacrament meetings and sometimes even while ward members were partaking of the ordinance of the sacrament.[110]

Church apostle Elder Charles A. Callis of the Quorum of the Twelve visited Vegas in 1941 for a quarterly conference. He spoke to more than five hundred church members about the tremendous need for Latter-day Saints to be loyal and supportive of the US government during the wartime era.[111] Church dances were also held to help distract local citizens from their wartime worries.[112]

The war continued, and the Las Vegas Ward commemorated the centennial anniversary of their Relief Society, the church's women's organization, in 1942.[113] Local Latter-day Saint women were busy preserving their pioneer history during the war era. Just two months after the bombing of Pearl Harbor, in early 1942, the Daughters of the Utah Pioneers of Las Vegas met together for a convention. They felt fortunate to have the founder of this organization, Kate B. Carter, as the main speaker. Carter had traveled from Salt Lake City, the DUP headquarters, to participate. The press noted, "The subject of the meeting…was the early history of Las Vegas which is so full of romance."[114]

The Relief Society organization not only preserved history but was also known for its local charitable acts. The *Review-Journal* observed, "One of the finest examples of co-ordination by the 'haves' to benefit the 'have nots' is the L.D.S. church relief society. This organization has been developed to a high degree of efficiency through the years, until today it represents several industries in miniature, formed to produce the most for the least to benefit less fortunate members of the church."[115]

During this era, the church and its organizations continued to grow and progress. For instance, the *Review-Journal* headlined an article about a stake conference "Church Meeting Is Largest Ever Held in Vegas." Each of the four sessions of the Moapa Stake conference was devoted to the theme of "building the home," and a choir of sixty members of the Singing Mothers participated. An extra incentive to attend the gathering was the visit of general authority LeGrand Richards, the church's presiding bishop, who traveled to the event from Salt Lake City. Bishop Richards discussed the challenge of the war in relation to family life and encouraged local church members to cleave to their ideals. He stated, "There is an excuse for an adjournment of politics, but not of religion during the war era."[116]

When the war concluded, Bishop Reed Whipple of the Las Vegas Ward announced that the ward would host a homecoming party for those who had served in the military. From his ward alone, 103 men had served in the armed forces.[117] The following year, in 1946, the Las Vegas and North Las Vegas Wards combined to present an evening Christmas program at their shared church building, open to the public. A chorus of 80 members joined together to sing hymns from Handel's inspiring *Messiah*.[118]

POSTWAR GROWTH TO STAKEHOOD

After the war concluded, the Vegas Saints continued to be mentioned in the local news and still invited servicemen to activities.[119] Along with weekly church meeting times, other events were published. For example, in the spring of 1946, the Saints held a banquet attended by more than 250 members of the North Las Vegas Ward. Bishop Johnson E. White conducted the banquet and was assisted by the Relief Society. The banquet was followed by a ninety-minute program that included music and dances.[120] There is also evidence that the Saints were involved in social events hosted by the city. For example, in back-to-back years (1937 and 1938), the local Las Vegas Daughters of the Utah Pioneers camp won second prize for their floats, depicting Latter-day Saint transportation used for the trek west, in the annual Las Vegas rodeo festival known as the Helldorado Oldtimers' Parade.[121]

A decade later (1947), the Saints' float won first prize in the parade.[122] In 1950, the press again reported on the Latter-day Saints' participation in the parade with "hand carts used by the Mormon pioneers who pushed their way westward."[123] Several years later, honors were again bestowed for another float depicting the arrival of Latter-day Saint pioneer settlers, erected by local members of the Daughters of the Utah Pioneers.[124] During this era, the Saints continued to publicly advertise their Sunday church meeting times as well as midweek activities for children and youth in the afternoons and evenings.[125]

In 1947, the Charleston Ward was created from the First Ward, with Philip H. Empey called as bishop. The *Las Vegas Age* advertised the three Las Vegas wards side by side with their respective meeting times.[126] Thomas L. Adams replaced Reed Whipple as bishop of the Las Vegas Ward, and due to the abundant usage of the ward building, Adams undertook a major project to renovate it. However, the most important project during Adams's service as bishop occurred in the fall of 1948, when the first Las Vegas Latter-day Saint religious education seminary program was formed. By the dawn of the 1950s, the population of Las Vegas was near-ing 25,000,[127] and it was estimated that by 1948 there were about 2,560 people on the Latter-day Saint membership records,[128] a little more than 10 percent of the area population, with four operating chapels in the Vegas region. J. Harold Brinley, a former bishop and professional educator, was appointed as the first seminary teacher.[129] This southern Nevada educator touched many lives, and decades later a middle school in northwest Las Vegas was named after him.[130]

In late 1949, President David O. McKay dedicated a new church build-ing in Las Vegas, at the corner of Eighth and Linden.[131] This grand event was announced to the Vegas community in the *Review-Journal* two weeks before the building's dedication: "LDS to Dedicate New Ward Church." The article noted that the building commenced in February 1948, cost about $240,000 to construct, and would primarily serve members of the Las Vegas Second Ward; membership in the Vegas region had risen to 1,400 total members.[132] This same day, Florence Lee Jones, reporting for the *Review*, wrote that the new edifice was a "testimony to the faith of the Mormon people in the future of Las Vegas" and provided a detailed description of the building. Jones explained that the chapel could seat 350 people and that an additional 1,250 individuals could be seated in the cul-tural hall, which would also be used for recreational activities.[133]

Erecting meetinghouses brought the church members together both physically and socially. Former Nevada state senator (1984–2003) and life-time practicing Latter-day Saint Ray Rawson recalled that when church buildings were erected, "there was a camaraderie, there was a brother-hood. Men that were lawyers and doctors and schoolteachers worked right alongside the carpenters and the plumbers." Rawson remarked, "I remember those days very fondly. You developed good, close friend-ships, and they have lasted lifetimes.... There was a sense that we were invested.... Everybody was there to save the ship."[134]

The following year, the Las Vegas Third Ward was created, with Thomas Gay Myers as bishop.[135] Two years later, the Las Vegas Ward had more than 1,200 members, and Myers replaced Bryan L. Bunker as the president of the Moapa Stake. Meyers envisioned increasing growth in the Las Vegas area as a result of the erection of the atomic-bomb area at Frenchman Flat.[136] With the increase in ward members, Bishop Dan-ford B. Crane, who replaced Myers, wanted to make sure that every home in the First Ward was visited at least once annually. He and his counselors (Marion B. Earl and Lawrence Long) figured out a plan for doing so. They would visit twenty-five families each month; the bishop visited nine families, and each of his counselors visited eight. Earl described the care provided for each church member: after making a list of all ward members, they "took turns each month phoning each member on his birthday." He explained, "We held our bishopric meeting early each Sunday morning in the Bishop's home. At the end of each meeting we telephoned each Aaronic Priesthood boy who had an attendance problem and arranged to pick them up for Priesthood meeting." Earl also remembered, "We undertook a major overhaul of the building." In addition, he wrote, "Welfare was stressed. The ward had a vegetable garden on the welfare farm."[137]

Not only did the vegetables multiply, but two years later, the Latter-day Saint population had grown to the point where the formation of a new stake was under serious consideration. Since the first Las Vegas Branch was created in 1915, the Saints had fallen under the jurisdiction of the Moapa Stake, formed in 1912.[138] Andrew Jenson, church assistant historian, observed that by 1930, the Moapa Stake consisted of nine wards: "Alamo, Bunkerville, Las Vegas, Littlefield, Logandale, Mesquite, Overton, Panaca, and Saint Thomas…also two organized independent branches, viz.: Pioche and Caliente."[139] Two dozen years later, the Las Vegas Stake was about to be created.

By the spring of 1953, the Moapa Stake had a membership of more than seven thousand. The increase in the stake's population made it difficult to accommodate the large number of members attending the quarterly stake conferences. The *Las Vegas Review-Journal* caught wind of this and noted that because more than three hundred people had been turned away at each of the past three Moapa Stake quarterly conference meetings, local church officials had requested and received permission to use the telecasting equipment and skilled workers from KLAS-TV for broadcasting.[140]

CREATION OF THE LAS VEGAS STAKE (1954)
AND CENTENNIAL EVENTS

The following year, in 1954, the problem was at least temporarily solved when the creation of the Las Vegas Stake, formed from the old Moapa Stake, officially organized by Apostle Harold B. Lee, was announced at the Moapa Stake conference held in Overton, Nevada, on October 8. The new Moapa Stake, with Grant M. Bowler called as president, included the Logandale, Mesquite, Overton, and Bunkerville Wards. The wards that remained in the old Moapa Stake (renamed the Las Vegas Stake) were "Boulder City, Henderson, Henderson Second, Kingman, and Las

Vegas First, Second, Third, Fourth, Fifth and Sixth." President Thomas
Gay Myers and his counselors, Robert L. Bunker and Thomas L. Adams,
were retained as the presidency of the Las Vegas Stake.[141] At the time of
the division of the Moapa Stake, there were fifteen wards and a total stake
membership estimated at 8,895 people.[142]

The following month, church president David O. McKay dedicated
a new building for the Las Vegas Fifth and Sixth Wards of the Las Vegas
Stake.[143] President McKay spoke at length to the Vegas Saints. Among
other things, President McKay stated that he had recently watched the
film *Fabulous Las Vegas* and had wished "there had been flashed upon the
screen...one of the seven organized wards in Las Vegas." He also noted
that it had been a century since Brigham Young had sent church members to settle in the area in 1855.[144]

This same year, 1954, Brigham Young and the early Vegas pioneer
Saints were remembered at a centennial pageant titled *Destination Vegas
Valley*, performed locally at Cashman Field several times for the general
community. BYU professor Dr. L. B. Woodbury directed the production,
which featured a 150-voice choir and a cast of 200 local church members.[145] The pageant portrayed a century of Las Vegas history in "a three-
act panorama drama."[146]

The complementary centennial dance festival carried out the same
week was viewed by a crowd of about 4,000 who watched Latter-day Saint
teenagers gathered from southern Nevada, Arizona, and Utah perform at
Butcher's Memorial Field on the Las Vegas High School campus.[147] These
centennial events signaled that the church had finally come of age one
hundred years after the erection of the old Las Vegas Mormon Fort. The
festivities also seemed to bring the Saints closer to community members
who attended these events. Evidence suggests that such invitations and
kindness were reciprocated. In fact, Bishop Arden J. Sampson of the Las
Vegas Second Ward informed his congregation that the *Las Vegas Review-
Journal* had kindly donated $100 to their Sunday-school library.[148] During
the 1950s, baccalaureate services were held at Las Vegas High School, highlighting both the religious and the ecumenical nature of the community
as varied faiths united to celebrate the graduates.[149]

Throughout the 1950s, many young Las Vegas Latter-day Saints continued to serve full-time missions in the United States and around the
world. These missionaries wielded an influence for good beyond the
Vegas region and also brought back with them service experience that
often strengthened their own local communities.[150] As 1955 concluded,

Las Vegas Stake president Thomas Gay Myers announced the construction of four new Las Vegas church buildings, commencing the following year.[151] Myers reported that the Latter-day Saint population had increased to about 6,400 members, a 10 percent increase from the previous year.[152]

ADDITIONAL STAKES AND CONTINUED GROWTH

Growth continued, and about eight months after the announcement of the new church buildings, the Lake Mead Stake was organized (August 19, 1956), with headquarters in Henderson. James I. Gibson was called to preside over members in the new stake boundaries, which included the First, Second, and Third Wards of Henderson and the Boulder City Ward, which were taken from the Las Vegas Stake, and the Kingman Ward and the Needles Branch from the California Mission.[153] Several months later, Reed Whipple replaced Thomas Gay Myers as stake president when Myers moved to California.[154] By this time, the Las Vegas Stake Welfare Farm was flourishing,[155] and church general conference sessions were being broadcast to dozens of television and radio stations in nine western states (including Nevada).[156]

Four years later, the Las Vegas Stake, with more than 9,000 members, was again divided (November 6, 1960) to create the North Las Vegas Stake before a crowd of more than 3,000 Saints assembled at the Las Vegas Convention Center. Members sustained William Lorin Taylor as the North Las Vegas Stake president. He was set apart to that calling by Elder Howard W. Hunter of the Quorum of the Twelve Apostles. The new stake comprised the Las Vegas Second, Fourth, Seventh, Eighth, Tenth, Eleventh, and Thirteenth Wards, for a total population of 5,142 members.[157] During Taylor's service as stake president, a Spanish branch was also organized in the North Las Vegas Stake. Among its early leaders was a branch president named Compose.[158]

From 1954 to 1960, three new stakes were organized in Clark County. A century after 30 missionaries were sent to establish a settlement at Las Vegas, the population of the Saints in Clark County reached about 17,000.[159] With several stakes in the Las Vegas region, by the end of 1960, the Saints were firmly planted in the southern Nevada desert and would flourish for decades to come. Their stabilizing and refining influence would eventually spread throughout the Vegas Valley and metropolitan region as demonstrated by the thematic chapters that follow.

3

Ignorance, Education, and Cultural Refinement

Where there's a lot of darkness, there will be a lot of light.
They are always proportional.

—Nathan Noor, UNLV student and Las Vegas Institute of Religion graduate

INACCURATE OUTSIDE OPINION

Many people who live in Las Vegas feel that outsiders have an inaccurate view of the area. There is a misleading image that many visitors find titillating, and then again there is factual reality for those who actually live in the city.[1] For example, former Nevada state archivist Guy Louis Rocha explained that while he was a student at Syracuse University in New York, students asked him questions like, "You live in Las Vegas? You're kidding. People don't live there. They go there. Where did you live? In a hotel?" Rocha remarked, "The only image of my town was one long strip of casinos, hotels, and motels, and mobsters running amok."[2] Elaine Kennedy, a Latter-day Saint Vegas resident since 1952, recalled that when she and her husband traveled with groups of people, she was hesitant to say where she was from: "I never said we lived in Las Vegas, Nevada because the precept of people of Las Vegas, Nevada was the strip and what it all entailed.... And they didn't realize that families lived in Las Vegas, that we had beautiful churches, beautiful homes;…we didn't spend a lot of time in the casinos or on the strip, [but] we did enjoy…the entertainment."[3] Although Vegas locals are often disappointed by such ignorance, they understand the reputations relative to the Strip, and are also quick to point out that the Strip is not technically part of the city of Las Vegas.[4]

Claytee D. White, educator and resident of Vegas for decades, and not a member of the Latter-day Saint tradition, explained, "People outside of Las Vegas see us as these unusual people who chose to live in Sin City, and they mean it with every fiber of their being." Yet White, whose spiritual life comes first, has chosen to view Vegas through a different lens. She regards her city as a place "where we get to mingle with people from all over the world. People come here, and they don't just come for gaming and entertainment, but they come for all kinds of business.... You

Claytee D. White, 2020. Photo by Martin Andersen.

could be any place on earth, but Las Vegas has it all…. The opportunities are amazing." White also noted, "When communities are constructed, churches and schools are important; that's part of the contractor's, the architect's vision and mission to make sure that there are churches there that will represent the community…. Our spiritual life is so important."[5]

Stanley A. Steward echoed White's opinion: "When thinking of Las Vegas, images of gambling, casinos, showgirls, world-class entertainers, and dazzling lights come to mind. Few people associate religion with 'Sin City.' However, Las Vegas includes a vibrant religious community that has always existed on the shadow side of the neon."[6] Steward added, "The Las Vegas area has historically been home to myriad religious communities…. When the entertainment industry became the backbone of the local economy, it only enhanced the need for religious leaders and institutions to sustain the effort of maintaining a spiritual presence in Las Vegas."[7]

Matthew R. Davis observed, "To be sure, the mythical nature of Las Vegas as 'Sin City' colors the spiritual lives of its citizens like no other city in America."[8] He added, "For decades, Las Vegas has exploited its moniker 'Sin City,' and either deserved or not, this 'maverick' image has proven to be an irresistible lure for generations of tourists from the rest of America. The image of Babylon in the desert is almost biblical and conjures up certain other myths pervading the region, such as the West's lack of religious diversity, issues of cooperation between religious groups…and the degree to which religion has to mold itself to thrive in a place such as Las Vegas."[9] Davis argued, "Las Vegas provides an excellent arena in which to study religion as a theme in the West, specifically how it acted as a socializing and organizing force in laying much of the early Las Vegas infrastructure."[10] Nevada historian Eugene Moehring asserted that in Las Vegas, "as it had been in Nevada and the West, religion was an integrating force which glued the young community together. On a desert frontier beset by violence, hard drinking, and prostitution, religion provided a measure of social control."[11]

Carolyn Goodman, current mayor of Las Vegas, remembered that when she moved to Las Vegas, it was viewed "as Sin City, with all this negativism." Yet, she added, "now we have the non-profits and our faith-based leaders, all of them, working together.... The reality is, the good far outweighs any of the negatives, and it's just beautiful to see how the different faiths are united."[12]

Senator Ray Rawson stated, "My relatives in Utah couldn't believe a family could be raised in a place like Sin City. That just isn't Las Vegas. This is a wonderful place to raise a family. Our schools are good. Everything is out in the open, so kids have to make a choice in their lives very early, and it seems like that makes them stronger." Dr. Don Christensen related, "The overriding reason we came to Las Vegas was because my family would be better off raised here. Being in the mission field, where I was a minority, was more challenging. In the small [Utah] town where I grew up, you were Mormon or nothing—it was that dominant. That's not the most healthy environment; you don't have to stand up for your beliefs."[13]

North Las Vegas mayor John Lee remarked, "I think the moral values that the community has here is in large [part]because of the religious people that live in this valley here. And that the LDS church is arm-in-arm linked to every good organization."[14]

David Littlejohn, who led an academic team that interviewed Vegas residents, observed, "We heard over and over of the vitality of the churches in Las Vegas—in particular of 'my' church or synagogue, which for many recent residents...has become the single most important force in their lives. Although most of those who identified their denomination were main-stream Protestants, a sense also emerged that the presence of so many family-centered and morally disciplined Mormons and Catholics helped to create the strong sense of community they craved."[15]

University of Nevada, Las Vegas, history professor Mike Green observed, "You go right off the strip, you're in neighborhoods, apartments, houses. There are churches, schools, restaurants, everything you associate with any normal place in America; even if you don't think Las Vegas is a normal place, we're likely to have it. That's one of the things that tourists don't usually know, but if we as Las Vegans tell them, then we lose some of our attraction. They'd rather think this is this unique outpost. And Las Vegas was and is in certain ways an oasis in the desert. Well, the strip is the oasis within Las Vegas for the visitors."[16]

LAS VEGAS NEIGHBORHOODS AND LATTER-DAY SAINT INFLUENCE

Professor Rex J. Rowley, author of *Everyday Las Vegas*, stated, "Las Vegas is a uniquely instructive place to explore religious experience. Religious and nonreligious locals alike often claim that local life in this tourist town is 'separate' from the Strip and what it represents. This insider/outsider binary is, indeed, one of the city's defining characteristics."[17] Rowley further noted, "A number of institutional religions in the city…espouse principles that stand in opposition to temptation and allure promoted by Sin City, and many local believers strive to avoid the vices in their city." The Latter-day Saints are one of these groups who strives to avoid the unseemly and promotes virtue and goodness through their thirst for education and desire for refinement.[18] With reference to the Church of Jesus Christ of Latter-day Saints, Las Vegas local Yvonne Jacoby observed, "The Mormons set the standard for what church should be in Las Vegas," adding, "The Mormons are very family-oriented. Without their powerful voice a lot of people might think that topless dancing was an acceptable occupation."[19]

Interviews conducted with the public at large indicate that for many, first contact with Latter-day Saints often occurred in a neighborhood or local community setting. The Buckley family remembered, "[When] we came up here there were people with lots of kids. We thought they were all Catholic and then we found out about the Mormon Church. Yes. That's the first time we ever met Mormons here. I didn't know what a Mormon was. I lived in a Catholic ghetto all my life. It was wonderful— you couldn't bring me back to California today."[20] Joseph Thiriot, a Latter-day Saint who moved to Vegas in 1940 at age thirty-four, observed that there were only a few other churches in the area at the time, the Baptist, Methodist, and Catholic churches, and Thiriot did not let denomination keep him from community. In fact, he sang in a quartet "at all the churches."[21]

The sentiment of one for all and all for one is widely evidenced throughout the first half of the twentieth century, according to articles printed in the *Las Vegas Age* (1905–47). Particularly striking is that not one single piece of anti-Latter-day Saint literature appeared in this popular local newspaper during these early decades of the church's presence in Las Vegas.[22] Frank Cope, whose parents relocated to Las Vegas from Kansas in 1930 when he was only an infant, felt that during these early years problems between the Latter-day Saints and others did not exist. He remarked, "In fact, I don't recall any problems between anybody. In those days, everybody knew everybody, and everybody was friends." Cope recalled that the swimming pool at the "Old Mormon Fort" site on the Las Vegas Creek was a popular spot for community members at the time.[23] Others also remembered the swimming pool on this property, now a state historic park.[24] This venue would have attracted citizens and families from varied cultures and faiths and exposed them to the foundation of Latter-day Saint history in this desert region.

Las Vegas resident Mary Hausch recollected that the Latter-day Saints played a "pivotal part" in her neighborhood. She remembered that Rulon Earl, a devoted Latter-day Saint, was "a one-man neighborhood watch" and that the Earl family "were great neighbors."[25] Barbara G. Brents recalled, "The Mormons were very, very influential…and all of the kids in the neighborhood would join all kinds of activities at the church, whether they were Mormon or not. So it was a very influential church."[26] The church provided youth with an alternative to undesirable activity on the Strip, including educational classes on Sundays and primary activities during the week for ages three to eleven and activities for teenagers, known as "mutual."

While many outsiders deem growing up in Las Vegas undesirable, the locals seemed to love growing up in this metropolitan region. Although some areas in Vegas offer worldly ways, the disparity between the seemly and unseemly is evident throughout the city. Gloria Alger, a Latter-day Saint born and raised in Las Vegas, asserted that southern Nevada was a good place for families, as there was a stark contrast between the ways to live your life: "You don't have to go out behind the barn to see a drunk. You go down to Fremont Street and there he would be laying in the gutter. You wanted to see a prostitute, go down there and see a prostitute. You want to see any of this, it's right there." Alger continued, "In Las Vegas there's no people walking the fence.… Where in other parts of the country they go to church because it's a social thing to do whether you're living your religion or not.… I told my children…I don't want you to be a Mormon because I'm Mormon. I want you to be a Mormon because you want to be one."[27]

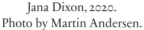

Jana Dixon, 2020.   Heidi Gresham Wixom, 2020.
Photo by Martin Andersen.   Photo by Martin Andersen.

Jana Dixon, Nevada's 2018 mother of the year[28] and a lifelong Las Vegas Latter-day Saint, has had many frank discussions with her five boys about what was proper and what was not. Dixon stated, "I think raising children in Las Vegas is very unique. It provides you an opportunity that they can see black and white…because it's so blatant in your face; I mean, behind every taxi cab or billboards, wherever you go, you're going to see things. So, there would be lots of discussions about…what's appropriate." She added, "I think living in Las Vegas and being a parent has its challenges.… In Las Vegas you're consciously aware because it is known as the Sin City effect, that you're constantly battling. You're walking out with your armor on every single day."[29]

One like-minded Latter-day Saint who battled to maintain a high ethical standard in her Spring Valley neighborhood is Heidi Gresham Wixom. During the midsummer of 1993, Wixom challenged a sexy business called "A Little Off the Top," an erotic salon where topless stylists cut hair wearing only alluring panties. The salon was placed strategically across the street from a car wash named "G-String Car Wash," which employed young women who were scantily clad in bikini tops and G-strings. The salon owners, wanting to capitalize on the setting, tried to push the envelope a bit further, meeting firm resistance from Wixom. "'Each community has a right to define community standards. That's what we are trying to do,' said the mother of five girls and the driving force behind the petition drive." To her credit, Wixom and two other women managed to gather four thousand signatures from their neighbors, which led to the salon's closure after several months of operation.[30] Heidi's husband, Mike, a local attorney, wrote the bill that Heidi presented to the legislature, and, amazingly, the bill passed in just three days, shutting down the salon and other businesses like it in their neighborhood. A new statute was also enacted to prohibit future similar business practices.[31]

Heidi's policy-changing experience prepared her for her next community campaign. About a dozen years after the salon's closure, she decided to do something about the lewd Vegas billboards. Wixom, then a middle school teacher and community activist, led another successful charge to eliminate offensive signage, stating, "We shouldn't be forced to throw a quarter on the floor when we pass a billboard and want our kids to divert their eyes.... People forget this is not just a tourist attraction. We are home to a million and a half people, where we live and drive and take our children."[32] Currently, Wixom is actively involved in an advocacy organization called "Power2Parent," whose mission is "to inform, organize, and mobilize parents and community members for the fundamental protection of parental rights."[33]

Other Latter-day Saints have also campaigned to keep a watch on local communities. One example is Sandra Heverly, a survivor of two automobile accidents involving a drunk driver. Heverly established the Mothers Against Drunk Drivers speakers bureau and personally delivered more than two hundred talks on drunk driving, earning her an award for her diligent efforts to protect the Las Vegas community.[34]

Another resident who made a difference at the dawn of the twenty-first century is Latter-day Saint attorney Ron Madson, who led a fight against casinos spreading into neighborhoods, likening "gambling [to] a tumor in Clark County's body politic." Madson was pictured in the *Review-Journal* leading a community group discussion at Hayes Elementary School, examining options for keeping casinos out of local Spring Valley neighborhoods.[35]

Joyce Haldeman, a Latter-day Saint who moved with her parents to Las Vegas in 1962, also took a stand against the encroachment of casinos into local neighborhoods. She remembered her discontent upon receiving the disturbing news that a casino was going to be built near where she lived. The Haldemans decided to have a family protest. Her ten-year-old son was quoted in a news clipping, stating that he thought the casino would be bad for their community.[36]

In the late 1970s, another controversial issue affected the Las Vegas community—the Equal Rights Amendment (ERA). Like Haldeman, a number of local Las Vegas Latter-day Saint women led their families in

Joyce Haldeman, 2020.
Photo by Martin Andersen.

taking a firm stand against the amendment; they believed in equal rights, but they did not agree with what they perceived was the amendment's hidden agenda. Resident Janet Brigham wrote, "In the final weeks before the [1978] election…concerned members campaigned as families…the day before the election. The family home evening activity for many was to walk throughout Las Vegas residential areas and distribute anti-ERA literature and discuss the amendment with interested citizens. The final statewide vote was two-to-one against the amendment."[37]

One catalytic Latter-day Saint woman who campaigned strongly against the ERA amendment was Judie Brailsford-Marcucci, who encouraged women such as Wixom and Haldeman to get involved in the community (both women actually worked for Brailsford-Marcucci's consulting firm for a time). Brailsford-Marcucci was also involved with another mover and shaker named Lisa Mayo-DeRiso, and together they took a firm stand on moral issues in the marketplace. This Latter-day Saint/Catholic team was a powerhouse. Mayo-DeRiso stated that since her family moved to Las Vegas in 1986, the Latter-day Saint community had been leading the way to address "quality of life" matters. She said, "Judie Brailsford and I took on the gaming companies with SB287, a neighborhood protection bill; we took on billboards, liquor stores and gaming near schools, cannabis dispensaries near churches and neighborhoods, and more. If not for the activism of the LDS community, our kids and neighborhoods would be negatively impacted by these noncompatible uses."[38] Brailsford-Marcucci remembered that she and Mayo-DeRiso realized that they had

Judie Brailsford-Marcucci, 2020.   Lisa Mayo-DeRiso, 2021.
Photo by Martin Andersen.   Photo by Martin Andersen.

to put a stop to large casinos bleeding into family communities. Together they gathered twelve thousand signatures and successfully kept casinos outside of residential areas.[39]

Latter-day Saints continue to stay involved in such issues and join hands with their neighbors who share the same values. Though they realize they cannot rest on previous efforts, their work has kept most neighborhoods in the Vegas Valley and outside the major hotel and casino district generally safe and family friendly.

SEMINARY: A RELIGIOUS EDUCATION PROGRAM FOR YOUTH

Seminary, a Latter-day Saint religious weekday education program, has also helped to keep Latter-day youth insulated from worldly influence. The seminary program reached Nevada in 1937, at the Moapa Valley High School in Overton, where 85 percent of the students were enrolled. Over time, other seminaries were instituted in various parts in the state, including Las Vegas.[40] The *Church News* reported on the opening of the first Las Vegas seminary, which opened in November 1948, under the direction of J. Harold Brinley, a member of the Moapa Stake presidency and the seminary principal. About fifty seminary students were attending class five days a week, beginning at 7:40 A.M., in the Church Welfare Building, located at Ninth and Clark.[41] During these early years, students were released from their studies at school so they could attend the hourlong seminary class.

In June 1954, Nevada's attorney general ruled against seminary classes being held during regular weekday school hours.[42] Therefore, in the fall of 1954, the Nevada state superintendent of schools informed the Moapa Stake that school funding would be withheld unless the seminaries ceased holding release-time classes during the school day. Notwithstanding this government stipulation, a modified seminary program was configured and continues in Nevada and in other states where release-time seminary is not permitted. Rather than attending seminary class during school hours, Latter-day Saint youth now attend weekday early-morning seminary classes. This program runs in conjunction with the school year throughout high school. Dedicated volunteer teachers serve without monetary compensation to tutor these seminary students.

In the early twenty-first century, release time for seminary was again discussed as a possibility. Ruth Johnson, a Latter-day Saint and former Clark County school board member, recalled that when parents were asked about the possibility of release time versus early-morning seminary, the general response was, "Actually we think the sacrifice that our kids are making to get [to the] early morning program is bringing blessings into their lives that they wouldn't otherwise get, and we don't want to do release time."[43] Ray Rawson said, "Seminary is indispensable,...and I've always sensed that the kids that had to get up and go to seminary at six in the morning valued that maybe more than some kids that just had it as part of their school."[44] Tami Hulse taught seminary in Vegas for more than a decade. She believed that seminary helped form a camaraderie among Latter-day Saint youth that carried over to campus and that it created a determined work ethic, providing students with a spiritual injection each day before they entered the school grounds.[45]

While serving as a Clark County elected official on the school board, Mary Beth Scow also influenced Henderson youth as a seminary teacher. Scow said, "I taught seminary for eight years, almost the entire time I was on the county commission [2010–17] and a couple of years while I was on the school board.... I would always tell my students what you're learning here is fortifying you to go over to that high school and to be able to face the things that you're gonna hear, the things that you're going to see." Scow further noted, "I had an experience one time with our principal at the high school because I was on the school board at the time, and...he said, 'I just have to say, sometimes I come out to watch your kids come over here because they are a light to my school, they come over here and they help. They help the teachers, they help in the classrooms; they are a light to my school.' So, I always tell my kids that they're a light. They can each be a light in everything they do."[46]

Tammy Stout, volunteer head supervisor for the Shadow Ridge seminary program in Las Vegas, echoed this sentiment, noting that the Latter-day Saint youth illuminated their high school environment: "[The administrators] have commented to us on numerous occasions that when our seminary is dismissed and as they are walking over…one block to the high school that they will get on their radio and say, 'Do you feel it?' and they will say, 'Yes, they're on their way.' Meaning, they can feel the spirit…of these seminary students as they walk onto that campus and the goodness that they are bringing to that high school."[47]

Mark Albright, an experienced local church leader, further commented on the influence these seminary students have on local high school campuses throughout the Las Vegas region. He recalled, "I've talked to a number of teachers and principals that have told me that when you look at the student body leaders, the student council leaders, the majority are LDS in the high schools…. They're the leaders on teams, the athletic teams, the clubs, student council. They're just a great influence."[48] Sheila Moulton, a veteran Clark County School District Parent-Teacher Association (PTA) member, said, "When I'd walk into Las Vegas High School or other high schools, there would be on their displays…the student leaders of the school, and many of them were LDS."[49] One seminary teacher mentioned that when a local high school football coach learned that two of her students on his freshman football team were Latter-day Saints, he promptly informed the boys that they would be giving the weekly team prayers before each football game during the season.[50]

North Las Vegas mayor John Lee remembered the Latter-day Saints at his high school: "They were usually in the smartest clubs. They were elected to things,…and the rest of us just kind of followed along;…we knew dang well…they should be the president of the school because they would do the job instead of just goofing around. So, they held a lot of position of leadership within our schools."[51] Former Nevada governor and US senator Richard Bryan, an Episcopalian, likewise remembered the Latter-day Saint influence at Las Vegas High School and even recalled the names of the leaders when he was a student in the 1950s:

> At the high school level, many of the leaders, class leaders, were members of the church, and many of them were class presidents and were student body presidents. I can only recite my experience at Las Vegas High School. Don Ashworth was elected student body president the year that I graduated my school. Billy Hardy was a

class president; Larry McDonald was a class president. Jan Stewart had been student body president a couple of years, the year before I was a senior. So there were a lot of class presidents that were members of the LDS church, and they were very well liked, and they were very popular.[52]

Joshua Popp, a recent high school graduate from Shadow Ridge High School, thought the Shadow Ridge seminary program and teachers were inspiring and influential. However, he also admitted that the early-morning seminary classes before school required a bit of effort, but the return was worth it as it provided "a great kick-start for the day for the kids and prepared them just going into the world."[53]

The high schools and seminaries appear to enjoy a synergistic relationship, as Latter-day Saint young people place a high value on education and frequently fill high school leadership positions.[54] Popp explained that during his high school experience, the student body president and the majority of the student council were Latter-day Saints and wielded a tremendous positive influence on the student body. Students were made to feel welcome and that they belonged. Many positive and uplifting messages flowed from these student leaders at Shadow Ridge High School.[55]

Paige Smith, a member of the Catholic Church who has taught at Shadow Ridge High School for seventeen years, stated, "When Shadow Ridge first opened, the church wasn't built yet, so they had seminary in my classroom.... I think having seminary before school was great for the kids because they get a little bit of that moral compass...that can kind of guide them through the day." When asked about the influence these Latter-day Saint seminary students have on the Shadow Ridge campus, Smith added, "I think they absolutely make a difference.... They're very involved in student council,...and they're kind of the driving force.... I think they provide good leadership.... I know that others look to them as leaders and as role models."[56]

Not surprisingly, parents of these Latter-day Saint youth are known to lend immense support to the local schools. One academic observed, "Mormons in Las Vegas strongly support local public schools. Actually, the relationship enjoyed between the Mormon seminary program and local high schools illustrates the influence of the Mormon Church on education in the area. When high school sites are designated, LDS leaders work to ensure that a chapel is nearby, usually within walking distance."[57]

Tom Tyler, a former Nevada area director for the Latter-day Saint Nevada Church Educational System, confirmed that local church leaders had church buildings built "right across the street from the high schools."[58]

Tammy Stout explained that early-morning seminary classes are held at a church stake center close to Shadow Ridge High School, beginning at 6:00 A.M. during the school week. She pointed out that 26 teachers teach nearly 430 students in nineteen classes, with the number of students enrolled increasing. When the volunteer teachers finish their classes, she added, "they head off and have their job and go home and wrangle their own children."[59]

Robin Dixon, who spent her youth in Las Vegas and later raised her children there, observed as a former seminary student and teacher that seminary is key to helping young people make good choices. She explained, "The city is a city of black and white; there is no gray.... That's why I think I stayed to raise my children here;…it made my children stronger.... Those seminary moments that you have with your teachers and the people that are with you…insulate you against the evil that you see at school and hear at school.... I truly believe that seminary is key to a foundation for any youth."[60]

Another Latter-day Saint mother, Cristi Bulloch, remarked that living in Las Vegas is kind of like the tale of two cities: "We have what everyone else knows Las Vegas is: gaming and all of what goes along with that, and then we have wholesome family life: soccer moms, PTA, lots of musical events and opportunities, a great community that offers a lot for families. It's been a great experience here raising children; the LDS kids seem to be the leaders in the school,…and I think they're influenced greatly by wonderful seminary teachers."[61] Bulloch reported that her two daughters didn't mind missing school when sick, but they begged to attend seminary on those days. She also observed that seminary has been instrumental in missionary efforts and fellowshipping. Many friends of the non-Latter-day Saint kids attend various church activities as well as seminary classes. Friendships have multiplied, and considerable conversions have resulted.[62]

David Dixon, sixty-year resident of Vegas, reflected on parenting five boys in this region:

> Raising a family in Las Vegas,…you have such opposition that you face readily on a regular basis. You see it every single day, and so you have to be proactive when you are trying to teach and train your

Cristi Bulloch, 2020.   David Dixon, 2020.
Photo by Martin Andersen.   Photo by Martin Andersen.

children on what is right and what is wrong because things are so prevalent and obvious in front of your eyes on a daily basis as to what you might see and hear. And so, from that aspect, it gives you an opportunity to really teach the gospel because you can frame things in such a way that it's easy to make these comparisons.

With reference to the church seminary program, Dixon added, "There are several of these high schools that are very near the chapels where the kids attend seminary, and so at 6:45 in the morning there's this army of 350 or so LDS students that are walking to the high school, and then many of the instructors and teachers and principals and leaders of the local school are very impressed that you have this army of righteous, good, bright kids that are coming to school. They're serious about their education."[63]

Former Clark County School Board member Ruth Johnson reported that while serving on the board (1997–2008), and at the same time serving in a stake church assignment, she interviewed several principals in the Las Vegas region. She wanted to know how they believed Latter-day Saint youth had contributed to their high school campuses. Johnson described their experience: "Every single one of them said, without a doubt,…'We would not be the school that we are without our LDS population. Those kids are strong, they know what they stand for, they have values, they look out for other people, they serve in community involvement and in service projects and service clubs. They're the leaders on our sports teams.… They are strong, they are dedicated, their families are committed to the school, and we would not be the same without them.'"[64]

Johnson reported that several principals stated, "Unequivocally they would not have the school leadership that they had in the student body presidency. They would not have the service projects and service opportunities without the LDS kids. And they would not have had the leadership and the sportsmanlike conduct taught by example without the LDS kids."[65]

Eileen Ludwig, a veteran volunteer seminary teacher for three decades (1970–2000), was an eyewitness to the fruits of the seminary program. Reminiscing about the students she taught, Ludwig remarked, "There are now firemen, policemen, lawyers, teachers, nurses, building contractors, auto mechanics, plumbers, air conditioning technicians, doctors, carpenters, musicians, and many more professions who have passed through my classroom. More importantly, there are stake presidency members, bishops and bishopric members, gospel doctrine teachers, Scout leaders, Primary presidents, Relief Society presidents, and many, many, missionaries who were in my classes."[66]

Mark Hutchison, former lieutenant governor of Nevada (2015–19), who attended seminary in his youth, taught in the program for eight years, and also witnessed six of his own children participate in seminary, stated, "I think seminary…insulates those of us who grew up here and my children and continues to insulate the youth of today in Las Vegas in being able to fellowship with like-minded saints and youth…. Every morning they get up and they have like-minded Saints and this energy of righteous youth that prepares them then as they go into their high schools and some very challenging circumstances."[67]

Latter-day Saint Kyle Stevens, account representative at Brady Industries, spoke of the distinction of these church youth who rise above such trying conditions: "Raising your children in Las Vegas, there is a contrast to some extent. We think about it. Sometimes it's profound…. But the young people that attend these seminaries…are as fine a young people as you'll see, as you'll come across in the church without a question. We've raised really fine young people, missionary young men [and] young women in this community."[68]

Community expectations trail Latter-day Saints, both young and old. William "Will" Stoddard, influential Latter-day Saint leader and local attorney, said, "People in Las Vegas know who members of The Church of Jesus Christ of Latter-day Saints are, and they expect them to behave as such…. People know the church is strong here. They expect people to live their religion, and they do…. My sense is that if you're trying to figure out whether you can raise a good family in Las Vegas, it may be that you can raise one…easier in Las Vegas than you can in other places just because of what people expect of you."[69]

Expectations were exceeded for one Wildcats baseball player at Las Vegas High School. Bryce Harper, who took advantage of seminary while attending high school, is now playing for the Philadelphia Phillies and is in his third year of a thirteen-year contract worth $330 million. At the young age of sixteen, Harper was featured on the cover of *Sports Illustrated* (May 2009) with the headline "Baseball's Chosen One." Among other things, it is now known to the general public that Harper attended Latter-day Saint "religious education classes nearly every morning." This early-morning seminary instruction certainly helped solidify praiseworthy principles that have remained with him to the present.[70]

Another Latter-day Saint Vegas athlete and former seminary student featured in *Sports Illustrated* is Aaron Fotheringham. This talented young man, disabled from spina bifida since birth, is known internationally for his acrobatic performances, including the incredible act of doing a back-flip in his wheelchair. This fearless feat has etched his name in the *Guinness Book of World Records.* Aaron was also given the key to the city of Las Vegas and a medal of honor for his accomplishments.[71]

INSTITUTE: A RELIGIOUS EDUCATION PROGRAM FOR YOUNG ADULTS

Post–high school Latter-day Saint young adults enjoy instruction equivalent to the seminary program. Many universities and colleges throughout the country offer Latter-day Saint Institutes of Religion near their campuses. The Las Vegas Nevada Institute of Religion is within a stone's throw of the UNLV campus. One author noted, "The Church approved the purchase of a building site for an institute…near the Nevada Southern University of Las Vegas Nevada [now UNLV] on November 17, 1958."[72]

Decades later, the institute has blossomed. David Rowberry, an institute director from 1993 to 2006, remembered, "We were excited when we were asked to come to Las Vegas to direct the institute program.… But we came here with a question in our heart: Could you raise kids in Las Vegas?…This has become our home. We have seen marvelous, marvelous Saints here, and as we came to the institute, we found marvelous young people.… This is a booming Latter-day Saint community."[73]

Within a half-dozen years of Rowberry's arrival, he was instrumental in recruiting a thousand students to enroll in institute classes in various pockets of the Las Vegas Valley. Rowberry was impressed with the influence the Latter-day Saint and non-Latter-day Saint young adults were having on the community and vividly remembered former UNLV president Kenny Guinn[74] asking him, "Would you train the student body officers at UNLV using your institute council?…I know these young people, we need that." Rowberry and his institute council happily consented and provided proactive leadership training for the UNLV student body leadership.[75]

Another example of outsiders noticing the Latter-day Saint young adult students occurred while bricklayers were constructing part of a UNLV campus dorm building just across the street from the institute. Rowberry explained that the workmen would see the students entering the institute building and exiting with what they referred to as a glow. They came into the institute to ask Rowberry why. The result was that one of the bricklayers later joined the church and the other became a great friend.[76]

The current institute director, Bruce W. Hansen, began teaching seminary in Las Vegas in 1983 and a decade later was hired to instruct students at the institute. He has been teaching institute ever since. Hansen maintains that the institute is a Latter-day Saint missionary's dream come true:

> The institute building is at a great location; we're right at the heart of UNLV, and although this is private property, we own it. We have the chance to share the gospel by example and word on a regular basis. We get many people. Today we had a booth out front, we had a ping pong table, cornhole platform, and a big sign that says, "Download the Book of Mormon and get a free ice cream." We probably had half a dozen students come in here for the first time, have a good experience, ask more about the church, and hopefully our missionaries will have a chance to share the gospel with them in greater detail.[77]

Hansen explained that the institute's spiritual environment and the friendships visitors develop with the young adult Latter-day Saints have led to many baptisms. Regarding the well-known city slogan "What happens in Vegas, stays in Vegas," Hansen commented, "Well, one thing that doesn't stay here is the gospel of Jesus Christ. I have students who have served [missions] all over the world; they come back even [spiritually] stronger, they invite their friends [to institute], and we get convert baptisms on a regular basis."[78]

One of those young adult converts is Ingrid Zarate, a Latina from Mexico. Both as a seminary student and as an institute student, she drew strength from these religious programs and her fellow Latter-day Saint peers. Zarate observed:

> There is a difference in standards...The Church of Jesus Christ of Latter-day Saints uphold.... Not only did they uphold their academic standards but also their moral standards, and I saw that through the way in which they lived.... [I wondered], why are you waking up at 6 A.M. to do that [seminary class]? But when they share the benefit of that and when you see the joy that they have because they do that, it makes you realize that maybe you're the one, maybe you should also make that sacrifice, which, in fact, is a disguised blessing.[79]

Zarate further explained, "Living here...in Las Vegas, which is Sin City, you see a difference of culture all the time.... There are some people who don't dress modestly or who live with different standards,...so having the institute is definitely, like, a safe place that's cultivated within the university.... Not just us members realize that, but...all of our non-member friends, they come here because this is, like, a safe place for everybody."[80]

Nathan Noor, raised in a small town in northern Utah and a recent UNLV graduate, likewise benefited from the institute program. Noor previously served as president of the Latter-day Saint Student Association (LDSSA) and contributed to the UNLV campus activities and also helped make the student body aware of the Latter-day Saint presence via the institute. Noor, who thoroughly enjoyed his experience as a UNLV student and institute graduate, commented on the cultural environment of Las Vegas as a whole and wisely observed, "Where there's a lot of darkness, there will be a lot of light. They are always proportional,...and I feel that despite...the readily available temptations on the Strip, the Church gave me ample opportunities outside of those worldly pursuits to let me enjoy my life.... It's not about location, it's about intention, and regardless of whether you live in Las Vegas...or anywhere else, there will always be temptation, there will always be bad things available."[81]

IMPACT OF LATTER-DAY SAINTS ON SECULAR EDUCATION

Local Latter-day journalist and editor Charlie Zobell maintains that church members have been influencing education in Las Vegas since the legalization of gambling in 1931. He reasoned that the focus during the 1930s was on "legalized casinos,...and [citizens] could care less about schools.... So, who took care of that? It was the Mormons." They chose to shape education as both teachers and administrators and make sure their schools were built and received appropriate funding.[82]

For generations the general community has admired Latter-day Saint youth. Twelve-year-old Charlotte Conti was impressed with church members after moving from California to Las Vegas with her family in 1953. Looking back to her high school days a quarter of a century later, Conti remembered, "The Mormon people were very active in our school and in our class.... They were usually very musical or very outgoing." She added, "They were very active. The young people in the Mormon Church always seemed to have something to do.... And when your parents are both working, which mine had to when we first moved here, it was kind of a relief to have something there for me,...and I found...there were many things that I liked about their church a lot." Conti observed, "Most of your young leaders in your junior highs...come from very good Mormon families. They're taught from [church] Primary class on to be leaders, and they are good leaders.... Look right now down in your City Hall; look at all the Mormon people that are in there. Look at your attorneys that are Mormons;...there are a lot of them."[83]

This positive influence on the community has continued to the present day. One author noted that because local youth are enticed by high-paying jobs in the gaming industry, "Las Vegas and Nevada have the highest dropout rates in the nation. They have the lowest percentage of students going to college." By contrast, Latter-day Saints are taught to obtain as much education as possible and to avoid gambling: "Bucking the local trends, Mormon families account for a disproportionate percentage of college-bound scholars in Las Vegas. It is not unusual for half of a high school's valedictorians to be LDS, even though Mormons may account for less than 10 percent of the student body."[84]

Elaine Kennedy remarked, "When you were a Mormon growing up in Las Vegas, you were a Mormon, you were not a Jack Mormon.[85] You either followed what we believed and what we did, or you didn't. And the kids grew up with Mormon friends and were very active in school activities, being president of their high schools and different things like that. And so, the kids have always been very active in the church,...[and] I think the Mormons have always been highly respected."[86]

One Las Vegas resident wrote, "Community involvement, volunteerism, and organization are all tenets of the Mormon faith and directly impact how Mormons think the educational system in Las Vegas should be run.... The impact of Mormons on the education system in Las Vegas is widespread and notable."[87] Latter-day Saint parents are keenly involved with their children's education, especially the mothers. Cristi Bulloch observed, "The LDS women in the community have really gotten into the schools and worked, and I've seen it time and time again where somebody's the PTA president or the PTO [Parent-Teacher Organization] president. We've had a number of women that have been on the…Clark County school board and have really supported children in our community and done great things."[88]

One of these women is Joyce Haldeman. Haldeman recalled the opportunity she had in the early 1980s to make a difference while serving as a local PTA president. It was in vogue nationwide to have comprehensive health-care clinics in the schools. Haldeman commented, "[This] meant that they would provide access to abortions and birth control to children on campus. So, of course, the LDS community was very much opposed to that, and I was one of the people who was able to reach a compromise that was adopted by the PTA when they were developing their legislative platform. So we were able to do things like that; whereas the community was going in one direction, we could help maneuver it into a better compromise as we went forward." When her children were older, Haldeman was employed by the Clark County School District, which at the time was the fifth-largest school district in the United States. She enjoyed a good reputation for getting bond campaigns passed.[89]

Another mover and shaker in the school system was the previously mentioned Mary Beth Scow, former Clark County commissioner (2010– 17) and Nevada's mother of the year in 2009.[90] Scow was also a member of the Board of Trustees for the Clark County School District for three terms (a dozen years) before joining the Clark County Commission. During her years on the school board, Scow was known as one of the three "Mormon Moms." Reflecting back on this period, she recalled that Latter-day Saint mothers took an active interest in their children's education and made sure they were aware of what was going on in the classrooms and were apprised of school board policies so they could ensure that all children were treated fairly and that worldly practices did not creep into the curriculum. Scow was no exception.

While serving in the PTA, Scow realized that policies affecting the system were made on the school board level, which she later joined. Scow remembered, "When I was on the school board there were three of us that were members of the church, and we were known as the Mormon Moms, and a lot of times people would criticize us because we were just moms;

we had never been career women. We were all college educated, but none had ever had a real career, and so it was supposed to be a derisive term, the Mormon moms on the school board, and we knew full well about it."[91]

The two other "Mormon Moms" serving on the school board with Scow were Ruth Johnson and Sheila Moulton.[92] Johnson described how the three of them got the nickname "M&MS," an acronym for the Mormon Moms. Sheila Moulton brought a jar of M&MS to a PTA meeting and explained that just as each piece of chocolate had a different color, school-children had varied ethnic backgrounds and different needs begging to be met. Johnson said that after that presentation, the name "M&M's" stuck, which the three women happily embraced. Johnson affirmed, "We wanted to be those mothers who were known for standing for values, for caring for families, for making it possible for children to succeed and stay focused,…no matter what."[93]

In recalling the influence the Church of Jesus Christ of Latter-day Saints has had on secular education, former Nevada senator Harry Reid observed, "We have a significant number of schools that are named after teachers, LDS teachers and administrators."[94] Former Nevada senator Richard Bryan added, "I could go on and on and on about members of the church that have schools named after them in the community;…they had a very big impact."[95]

In fact, the names of thirty-five Latter-day Saint educators are etched on school buildings across the Clark County School District in the Vegas region.[96] Yet, Wendell Waite, a ninety-year-old Saint who spent his career as a Las Vegas educator, maintains that although the church in Vegas had "a big influence on education," unfortunately, in his estimation, it has diminished in recent years. Waite attributes this waning in large part to Californians, who, wanting to escape higher taxes, have migrated to southern Nevada and have brought with them their worldly philosophies and influence.[97] Church member Jeanette Clark, who pushed for a high standard of sex education in the local public school system, added, "With the growth in the community, the people coming in don't have the same values we have."[98]

ZION'S YOUTH SYMPHONY AND CHORUS

Despite the influx of more liberal influences, an inspiring community program is on the rise and is already having a tremendous positive educational and culturally refining influence. Zion's Youth Symphony and Chorus, cofounded by Latter-day Saints Terilyn Taylor and Jenny Jackson in 2003, is an innovative program for high school students between the

Zion's Youth Symphony & Chorus, Smith Center, 2019.
Courtesy of Elise Noorda.

ages of fourteen and eighteen years old. Taylor and Jackson, both violin teachers from Utah, moved to Las Vegas in the early 1990s and decided to launch a musical group titled the Deseret Strings, primarily for teenagers who were at a "critical transition" in their musical development. Later, Jeremy Woolstenhulme joined their team, and together they created a youth symphony and chorus.

Eventually, the prestigious Smith Center became the venue for their biannual concerts to audiences of four thousand, whom they inspire and leave spellbound. Taylor said that when they perform, their intent is to disseminate light and goodness by keeping the gospel of Jesus Christ their focus, making them distinct from other high school orchestras.[99]

Cofounder Jenny Jackson described a pivotal moment in the organization's early days, prior to Zion's Youth Symphony and Chorus. The Deseret Strings were playing at a Christmas fireside concert for the local temple workers. The featured speaker, Latter-day Saint Apostle Richard G. Scott, tapped Jackson on the shoulder after the performance and meeting concluded. Scott implored, "Sister Jackson, the youth of Las Vegas and the community of Las Vegas need this group. Please keep it going." After receiving this brief but meaningful counsel from a church general authority, Jackson said, "We felt like that was a real direction from Heavenly Father that we really needed to do something [more] with this." The rest is history.

Over time, the musically gifted Skouson brothers became integral to Zion's Youth Symphony and Chorus, composed of about three hundred young people. David Skouson directed the orchestra, and Jeffrey Skouson led the choir.[100] Jackson explained their harmony and mutual passion: "Having two conductors for Zion's Youth Symphony and Chorus has been really an interesting experience.... They kind of breathe the same air,...and you can see how they move alike.... They're separated by distance on the stage, they have monitors to see each other, but you can just see how their arms are in sync with each other, I mean, they're feeling it. It's been wonderful!"[101]

Jackson recognizes how the Skouson brothers have helped these young Latter-day Saint musicians and choir members realize their potential. Jackson recalled David Skouson imploring the orchestra to "bring your A game, your best work, your best concentration, put your cellphones away and leave the world outside and come in here and have a spiritual experience.... You're the salt of the earth."[102]

Wendy Randall, a gifted artistic designer who has worked behind the scenes with the Skouson brothers on their productions, stated, "Las Vegas is the entertainment capital of the world, and I've lived here my entire life. I've seen...many people in our city using their God-given talents to advance things that are opposed to God. Zion's youth uses God-given talents to advance God and goodness and light and beauty and all of the wonderful things that the Lord has blessed us with."[103]

David Skouson described how wonderful it is to see these young people blossom, even those within his own household: "You can't be involved in something like this and not have it affect you personally, and...it affects my family too. My children, all three of my children have gone through this program,...and they've all been section leaders and have been integral in this group, and I watch how that pushes and affects them and gives them strength."[104]

Jeffrey Skouson stressed that the unique nature of the organization is its focus on service. Speaking of the talented youth musicians, he explained, "They get a chance to give something back to the community through this medium of music.... They're doing things that are probably a little beyond the typical reach of a fourteen-year-old. And we love that. And our motto has always been...'We can do hard things.'...And they know that now. They've proven that to us."[105]

These young people have also demonstrated that despite these challenging times, they can do hard things, generating hope and inspiration. Many of these performers also spend their early mornings in Latter-day Saint seminary classes across southern Nevada in addition to the many hours they devote to their academic studies and extracurricular activities.

Evidence indicates that their sacrifices and concerted efforts have yielded fruit. Elise Noorda, executive director of Zion's Youth Symphony and Chorus, said, "I've seen and heard over and over stories about people that bring their friends, their neighbors;…they trust what Zion's Youth does, and so more and more they bring their friends,…and we've heard…about people that have been touched, people that have been baptized, people that just understand more deeply that we are truly disciples of the Lord Jesus Christ, and maybe [negative] things that they've heard or understood before just can't be true."[106]

4

Business and Entertainment

I think the Mormons have the most integrity
of any group in the country.

—Howard Hughes

Latter-day Saints positively benefited from the economic development of southern Nevada, and they gave back to local businesses and the entertainment industry. Mercantiles such as the early-twentieth-century Clark Forwarding Company benefited faithful church members, and, in return, these employees provided honest work, shared the gospel, and influenced the moral integrity of the business. Saints also found work with the early railroad companies, surveying and laying track. A prominent stimulus for the economy was launched in 1931, when the gaming industry became legalized. Although it would take time for gaming to fully mature, other immediate gainful opportunities developed simultaneously.

HOOVER DAM CONCEPTION AND EMPLOYMENT

The same year that gaming was legalized, in 1931, Latter-day Saint W. (William) H. Wattis signed a major contract to construct the Boulder Dam, later renamed the Hoover Dam.[1] Wattis was a native of Utah and co-owner with his brother of Utah Construction. There was no doubt Wattis was also a dyed-in-the-wool Latter-day Saint with deep roots. His grandfather and family immigrated to Nauvoo, Illinois, in 1841 after being taught and converted by Apostle Wilford Woodruff.[2] Wattis became well connected with other church general authorities, playing golf with Charles W. Nibley, Reed Smoot, and even President Heber J. Grant.[3]

In order to construct this behemoth dam, William Wattis led the effort in forming a consortium called Six Companies, which agreed to erect the dam with a bid of $48.9 million.[4] Tragically, just six months after the contractual deal was in place, Wattis, president of Six Companies, succumbed to cancer, and Marriner S. Eccles, also with a long generational church heritage, took over to preside over Utah Construction.[5] Four years later, the Hoover Dam was completed, and Six Companies made a profit of more than $10 million, or about 21 percent of their bidding price.[6]

Due to the necessity of housing thousands of men who would be working on the dam project, the federal government erected Boulder City, located about twenty-five miles southeast of Las Vegas. With a population of about five thousand, Boulder City was promoted as a model town, a "moral Utopia," by the Department of the Interior. This instant city offered dam employees housing and medical benefits as well as recreational and shopping accommodations.[7]

One author recognized the special lure and attraction the city held for Latter-day Saints after gaming was legalized throughout the state of Nevada: "As a federally run town, Boulder City offered one distinct advantage for the Saints: Gambling was forbidden," adding, "To this day, it remains the only city in Nevada without a single slot machine."[8] The unprecedented employment drought due to the woeful era of economic depression brought Latter-day Saint families to gaming-free Boulder City in the early 1930s for work. After the dam was completed, many of these families remained in their adopted city, and eventually the number of Latter-day Saints swelled. To make church services more convenient to local members, the Boulder City Branch of the Las Vegas Ward was formed on April 24, 1932. Local church leaders prioritized finding a suitable location for the Saints to meet. One local newspaper announced that the Boulder Branch members were meeting at the Park funeral parlor.[9] Six weeks later, news was published that more than thirty Latter-day Saint women from the Church Relief Society organization met in Boulder.[10]

With the first church building in Las Vegas unoccupied, due to the erection of another more spacious building, the Boulder City Branch presidency made a visit to Vegas the following month to see if they could purchase that first framed meetinghouse. At a cost of $1,750, the Las Vegas church building was moved in pieces and reassembled in Boulder City. However, the building was not dedicated until nearly two years later, when the total cost of the meeting house was paid in full. Church president Heber J. Grant dedicated the Boulder City church building on March 25, 1934, and spoke at several additional meetings, along with Apostle John A. Widtsoe, to nearly two hundred Saints.[11]

During the early years of the 1930s, some Latter-day Saints traveled by train or automobile from the city of Las Vegas and other small towns to work at the dam. One such church member was John Laurence Stapley, who lived halfway between Las Vegas and Boulder City at the time.[12] Mark Dixon, grandson of Stapley, said, "My mother was born here in 1932. Her father, John Laurence Stapley, ... came here as they began construction on the dam looking for a job. You couldn't get a job with Six

LDS Boulder City Meetinghouse dedication, 1934.
Courtesy of S. Mahlon Edwards.

Companies…unless you knew somebody. He had a cousin named Richards who was working here who got him hired. He started out on the cliffs in Black Canyon knocking rocks off, finished as a concrete foreman."[13]

Another Latter-day Saint who worked on the dam was Glenn Waite, who drove a Model-A Ford about twenty-five miles back and forth from Las Vegas to the work site each day. Waite was also employed in concrete work. His son Wendell remembered his father's work mask being covered in cement dust when he returned home each day.[14] Little did John Stapley and Glenn Waite know that a half century later, their grandchildren (Jana Waite and David Dixon) would cement their relationship in marriage and raise a big family in Las Vegas. Waite, Jana's grandfather, gave a detailed account of his job description, workweek, and pay for the three years he worked on the dam: "The job I had at the dam was helping unload cement. They ran three shifts, and they paid us $6 per day. This was big money at that time. We worked 8 hours per day, 7 days a week (no overtime pay, just $6 a day)…. It was hard work. There were four men to a shift. The men would unload ten train car loads of cement in 8 hours…. We would unload 30 carloads a day. So, you can see how much cement went into the dam every 24 hours, day in and day out."[15]

After the dam's completion, some stalwart Saints launched business ventures in Las Vegas. For example, Chauncey Riddle's family closed their touring company and opened a local taxi business known as "Yellow Cabs."[16] M. J. Christensen opened what became a successful family jewelry business on Fremont Street.[17] These family businesses provided some balance to the up-and-coming gaming industry, and their integrity did not go unnoticed by others not of their faith.

During the mid-twentieth century, Eric Christensen commented on what life was like for his influential family and other church members: "The early Saints from my grandpa and my dad's era were integral to the growth of Las Vegas. My grandpa was president of the Chamber of Commerce.... My dad was part of scouting forever, and again my uncles were heavily involved in politics and the judicial system here in town." Christensen added, "It was a small community, tight-knit, sweet people.... Vegas was starting to be a boom town, as compared to Utah where they were from.... Vegas had the Air Force base, and they had the dam...and so it was a growing place. The railroad was becoming a key factor in its growth, and then of course the gaming industry was ramping up at the time too."[18]

HOWARD HUGHES AND THE "MORMON MAFIA"

Howard Hughes represents perhaps the most famous example of the link between the gaming business and Latter-day Saints. Hughes is often remembered as the eccentric who spent several years holed up in the City of Lights (1966–70). Stanley Steward, author of *Where Sin Abounds: A Religious History of Las Vegas*, observed, "Howard Hughes' posture towards Mormons exemplified the attitude of other local business leaders. He sought out the Mormon employees because he believed they could be trusted. There existed a dialectical relationship between Sin City and Mormonism. The Mormons provided integrity, skill, and a work ethic that was valuable in the burgeoning tourism industry, and the city's strong economy provided lucrative financial opportunities for many Mormon residents."[19]

Noah Dietrich, who worked for Hughes for three decades, recalled Hughes telling him, "I think the Mormons have the most integrity of any group in the country. They take care of their own people, and they won't accept help from charity or the government. And I like they don't drink liquor. You can trust them."[20]

It was common knowledge that Hughes had employed Latter-day Saints as personal aides because of their honesty and work ethic. An article in the *Church News* titled "Howard Hughes Picks Mormons for

Efficiency" noted, "Film and aviation tycoon Howard Hughes has sur-
rounded himself with 'a group of young assistants almost all of them Mormons,' says the current issue of Look Magazine. An active Mormon…tends
to be a man of integrity who devotes himself slavishly to his job. He nei-
ther drinks, smokes, nor gambles. 'This is exactly what Hughes requires
amid the temptations of Las Vegas…. These assistants work 24 hours a
day.'…Their job is to do whatever Hughes tells them to do."[21]

Latter-day Saint Frank William "Bill" Gay is credited for pulling
together a small group of fellow Saints employed by Hughes, referred to
with tongue in cheek as the "Mormon Mafia."[22] Gay fell in with Hughes
when the billionaire needed a full-time assistant who could supervise
his office in Hollywood on Romaine Street and also travel with him as
a personal assistant. His secretary brought Gay to Hughes's attention.[23]
One Hughes biography summarized the circumstances as follows: "Gay,
a lanky twenty-seven-year-old, had taken the…job to earn money to return
to college…. While he and his wife were visiting parents in Los Angeles
in the summer of 1947, Gay learned of the Romaine Street job [in Holly-
wood] from his wife's uncle, Wendell Thaine, a close friend of Nadine
Henley's [Hughes's private secretary]…. That fall he worked with her….
Polite, efficient, and hard-working, Gay quickly earned Miss Henley's
respect…. Gay would be ideally suited for the job, she told Hughes."[24]

Gay worked for Hughes for more than three decades (1947–78), which
included the Las Vegas years (1966–70) wherein expensive purchases were
made.[25] During his years in Vegas, Hughes bought the North Las Vegas
airport as well as the following casinos: Castaways, Desert Inn, New Frontier, the Sands, and the Silver Slipper on the Strip, as well as Harold's Club
in Reno. By the mid-1970s, it was estimated that 17 percent of Nevada's
gambling assets came from these Hughes-owned casinos.[26]

E. PARRY THOMAS

One catalytic Latter-day Saint banker who advised Hughes with his Las
Vegas business transactions was E. Parry Thomas. Thomas began run-
ning the Bank of Las Vegas in 1955 and was a tremendous stimulus to the
Vegas economy for decades. By 1977, Thomas was UNLV's choice for most
"Distinguished Nevadan." Although Thomas viewed himself simply as a
"very community-minded banker," he was widely referred to as "Mr. Las
Vegas."[27] Bob Maheu, a close confidant of Hughes who handled all busi-
ness transactions during the years the eccentric billionaire lived in Las
Vegas, said, "I don't know how many occasions Howard would tell me

E. Parry Thomas, 1981. Special Collections
& Archives, University Libraries,
University of Nevada, Las Vegas.

he wished he had Parry working for him full time to solve problems. He just felt Parry was the brightest guy on the block who could work his way through every situation."[28]

A casino owner wanting to remain anonymous confided, "Parry Thomas was the perfect man for the perfect time. With his intelligence, distinguished looks, Mormon background, and instant likability, all the boys back in the day knew they needed Parry's loyalty to achieve their dreams, and if they crossed him, their long-term chance of success in Las Vegas was minimized."[29] Senator Harry Reid said of Thomas, "He could be the lead in any movie. He was handsome beyond all imagination, and he dressed accordingly." Reid explained that Thomas, a banker from Salt Lake City, grew wary of arranging loans for southern Nevada operations because of the gaming issue. Reid added, "He had to figure out unique ways of doing it. So he set up a bank in Nevada, and he made the loans himself. He personally came to the legislature in 1969 and advocated corporate gaming, which got the mob out of gaming. So, E. Parry Thomas is responsible for much of the growth in Nevada."[30]

E. Parry Thomas, Jerry Mack, and Steve Wynn. Special Collections &
Archives, University Libraries, University of Nevada, Las Vegas.

Thomas also found immense success in forming a business partnership with Jerry Mack, son of Nate Mack, who Thomas perceived "was
without question the most influential of all Jewish people in Las Vegas."
Thomas related, "He told me he liked how I was handling things at the
bank and that he'd like me to become partners with his son Jerry.... About
two weeks later, Nate sat down with Jerry and me, and he said, 'You guys
just bought eighty acres,...now you take it from there.'"[31] Together they
formed a successful alliance built on trust and wise stewardship that
lasted the duration of their business careers. Thomas explained, "Jerry and
I decided early on that the best way for us to operate was not [to] get in
each other's way.... Jerry would run anything to do with real estate,...and
I would run the bank."[32] Regarding the famous Thomas-Mack combination, Harry Reid remarked, "They were an unmatched pair. Parry Thomas,
Mr. Hollywood, Jerry Mack, Mr. 'I slept in my suit today,'...was a financial genius."[33]

Culling from his own faith tradition, Professor Mike Green added a
Jewish perspective, when he keenly perceived the commonalities between
Thomas and Mack: "There's a connectedness between Mormons and Jews
if you stop and think about it. Both of them being forced out of places
they were living, both of them having to move around a lot, considerable
oppression, and a considerable amount of misunderstanding or ignorance

of just who they are and what they do. And in Las Vegas, you see this merging,…Parry Thomas handled the banking, Jerry Mack handled the real estate,"[34] an enduring, elite, winning combination. Thomas was known for his finesse in navigating diversities in the art of the deal. He said, "I work for the Mormons until noon, and from noon on for my Jewish friends," meaning his casino associates.[35]

Matthew R. Davis wrote, "The ability of religious groups to cross their own spiritual barriers in order to grow the city and their communities provided much of the early infrastructure of Las Vegas. UNLV's campus is the result of the Mormon-Jewish collaboration and partnership of Parry Thomas and Jerry Mack, a partnership not likely to have happened in a place like New York City with already defined religious and social parameters."[36]

Billionaire Steve Wynn expressed, "Parry Thomas and Jerry Mack were legitimate guys who understood how to operate in an edgy environment." Wynn observed, "They always maintained their legitimacy and dealt with edginess professionally. There is no question that they moved gracefully and profitably on the edge. By that I mean they always knew where the line was and they didn't cross it. But they stayed right up against it because that's the only way they could have pulled this industry [gaming] in the modern era."[37]

Regarding this tenuous balance-beam walk, Parry Thomas once said, "The gaming industry is a business and its one of the most productive businesses in the world, but certainly it is critical in Nevada and especially Las Vegas.… It has to be recognized by the public that eighty percent of

Professor Michael Green, 2020.
Photo by Martin Andersen.

the employment in Las Vegas is connected directly or indirectly to that industry."[38] Most Las Vegas residents understood that the gaming industry was precarious and its environment dicey. But Thomas and Mack were willing to take the risks to help the city grow. Their unique religious backgrounds and family traditions infused them with deep-rooted stability and confident identity.

Mike Gaughan recalled, "Parry was the first and only banker you could get money from in the gaming business."[39] Reflecting back on his early years in Vegas (1954), Thomas stated, "Gambling was illegal in forty-seven states back then, and their instructions to their [bank] branches in Nevada were that you don't do business with gamblers.... What I used to say to my superiors in Salt Lake at the time was that it was very simple: We were a community bank and it was our business to serve the public in the Las Vegas community. We should serve all legal entities, and gambling was not only legal in Nevada, but it was the main industry."[40]

Thomas would argue that along with the risks associated with the gaming industry, there were certainly dividends for the community, not the least of which was employment opportunities for families. Thomas once remarked, "I spent more than half my life finding money for Las Vegas."[41] Aside from finding money for the community's benefit, the Thomas-Mack duo also donated money from their own pockets to improve the city. Nowhere is this more evident than the millions of personal dollars poured into the development of what would become the University of Nevada, Las Vegas. The UNLV Thomas & Mack Center stands as a daily reminder of their long-lasting contribution to the campus.[42] Tom Thomas recalled that his father "had with Jerry Mack, almost single-handedly seen to it that Nevada Southern University would have the vision, and the land, to grow into UNLV, a respected state university that would become the cultural heart of the city."[43]

Reflecting on other business transactions of his influential father, Tom Thomas stated, "This was a man who structured the financing and served as chief adviser and go-between for all of Howard Hughes's hotel acquisitions in Las Vegas...and had worked individually with a diverse and motley assortment of casino owners and political bigwigs to help Las Vegas transition from an easily stereotyped Mob town in the 1950s and '60s to [the] darling of corporate America in the 1980s."[44]

Several years before Parry's passing, his son Tom recalled his father's Latter-day Saint family values and contributions to the church: "Raised in a strong Mormon family, Parry had been a devout church-going Mormon

Tom Thomas, 2020. Photo by Martin Andersen.

until the age of fourteen, and although he hasn't participated in the rituals of the church since his teen years, he credits the religion with providing him the moral and ethical fundamentals that have guided him through his life. He has consistently answered calls from the church since then, whether it be for financial assistance or helping a brother in the faith through a difficult time."[45]

Tom Thomas explained, "Although he wasn't a churchgoer, he was held in very high regard in the LDS community."[46] Years later, in an interview, Thomas offered further insight into his father's ethical roots: "My father's background in the church and maybe even more importantly the impact of his mother and the example that she was of service and leadership in the church…shaped much of who he was."[47]

Another of Parry's sons, Steve Thomas, recalled, "Although Dad was not a churchgoer, a lot of how he lived his life was very much in keeping with all the precepts of the church. There was always in my opinion more Mormonism in my father than non-Mormonism going on. The adage of stewardship and giving back to the community and living our life with integrity and taking care of your kids. Family comes first."[48]

Evidence that the parental investment paid off might be inferred from the fact that both Tom, a successful attorney-businessman, and his brother Steve, an orthopedic surgeon, have served as bishops and have continued the Thomas family legacy of integrity and trust, rooted in their church values.[49] Brian Greenspun, chief executive officer, publisher, and editor of the *Las Vegas Sun*, observed, "With all Parry Thomas has done in Las Vegas, I'd say his greatest contribution to the city is his family. He and

Peggy have raised bright, hard-working, responsible, ethical people who are still working and sharing his legacy in this town.... When parents raise good, honest, devoted members to a society, that's a much greater gift to a community than anything else they could do, because the ripple effect of those good works reaches so many others."[50]

RISKS POSED BY THE GAMING INDUSTRY

It is no secret that the gaming industry saturates the Vegas environment, and adapting to this unique crucible encourages an uneasy truce for many believers and their religious leaders. Lori Leibovich observed, "The ubiquity and power of the gaming industry make it impossible for religious leaders to condemn it without offending someone in their congregation. Moreover, relationships between religious groups and the casinos are mutually beneficial." However, the Church of Jesus Christ of Latter-day Saints has taken a stand against gambling, but has made concessions over the years with regards to church members employed in gaming, though it is discouraged.[51]

As early as 1925, a year after the First Las Vegas Ward was established, the church's First Presidency issued a statement warning that the purpose of gambling was to "encourage the spirit of reckless speculation, and particularly to that which tends to degrade or weaken the high moral standard which the members of the church, and our community at large, have always maintained.... We therefore advise and urge all members of the church to refrain from participation in any activity which is contrary to the view herein set forth."[52]

This tight grip loosened after the state of Nevada legalized gaming in 1931. The previous year, local church member Ira Joseph Earl had opposed this legislation. One author wrote, "Earl was an unreconstructed Mormon from the old school.... Through the first half of the century, Church members recall that involvement in gambling was grounds for denial of a 'temple recommend.'"[53] Latter-day Saints have wrestled with this moral dilemma for decades. The gray areas surrounding gaming employment raise innumerable soul-searching questions: Do I follow the majority in embracing gaming employment, or should I try to find another job outside of the industry? Or if I work for the gaming corporations, where are the lines not to cross so I can remain in good standing with my faith?

A twenty-three-year-old Latter-day Saint, McClain Bybee, experienced this inner turmoil when he worked for the Sahara Hotel & Casino from 1966 to 1974.[54] In the first year of Bybee's employment at the Sahara,

McClain Bybee, 2020. Photo by Martin Andersen.

Dr. Samuel Davis, an optometrist and stake president of the Las Vegas North Stake, shared with the local press the church's position on gaming: "Anything that urges a person to get something for nothing we don't sanction. We live with it [gambling] but we're not part of it."[55]

Notwithstanding this hard-line proscription, somehow young Bybee found a way to work within the industry as an employee without letting it become a part of his personal life. Commencing as a Sahara hotel clerk, he impressed his employers and soon became an administrative assistant to Joseph Rosenburg, a "head honcho" at the Sahara. Bybee recalled that one day Rosenburg asked him if he had a Latter-day Saint temple recommend and was worthy of it. Bybee replied that he was. Rosenburg then stated, "If you are disloyal and unfaithful to your God, then you'll probably be disloyal and unfaithful to me, and I can't have you work for me."[56]

Bybee stayed true to his faith and quickly ascended the corporate ladder. In less than three years, he was appointed a manager at the Sahara, second in command. He looked so young at the time that the administration required him to grow a mustache. Although Bybee was valued by the Sahara organization as a capable administrator, his conscience gnawed at him. He felt he should separate himself from the environment surrounding the gaming industry, and so he left in 1974, even though the Sahara hotel administration offered to double his pay if he would stay. The following year, Bybee was called to serve as a counselor in the first Las Vegas Mission presidency (July 1975) and was never again involved with any aspect of casino life.[57]

For many Latter-day Saints employed by the casinos, feelings of apprehension and concern that their spiritual integrity may become tainted to some degree by their association with gaming were a common reality. Was it better to work inside or outside the casino? Was it crossing the line to work in "the pit" on the casino floor? Would gaming positions jeopardize being considered for potential church leadership positions or receiving the Melchizedek priesthood?[58] And could having gaming jobs mean church members could be denied admittance into sacred Latter-day Saint temples?

Authors Bob Gottlieb and Peter Wiley, not Latter-day Saints themselves, observed the effects of the church's guidelines on participating in the gaming industry. Latter-day Saints had been counseled to avoid gambling. Regarding which specific gaming positions the church discouraged, they explained, "These are the jobs such as dealers, cocktail waitresses, pit bosses, and even dancers, all of whom are visible participants on the floor.... If LDS members persist in that area of employment they are told that they may not be ordained to offices in the Melchizedek Priesthood, nor appointment to an administrative position in the church, nor most significantly, be issued temple recommends or be allowed to have a temple wedding." The exception, according to Gottlieb and Wiley, was that "church leaders do not counsel their members to stay away from casino management positions."[59]

During the mid- to late twentieth century, church policies related to baptism, receiving the priesthood, and temple worthiness were reviewed and modified. For example, Elder LeGrand Richards of the church's Quorum of the Twelve Apostles sent a letter to the president of the Las Vegas East Stake (November 23, 1965) indicating that the First Presidency and Council of the Twelve felt that those who were "working in the casinos and gambling places" should not be allowed to receive temple recommends. "They felt that the saints should be willing to try and find remunerative work in other fields rather than to engage in throwing of dice, the dealing of cards, the spinning of the roulette wheel and directing the casino games in these places." Richards added, "This seems to accord with the instructions that you have had in the past."[60]

The following year (August 30, 1966), the First Presidency reiterated their position on the issue to stake presidents in the Las Vegas, Reno, and the California missions:

> Inquiry has been received from the presidency of one of the stakes
> in Las Vegas regarding the attitude that the Church should assume
> in the matter of appointing to administrative positions or issuing

temple recommends to employees in gambling casinos, more specifically employees who are dealers, pit bosses, cashiers in teller windows, change girls, bartenders, cocktail waitresses and cigar and cigarette girls.... We do not want any of our members participating in these gambling dens...and advise that we should not appoint to administrative positions nor issue temple recommends to people in these gambling places whose employment requires them to meet the public and participate in the manner indicated. We hope that our brethren and sisters can find employment in a more desirable environment.[61]

A little more than a decade later (May 18, 1977), the First Presidency issued another letter to the stake presidents in Las Vegas and Reno, as well as to the president of the Nevada Las Vegas Mission, stating, "Inquiries have been made about the propriety of baptizing investigators who are employed in the so-called areas of gambling casinos.... Those who sincerely indicate an intention to leave such employment may be allowed to enter the Church by baptism if they are worthy in every other respect. However, if they are members and continue in such employment, they should not be ordained to offices in the Melchizedek Priesthood, nor appointed to an administrative position, nor be issued temple recommends." The First Presidency also counseled that "priesthood leaders should labor with such persons in a spirit of kindness and love to help them find employment in a more desirable environment."[62]

Three years later, in 1980, when the church commemorated the sesquicentennial anniversary of its establishment, local member Danford Crane reflected on a half century of Latter-day Saint history in Vegas since gambling was legalized and felt that somehow the church had managed to build a great relationship with the gaming industry while not compromising its high standards. Crane observed, "Gaming people have a good opinion and respect for the church, and we've learned to live with that estimation."[63]

Several years later, author Kenric Ward wrote, "By 1986, just as planning was under way on the Las Vegas Temple, priesthood leaders were instructed to issue recommends to 'all worthy members'—without regard to occupation.... In the absence of any ironclad written prohibitions, Mormons in Las Vegas did as the Las Vegans do—they went to work in...every facet of the gaming industry—from the countrooms to the boardrooms."[64]

Former Clark County commissioner Jay Bingham raised this rhetorical question: How can you be a Latter-day Saint and operate in a gaming town? Knowing full well while he was in public office that the industry brought $2 billion to the community, Bingham decided not to curtail employment in the gaming industry but rather ensure that he "regulated it honestly, with integrity." He added, "Maybe I don't like gambling, but it was here, and I wanted to make sure it was done right;…what we wanted to do was keep it clean."[65] Reed Whipple, a former member of the Las Vegas City Commission for two decades, had believed and followed the same protocol in working with the other commissioners to regulate gambling. Whipple said, "The Church has not gone along with gambling here,…but since it is here, Church members have tried to keep it under control and above board."[66]

ALTERNATIVE EMPLOYMENT OPTIONS

During the twentieth century, many Latter-day Saints found employment options outside the gaming industry and prospered. This included Latter-day Saint contractors hiring workers from the local labor union, but apparently church members did not take a lead role in organized labor such as the Culinary Union.[67]

One notable business operating in the mid-twentieth century was Vegas Village, an ambitious entrepreneurial endeavor that built a shopping center and completed other real-estate projects. This successful business plan was launched by a group of Latter-day Saint real-estate agents and investors and lasted several decades.[68] Ralph Harman, a faithful church member, was one of the founders of Vegas Village.[69] His son David Harman explained that people came from all over the Moapa Valley and even from California to shop at Vegas Village. He commented, "There was nothing like it…in that area. There were Safeways and other kinds of stores that were in the community, but this became an instant success…. On any given day,…the Vegas Village would have about 75 percent of shopping in Las Vegas, so, it was really successful."[70] David's sister Gayle Harman added, "Vegas Village was the first time that any store of that size ever came into Vegas. It was a big-thinking idea;…they always do things big in Las Vegas. And so, Vegas Village comes in with this big store, a very popular store." Yet after a successful run of more than a decade (1955–69), Vegas Village was sold to Continental Connectors as the decade of the '60s came to a close.[71]

Those not of the faith often recognized the high standards upheld by the Saints in various businesses such as Vegas Village that often echoed trust and stability in the marketplace as well as in the private lives of church members. One writer observed, "For Mormons, tithing was not optional…to enjoy membership in good standing. Besides the tithe, fast offerings, offerings for the poor, and dues for the maintenance of the ward were part of expected donations. With a solid financial base, expansion continued, and the Mormons eventually became one of the strongest religious communities in Las Vegas…. The Mormon message held particular appeal because of its emphasis upon socially conservative values, its help for the poor and needy, a strong family emphasis, and good strategic planning."[72]

Church members produced print media to encourage business networking. One author observed, "The LDS *Information Guide* as well as *Desert Saints Magazine* are two prime examples of where people can go for information about the LDS community, both from a business and personal perspective. The LDS Guide offers information on Mormon-run businesses that cover the entire spectrum. Mormon accountants, attorneys, counselors, landscapers, photographers, and swimming instructors can all be found in the Guide's business listings. Businesses like Cumorah Credit Union utilize these listings to drum up business from a primarily Mormon base."[73] According to Ed Kanet, who helped publish the *Guide*, the publication ran from 1990 to 2008 and was "an annual directory for Latter-day Saints in the greater Las Vegas area."[74]

Another successful unofficial Latter-day Saint publication was birthed from humble beginnings. Originally a twelve-page circular launched by Charlene and Richard Taylor, the *Beehive Standard Weekly* was first published in 1975, intended for the local women with whom the Taylors' worshipped. Soon the circular mushroomed, and church members throughout the Las Vegas Valley were reading business advertisements as well as friendly reminders to maintain the high standards and ethics expected of them both at home and in the workplace. The *Beehive Standard Weekly* was mailed to local church leaders and members and was distributed at a variety of Latter-day Saint gathering places: bookstores, family history centers, employment centers, and local stores and church offices.[75]

A decade later, the *Beehive Sentinel*, another Latter-day Saint publication, posted its own movie code and ratings to protect families from unseemly films. For example, *F* meant family friendly; *A* meant acceptable for adults, and *O* meant the film was objectionable.[76] "Lingerie for

LDS" was advertised, and announcements such as births, baptisms, missions, marriages, anniversaries, and even awards appeared in the issues on a regular basis.[77]

A not-so-subtle article capitalizing on the Latter-day Saint health code was boldly titled "Hire a Non-Smoker" and included the following list of reasons for so doing: "Non-Smokers have less absenteeism,...fewer illnesses,...fewer work accidents,...tend to be more productive,...have a better impression with the general public,...are less destructive of company property,...do not offend fellow workers,...are less subject to many occupational health hazards, [and]...can work around sensitive machinery." Finally, the article concluded, "At a time when there is intense competition for jobs, being a non-smoker can be a distinct advantage. Non-smokers should specify on their applications...'I DO NOT SMOKE' whether the question is asked or not."[78]

Some political groups discovered that articles and inserts in these local unofficial church newspapers had the potential to influence the Saints. For example, when Harry Reid ran for the US Senate, a cover story appeared in the *Beehive Sentinel* with a biographical sketch of his life and a Q&A with Reid.[79] Some church members, however, did object to being handed the paper as they exited worship services or finding the papers placed beneath windshield wipers on their automobiles.[80]

Regardless of occasional objections to distribution methods, the *Beehive Sentinel* remained popular among church members because it provided useful information such as reminders of upcoming religious and cultural events as well as targeted advertisements for local businesses.

By 1980, the sesquicentennial year commemorating the establishment of the church, Las Vegas businesses were well acquainted with the local Saints in their community and sent their congratulations via other local newspapers, including one article headlined "150 Years of Faith."[81] Also in this commemorative year, the *Review-Journal* published a complimentary article of the Latter-day Saint faith with the headline, "Church 'for All Ages' Not Just an Activity for Sunday."[82]

Mahlon Edwards is an example of the kind of Latter-day Saint who lived his religion seven days a week. He remembered how adhering to Latter-day Saint standards paid off for him while working for the Titanium Metal Corporation plant in Henderson both before and after serving a full-time church mission during the mid-twentieth century. Initially, Edwards was teased for refusing to engage in drinking alcohol, smoking, and viewing pornographic literature with his coworkers, although he still considered them friends. When he left to serve his mission, his boss

S. Mahlon Edwards, 2020. Photo by Martin Andersen.

remarked, "A Mormon who doesn't live his religion is one of the worst men you will find, but a Mormon who lives his religion is one of the best." When he returned from the mission field, Edwards was rehired at the Titanium plant on the same shift he had before he left. His previous foreman invited Edwards to eat dinner with the work team. Edwards shared his religious beliefs with them and reported, "There was a feeling of appreciation and understanding, although none of them were converted."[83]

Another Latter-day Saint, who like Edwards is not ashamed to share his beliefs in the marketplace, is David Dixon. Dixon's family moved to Vegas in 1959, and Dixon has made a successful career as a financial planner. Dixon keeps a copy of the Book of Mormon and the Bible in the reception area of his office, and from time to time clients ask about the Book of Mormon. Some have mentioned that they have seen *The Book of Mormon* musical. Dixon has given such clients a copy of the Book of Mormon and invited them to read it and remarked that clients often wanted to discuss it in subsequent meetings.[84]

Jay Bingham, a former member of the Clark County Commission,[85] observed firsthand the influence Latter-day Saints had on the construction industry. Bingham remarked, "Being in government for a lot of years you get to mingle with a lot of people outside of the church.... One of the phrases I heard when I was elected at a very young age [was]...'The Jews own Las Vegas, the mob ran Las Vegas, and the Mormons built Las Vegas.'"[86] Bingham noticed that many of the large contracting firms in the area are run by successful Latter-day Saint contractors who chose to make wise decisions in their youth and had a reputation for dependability, while other contractors squandered their money.[87]

Church members have also made their mark in practicing law and are known for their integrity. One such attorney was Thomas Steffen who had a stellar reputation that resulted in his appointment to the Nevada Supreme Court in 1982.[88] A fellow Latter-day Saint practicing law in Las Vegas for three decades, including two decades as a deputy district attorney, observed Steffen's exemplary behavior prior to his appointment in an unforgettable experience that has never been duplicated in his professional career: "We represented different defendants in a personal injury lawsuit and were walking to a deposition with them, talking to them as we walked. I was very pleasantly surprised when Tom Steffen suddenly stopped and faced his client, shook his finger in the client's face, and said, as best I can recall, 'I will not tolerate any kind of dishonesty. You tell the Truth!'"[89]

Speaking of the collective Latter-day Saint influence in the Vegas marketplace, Elise Noorda summarized, "Members of the church have been really involved in the community, in the schools, in government, in business, and they've set a good example. They've been friends to their neighbors and their coworkers, and they just established a presence. I would guess there's not very many people in Las Vegas that don't have a relationship with a member of the Church in some capacity."[90]

PROFESSIONAL ENTERTAINMENT

A handful of talented Latter-day Saints have found employment in the entertainment business of Las Vegas. They are known for the high standards they have adhered to in the midst of a nightlife that is fast paced and volatile.

Brandon Flowers

Brandon Flowers is clearly a rock star, but at the same time a faithful family man and an active, practicing member of the Church of Jesus Christ of Latter-day Saints. Flowers, a member of the rock band Killers, said in a CBS news interview, "I don't go to church because I got nothing better to do on Sundays. I really believe it!" He added, "I don't know what my life would be like without it. I think I would have been a casualty of rock 'n' roll."[91]

Gladys Knight

"Motown legend" Gladys Knight has had a tremendous influence as a gospel soul singer and is still a scheduled performer on the Strip. She began working on the Strip as early as 1967 and purchased a home in Vegas four years later.[92] But Knight's baptism into the Church of Jesus Christ of Latter-day Saints occurred three decades later, after observing the spiritual growth of her Latter-day-Saint-convert children, Kenya and Jimmy, and appreciating how they raised their children, her grandchildren.

After accepting invitations from Kenya to attend the church women's Relief Society meetings and later to take the missionary discussions, Jimmy baptized his mother, Gladys, in 1997. Regarding the bearing her membership in the church has had on her profession, Gladys said, "It didn't affect my career;...people pretty much expect me to walk my own road, and I've never regretted it once.... I feel like I am in the right place and I'm loving it."[93]

Knight has uplifted thousands through her upbeat soulful gospel music, and on the five-year anniversary of her baptism, she showcased an inspiring choir she had formed. Jamie Armstrong, former editor and author for LDS Living Magazine, wrote that Knight's desire to add "a little something" to Latter-day Saint church music "eventually inspired her to create an all-volunteer, multicultural Latter-day Saint choir that would bring a new level of energy and cultural awareness to traditional hymns. The choir, called the 'Saints Unified Voices,' is comprised of more than 100 people and has a two-fold purpose. First, they aim to spread the message of the restored gospel of Jesus Christ by providing an opportunity for people who wouldn't otherwise enter a Latter-day Saint meetinghouse to feel the Spirit. Second, they desire to help members of the Church embrace the cultural diversity of people worldwide coming into the Lord's Kingdom."[94]

Armstrong reported on the choir's tremendous success: "Gladys Knight & the Saints Unified Voices have released two albums. Their first, *One Voice*, won a 2005 Grammy Award for Best Gospel Choir or Church Album."[95] Knight explained the motivation behind the chorus: "The choir members are here because of their testimonies and their desires to serve the Lord.... They're not perfect, but they've got the vision and under-standing of our calling as a missionary effort, and they are dedicated to the work."[96]

Donny and Marie Osmond

What was scheduled to be a six-week show in Vegas for Donny and Marie Osmond mushroomed into something much bigger.[97] The Osmond two-some swept Vegas off their feet with their talent and charm. An article published in USA Today in November 2019 announced, "After more than a decade of performing in their iconic Las Vegas show Donny and Marie

Donny Osmond. Courtesy of Donny Osmond.

Osmond have taken their final bows. The brother-sister duo…wrapped their live show of the same name at the Flamingo Las Vegas hotel and casino.… The live 'Donny & Marie' ran for 11 years and 1,730 performances"[98] and several times was rated the number-one show in Las Vegas.

Good Morning America announced, "The brother-and-sister duo…were inducted into the Las Vegas Walk of Stars in October [2019], completing their residency at the Flamingo."[99] Donny Osmond described what occurred behind the curtains of their show:

> I go out there and have a lot of fun—it's a lot of work, it's a lot of stress. Traditionally, Marie and I, along with our dancers, will gather in a circle and have a prayer. Whoever feels like praying, including our dancers, will give a brief prayer and it brings such a wonderful spirit to what we're about to do for the next 90 minutes on that stage. Now having said that, I want to make sure people understand that we don't pray so when the curtains open up, we begin to preach. That's not what we do onstage. We get onstage and perform, but we

want that support from our Father in Heaven.... I feel that comfort and that strength every time I pray before the show.[100]

Marie Osmond spoke of the legacy that precipitated their unique stage traditions. "We brought 'sincere' to sin city," Marie said. "My father said, 'In scripture it says to dedicate everything you do to the Lord.' So every time, no matter what it was, we always had a prayer before going on stage. We do that in Vegas, Donny and I, we get our dancers together, and the dancers take turns, and we all do it, and I go, 'We're a family!' That's what we do; we dedicate this show to making our audience happy."[101]

Another man who greatly influenced Marie's life, besides her father, was church president Harold B. Lee. At the impressionable age of eleven, Marie had an experience with President Lee that affected the rest of her life. Marie recalled that President Lee counseled, "'You are going out into the world.' And he said, 'I'm going to give you a little advice.' He said, 'In any decision there [are] two choices. You either do it or you don't. Always make the choice that will take you closer to the celestial kingdom of God,'...and that has always stayed with me my whole life because maybe it's not the easiest choice, but you know it's the choice to make." Marie added, "And I've walked away from many things, parties where cocaine was dumped on the table from record companies, you know, to say thank you for your fabulous records and albums. I'm probably not the greatest celebrity because I don't party [laughs]. But I'm still here after five decades."[102]

Marie Osmond, 2019. Photo by Martin Andersen.

Donny reflected on his choices as a Las Vegas performer on and off the stage since he was seven years old:

> A lot of people think, how can a member of the church perform in a place called sin city,…and I've always said…you can choose to indulge in that or indulge in this…. I choose to play in Las Vegas, and there's nothing wrong with that; I don't gamble, I don't go to certain shows, I don't drink, I don't smoke, I don't do the drugs, those are all choices, but I still perform there,…[and] I choose to follow my Heavenly Father and his Son Jesus Christ.[103]

Performing in Vegas has rewarded the Osmonds with more than just monetary compensation. They have influenced hundreds of thousands of fans to make better choices. Donny shared this memorable exchange illustrating the lasting impact of the Osmond duo:

> After our shows in Las Vegas we have meet and greets and people come backstage, they want our autographs and pictures, what not, to tell their stories. And this really tall, burly man came up to me, and I thought, you know, he is a rock and roller and he is forced to be here because his wife dragged him here. But he said,…"I am a member of the church,…and I have you to thank for that." I thought, oh my goodness, what a compliment, that is better than a gold record.[104]

Other Osmonds have also performed in Vegas.[105] At age three, Donny and his older singing brothers performed with Andy Williams at the then new Caesars Palace in 1967, the same year Gladys Knight first sang on the Strip.[106] The talented Osmond family has left an indelible impression on countless people, both those who have watched them perform locally and audiences abroad. Journalist Sandra Widener observed, "The Osmond family has been a shining beacon of show biz respectability in a world of spitting Mick Jaggers and rock stars who bite the heads off chickens. And while the wholesome images of some celebrities turn out to be diametrically opposed to their private lives, the Osmonds are exactly what they appear to be."[107]

Amateur Entertainment and Recreation

While only a handful of Latter-day Saints have enjoyed professional entertainment careers in Las Vegas, amateur entertainment and recreational activities have been integral to the church from the beginning. To facilitate the Saints' propensity for activities, Las Vegas stake president Thomas

Gay Meyers purchased for the church ten acres of land from the Union Pacific Railroad in 1960. Construction commenced for a multipurpose church building, the Administrative Cultural and Sports Center, that would be utilized by two stakes during the 1960s. The structure seated up to twenty-five hundred people and boasted several ball fields on the same property.[108] Wendell and Bonnie Waite wrote, "The Administrative, Cultural and Sports Center served the two stakes well for several years. Many and varied activities were conducted, including stake conferences,…baptisms, dances, classes, dramas, recitals, musicals, Pioneer Day activities, basketball, softball, and volleyball games and other sports activities."[109]

Successful Latter-day Saint programs continued throughout the 1960s, including those by the "Singing Mothers." As previously noted, Church Relief Society choirs in various areas launched decades earlier performed under this same name for church conferences and music festivities. One "Singing Mothers" choir during this era even sang at the Relief Society general conference held in 1968.[110] Latter-day Saint Girls Camp was also held annually in the region.[111] The popular musical *Promised Valley* was performed by the combined Las Vegas stakes in 1961 and 1968 at the Las Vegas High School auditorium,[112] and stake Pioneer Day celebrations were held annually.[113] In the year 1963 alone, ninety-two separate entries were constructed for the "Big Mormon Parade" in honor of the Pioneer Day celebration.[114]

As the new decade approached, church membership in the stakes had multiplied and outgrown the Administrative, Cultural, and Sports Center. In 1970, the facility was sold to the city of Las Vegas and became known as the Reed Whipple Center.[115] Eric Christensen remembered some of the musicals, called road shows, that were staged at the center during this era. He recalled, "My wife's ward, their road show had a hundred and something kids in it. My road show in our ward had forty, fifty kids.… These productions were amazing." Christensen recalled with fondness the center having an abundance of indoor and outdoor activities.[116]

Road shows throughout the latter half of the twentieth century were popular among wards and stakes. Annual competitions were held each year to determine which ward had put on the best show. These competitive rivalries drawing ward and stake members closely together might best be captured via this homespun 1981 poem written by Jeraldine Wadsworth, road-show general chairman for the North Las Vegas Stake, called "Beware of Roadshowitis":

In our stake we are all good friends
Close as we can be…
Until it's roadshow time
Then love and friendship flee.

You will see each ward draw close together
Such exciting secrets they hide
Characters, scripts and music
In no one will they confide.…

And when the tallies are in and the show is over
Some will be glad, some will be mad, Some will be sad,
But in a few years
ALL will be glad!

For they will always cherish
The memories of that night so long ago
When all the wards of the North Las Vegas Nevada Stake
Worked TOGETHER to put on a tremendous roadshow![117]

5

Latter-day Saints
in Elected Office and
Community Service

They really were able to keep hometown values
staunch and foremost in Clark County.
—Joyce Haldeman, director, Greater Las Vegas Community Council

Latter-day Saints were considerably involved in public service capacities, both as volunteers and as elected officials, commencing in the early twentieth century. For example, Charles C. Ronnow, the first presiding elder of the Las Vegas Branch (1915), was also an active member of the Las Vegas Rotary Club and Chamber of Commerce. He also served on the Clark County Commission board and had served as a justice of the peace.[1] Ira J. Earl, appointed as the first bishop of the Las Vegas Ward (1924), was likewise heavily involved in shaping the community. Earl was named to the Las Vegas School Board (1931) and later served for two terms on the Clark County Commission.[2]

It was known that "'all Democrats in the southern end of the state looked to...[Earl] to help get them elected because his endorsement carried weight,' said one political observer at the time."[3] One author added, "Church members began to make their presence felt in civic affairs. Wendell Bunker was also a Clark County commissioner. Marion Earl served as justice of the peace.... Reed Whipple would become a fixture on the Las Vegas City Commission."[4] In addition, Whipple also served as president of the Las Vegas Stake for a record two dozen years (1956–80). He also "involved himself in charitable causes and served as president of the Boy Scouts' Boulder Dam Area Council—an organization largely supported by Mormon wards. Promoting a host of public works projects."[5]

In the fall of 1940, Berkeley Bunker's appointment as a US senator was the first time a local member of the church was recognized on both a state and a national level. The front page of the *Las Vegas Age* announced, "Berkeley Bunker Appointed to Fill Vacancy in Senate." Among other things, the article noted that thirty-four-year-old Bunker was the youngest member of the US Senate, adding, "The young man has been active in the leadership of the Church of the Latter-day Saints and spent 18 months on a mission to the southern states."[6]

A week later, and the night before Bunker's departure to Washington, the front page of the *Las Vegas Age* included an article headlined "Senator Bunker Given Farewell" and reported on the meticulous details of the grand event held at the "LDS Church." The highlight of the evening was Senator Bunker's farewell message: "There has long been conflict between religion and politics...but never conflict between Christianity and politics. One of my cardinal principles is that he who would be greatest among you, let him be the servant of all. I realize that a great opportunity has presented itself to serve a great and noble people." Bunker's intimate service to the local Saints in his ward prior to his senatorial appointment certainly helped prepare him for his new and high public service assignment. Bunker told the audience, "I never knew the heart beat of the people until I became Bishop of the LDS Church."[7]

The following month, a series of forthcoming radio broadcasts, titled *The Way of Peace*, by Senator Bunker's brother, was announced on the front page of the *Age*. Bryan L. Bunker, president of the Moapa Stake, would address the Vegas community to "discuss conditions and the great war from the religious angle."[8] In one of his broadcasts, titled "Put on the Whole Armor of God," Bryan Bunker encouraged Americans to "catch up spiritually" as a nation.[9] Included with the broadcasts were "musical numbers provided by talented members of the choir of the LDS church in Las Vegas."[10] The Bunker brothers demonstrate the constructive influence one can have as an elected officer, as an ecclesiastical leader, or simply as a citizen voluntarily engaged in community service.[11]

Although gaming was legalized across the state of Nevada in 1931, Latter-day Saint elected officials have tried to keep the vices, negative influences, and crime associated with gambling under control in order to protect their neighborhoods and keep their communities safe. Joyce Haldeman said:

> I think if there had not been the strong influence of members of the church here in Las Vegas it probably would've been a little bit different...about things that would be taught and would not be taught in the classroom, legislation that passed over the years or didn't pass because of the influence of members of the church. There were so many people who were members of the church who held

elected office during some of those formative years that they really were able to keep hometown values staunch and foremost in Clark County.[12]

Former Nevada state senator Ray Rawson asserted, "We have a definite separation between church and state, but that doesn't mean that the values that you learn at church don't have a place in government. We don't ascribe to an organized religion as being a state religion, but the values that we gain through our various religious beliefs are very important to the people in a community.... The LDS that have served in office, they're home centered, they're family centered, they have those values that will build good things for the community and help their children."[13]

SHERIFF RALPH LAMB

Bruce Woodbury recalled, "There were a lot of LDS people who had been in important positions in the community and public office. Sheriff Ralph Lamb was one of them.... Like every family some are more active than others in the church, but good people, and you could see the principles of honesty and integrity and respect for others and serving others that are in men like Ralph who took great care to make sure we were a safe community."[14] Woodbury continued, "Sheriff Lamb and his family came out of Alamo,...and the people I've known coming from that community are strong.... You can't bully them.... It's not a secret that we had organized crime...but he made it clear that you step over the line and harm our citizens, you're going to jail."[15]

One Latter-day Saint also raised in Alamo, but now a Las Vegas resident, described the Alamo cowboy Sheriff Lamb: "When he first started, the mob had a great influence on Las Vegas, and one of the things he did was he went directly to them. He said, 'Now here's the deal, I don't want any trouble in this town.' He said, 'If you're gonna kill people, you don't do it here,' and...the mob they never killed anybody in Las Vegas, they always took them somewhere else."[16] In describing Lamb, Senator Harry Reid said, "He was a pretty tough guy.... He had a tremendous influence here, but I don't think you need to look at the stuff he did as following the beatitudes."[17]

John L. Smith, southern Nevada native and local journalist, remarked, "This Cowboy sheriff...was a rough and tumble guy, but he also modernized the police department.... To shake his hand, it's like shaking the hand of a bear. He was a strong guy...comfortable in the saddle.... He

Sheriff Ralph Lamb. Special Collections & Archives,
University Libraries, University of Nevada, Las Vegas.

wouldn't kick your butt unless he had to, but if he had to, your butt was
in real trouble. That's the truth."[18] Former state senator Helen Foley said,
"Sheriff Ralph Lamb was a real cowboy, . . . and he had his own brand of
justice."[19]

Fred Kennedy, a longtime church member and Las Vegas resident,
recalled that Sheriff Lamb "was the type of person that didn't take any
hogwash off anybody. What he said, he meant, and he was good. He con-
trolled the city in a very good way. . . . When he would go to the casinos
sometimes, he would even carry his rifle with him, and he would talk
to them and know that they knew that he meant what he said, so they
didn't give him any problem."[20] Former Nevada senator Richard Bryan
said that during Lamb's years in office as a sheriff and elected chairman
of the board of licensing for gaming, he was "the most powerful political
force in Nevada."[21] Journalist Charlie Zobell confirmed Bryan's point by
explaining that the combination of his sheriff's badge and the authority

to determine gaming licenses made Lamb "the most powerful man in the state."[22]

During his tenure, Lamb operated within the general boundaries of the law but employed flexibility when necessary. Lamb enjoyed a long run as sheriff between the years 1961 and 1978, which gave him ample time to become somewhat of a legend. So popular were the stories circulating about him that in 2012 a TV show titled *Vegas* was created based on Sheriff Lamb, who was played by actor Dennis Quaid.[23] Like Parry Thomas, Lamb was not much of a churchgoer, but the Latter-day Saint principles of generosity, integrity, and courage taught to him by his parents in Alamo were not lost on the Vegas sheriff.

McClain Bybee, whose father worked for Sheriff Lamb, recalled, "He was a real cowboy,... and the mob respected him.... He got the job done."[24] Sheriff Lamb's niece Marsha Leason remembers him being very generous when as a young girl she was asked to collect ward building funds and Lamb donated a sizable contribution. On the other hand, Leason noted, "Uncle Ralph didn't put up with nonsense."[25]

Ralph Lamb. Courtesy of Marsha Scofield-Leason.

To illustrate her point, Leason recalled the story of Sheriff Lamb running members of the Hells Angels motorcycle gang out of Vegas. The gang promptly camped outside the city limits at Mount Charleston. This probably would have been agreeable to Lamb if they hadn't taken several women with them. The sheriff sent his deputies to gather the troublemakers and the women, who were then transported back into the city station, contained in a room, sprayed down with disinfectant, and sent out of the state. When the gang threatened to retaliate, Lamb was not concerned in the least.[26]

Leason also related a fun story that billionaire Steve Wynn told at Lamb's funeral, "where there was not a seat to be had."[27] Sheriff Lamb had invited Wynn to come out to the ranch to learn how to rope. Wynn came to the ranch, and Leason recalled that while they were roping, Wynn said that one of Lamb's intelligence officers drove out to inform the sheriff that a man from California lodging at the Stratosphere Hotel had put out a hit on the sheriff's life. Leason said, "Uncle Ralph sat on his horse for a minute, and then he took his white handkerchief,…wiped his brow, and then he says, 'Well, you go back and find him and tell him that's really not a good idea,' and then he said he went back roping. And that was it."[28]

Another niece of Sheriff Lamb, Laurie Bayne, described her uncle as kind but said that he "did not put up with people coming into Las Vegas that were going to have a negative influence on the community or on the city.... It was a different kind of world back then,…more of a kind of wild west mentality where you just threw people out of town…or put them in a car and had them delivered back to where they came from, and that was kind of how things were handled." Finally, Bayne tenderly recalled, "Shortly before Ralph died,…he called my son aside and asked him if he would please take care of his two boys after he was gone…and make sure that they went back to church and received the priesthood," again suggesting that the Latter-day Saint principles and doctrines were always at his core.[29]

Church member Ashley Hall, Las Vegas city manager from 1983 to 1991, remembered about Sheriff Lamb, "Ralph was a kind of a guy that would talk to you, and if you didn't understand, he spoke plain cowboy English." Hall said Lamb's attitude was "if you're gonna come here, going to cheat at the gaming tables and you're gonna rob and steal,…we're gonna find you, and…he wasn't above putting a bare knuckle right on someone's chin at times. He was that kind of a guy."[30] Journalist A. D. Hopkins wrote,

"Lamb never actually shot anybody in a lifetime of law enforcement, he said. People called him the cowboy sheriff, but gunplay was not his style. Fisticuffs were. Calf roping was and politics were. Lamb was sheriff for 18 years, longer than any Clark County sheriff...and was responsible for merging the sheriff's office and the Las Vegas Police department into the single police agency dubbed Metro."[31] Yet the last time he sought reelection as sheriff, Lamb was defeated and was prevented from continuing in office. Perhaps the cowboy-sheriff style did not appeal to the rising generation.

Like Sheriff Lamb, Ashley Hall ran into challenging situations, including dealing with a death threat for denying a man from running brothels in hotels within city limits. Fortunately, Hall managed to get this problem quickly resolved, and the troublemaker was forced to leave town. Hall remarked, "I've had my life threatened a couple of times because I wouldn't do [inappropriate] things that people wanted done.... And so that influence of not bending and bowing...I think we've [as church members] been able to keep Las Vegas from imploding.... I think the reason that Latter-day Saints have had such an influence in Clark County particularly is because professionally, educationally, administratively we have people who are capable, good people, and...they don't ask for bribes or kickbacks or anything like that."[32] On another occasion, Hall mentioned to a news reporter, "The LDS Church's influence...in the Las Vegas Valley has been paramount in keeping Las Vegas within certain bounds. I think you would find Las Vegas being much different than it is without the LDS influence."[33]

When describing what Las Vegas would be like void of any Latter-day Saint influence, Judie Brailsford-Marcucci, a Canadian migrant from Alberta, had an immediate one-word response: "Chicago." Brailsford-Marcucci, a sixty-year local resident, campaign strategist, and business consultant, is well known in the community as a mover and shaker. Bob Broadbent,[34] an influential Latter-day Saint who served on the Clark County Commission for several terms, got Brailsford-Marcucci involved in campaigning and said she was a natural. Brailsford-Marcucci emphasized the powerful influence church members have exerted on the Vegas community: "We helped elect every sheriff.... We helped pass three police bonds, and we have been very involved in the schools, and we have elected way more than what the percentage of our [LDS] people are. We have elected good people, LDS, Catholic,...those people who have those core values. We founded this community."[35]

Jay Bingham, 2020. Photo by Martin Andersen.

THE CLARK COUNTY COMMISSION AND OTHER ELECTED OFFICERS

Another avenue through which elected church members have shaped Las Vegas is service with the Clark County Commission. Each of the seven elected commissioners is responsible for supervising a district for a four-year elected term. A number of influential Latter-day Saints have served in this position spanning several decades. One former Clark County commissioner, Jay Bingham (1984–96), explained the power and authority of the commission: "All of the strip is in Clark County; it's not in the city of Las Vegas because the gamers didn't want the city to grow into the strip, so the county commissioners were the largest basically municipal government here. We were over water, sewer, zoning, airport, everything that had to do with the growth in this valley the Clark county commissioners had the say so on." Bingham also noted that two powerful Latter-day Saint senators, James I. Gibson and Floyd Lamb, helped to get approvals quickly in the state legislature to speed up needed building projects.[36]

Bingham continued, "In 1980 I was elected to the North Las Vegas city council. At the time the mayor was LDS, and there were two [LDS] city councilmen, out of five, and then in 1984, I was elected to the board of [Clark] County Commission. When I was elected, four members of the seven were LDS."[37] Bingham believed that a disproportionate number of church members were voted into these public service positions because the community felt they could trust Latter-day Saints: "They were good family people, and their morals were high, and what they said they delivered on, and that's one of the reasons why the Mormons were so respected throughout the valley and kept being reelected all the time."[38]

Any candidate requires deep resources and broad networking to run a successful campaign. Mark Hutchison, former state senator and lieutenant governor of Nevada, explained that along with actually filing to run for an elected office, effective networking is an essential factor in why so many Latter-day Saints are elected to office. Hutchison stated, "It takes a lot of resources, energy, money to run for office.... This is a political reality." He added that 85 percent of the candidates who have the most money and resources and the top networking system win. Hutchison stated, "Latter-day Saints have natural grassroots networks and resources available to them because they have people who embrace the same values that they're running on.... Latter-day Saints...say, 'Come embrace my candidacy because you embrace my values.' Those are reasons why Latter-day Saints are probably disproportionately engaged in and successful in elected politics in southern Nevada."[39]

Some candidates who have shared the values Latter-day Saints embrace have had great support from church members such as Brailsford-Marcucci, who campaigned to support candidates who had high standards and were men and women of principle. One such candidate was former county commissioner Aaron Williams, who was the first Black elected to the Las Vegas City Council in 1969 and three years later became the first Black to serve on the Clark County Commission.[40] Williams, a self-professed Baptist, clearly understood the electoral power Latter-day Saints wielded in getting him elected in Clark County.[41] Successful Latter-day Saint businessman Howard Bulloch put it this way: "The members of The Church of Jesus Christ of Latter-day Saints are really intertwined

Mark Hutchison, 2020. Photo by Martin Andersen.

Bruce Woodbury, 2020.   Mary Beth Scow, 2020.
Photo by Martin Andersen.   Photo by Martin Andersen.

in the fabric of southern Nevada, and sometimes they've been the bright colors of that fabric, and other times they pushed other people forward and have them be the leaders in the community, but they're intertwined in this community in a beautiful way in their involvement."[42]

One highly respected Latter-day Saint who has been heavily involved as an elected official is Bruce Woodbury, a former Clark County commissioner (1981–2009) who continues to hold the record for longest service as a Nevada commissioner. Recollecting his service as a commissioner, Woodbury stated, "I served for twenty-eight years…and focused a lot on issues like transportation.… I was the founding member and chairman of the regional flood control district, and…some people kind of called me the father of flood control and the transportation czar,…and the community was so wonderful to me and named the 215 beltway after me and three streets and a post office building."[43]

Another influential commissioner serving two back-to-back terms (2010–17) is Mary Beth Scow.[44] Scow served on the Board of Trustees for the Clark County School District for three terms and believed that her most important responsibility was "keeping pandora in the box." She kept gaming in designated areas and away from neighborhoods as best she could. In addition, Scow battled to contain medicinal marijuana businesses. She said that these "establishments wanted to be right by the Strip,…by the University [UNLV], in places where they knew eventually it would be recreational and they would be at an advantage in those locations." Scow added, "I worked really hard...to keep those establishments as far away from the university as I could.... We're in a fight to keep our community from being run over by wickedness."[45]

When asked why so many Latter-day Saints have been elected to public office, Scow remarked, "Members of the church have an interest in keeping their community strong and also to protect against some of the things that are happening in the world.... A lot of Latter-day Saints are interested in running for office for true reasons, and I think people see that. When you're somebody that's truly honest-hearted, you want to work for the benefit of the community. That resonated with people. There's a trust that people can feel, and I believe that's why we have so many members of the church that are elected officials."[46]

Mark Hutchison observed, "I think Latter-day Saints have been actively involved in politics and then have been quite successful in their runs for public office in Las Vegas and Clark County and Nevada because, for one thing, we actually file to run for office.... It's in the marrow of our bones to be engaged in good causes,...to confront challenging values by doing what we can to change those values."[47] Journalist John L. Smith supposed Latter-day Saints enjoyed success in political elections for two major reasons: organization and participation.[48] Another well-known journalist, Jon Ralston, added, "They're known as being influential, as pillars in the community, as politically involved."[49]

Consummate journalist Ned Day assessed the Latter-day Saints and the importance of securing the "Mormon vote":

> I like the Mormons. More accurately, I admire them. They stand as a shining example of what can be accomplished by adhering to certain principles. They take the time and energy of raising their kids, imbuing in those children a strong sense of values, a sense of right and wrong. They take the time and energy to get themselves involved in community activities that are designed to promote the general welfare.... People like the feisty and principled County Commissioner Paul Christiansen, like the thoughtful and yet compassionate Federal Judge Lloyd George, like the talented Aladdin President Richard Bunker,...the list could go on for a long time, but you get the idea.... All this explains why, in election years, smart politicians make no apologies for doing everything they can to count on the so-called "Mormon vote," an often unified, socially conservative bloc representing 25 percent of Clark County's registered voters.[50]

In 1988, one journalist observed that although the Latter-day Saint population might be small, it was "a significant factor when you consider the high percentage of registration and voter turnout among Mormons."[51] The following year, and just prior to the 1989 Las Vegas Temple dedication, Brailsford-Marcucci recalled that church apostle Neal A. Maxwell came to the area and was curious about the prominent role Latter-day Saints played in local civic affairs. He asked county commissioner Karen Hayes[52] and Brailsford-Marcucci, both Latter-day Saints, "how many people we had that were members of the Church that actually served in some elected position." Brailsford-Marcucci reported: "I think we had about 35 percent of county judges, and assemblymen, and county commissioners, and city councils, and mayors, and we were only maybe 18–20 percent of the population and he wanted to know how we did that." She also explained that they had a solid structure of organization that was probably due to the influence of Latter-day Saint church leader and state government leader James I. Gibson, who knew how to run campaigns, register people, and organize to get votes door-to-door to get candidates elected.[53]

James I. Gibson was indeed influential. He found a way to be a great leader in the church and state simultaneously. Latter-day Saint Kyle Stevens said, "I recall specifically that in the early '80s there was a general focus on some social legislation in the Nevada Legislature, and James I. Gibson at the time was back then the regional representative of the Church and a former stake president. He was a powerful state senator who led the fight on this particular piece of social legislation as a good, strong Democrat in the Nevada State Senate and was successful in that effort."[54]

Elected Latter-day Saints employed in key positions strongly affected the moral tone of the community and local neighborhoods. When Mahlon Edwards was a deputy district attorney, he occasionally advised and worked with the Clark County commissioners, a number of whom were members of the Church of Jesus Christ of Latter-day Saints. They, along with other like-minded people, wanted to keep a "tight control" on what he referred to as "adult businesses." Edwards said:

> I was involved in many cases involving disciplinary proceedings involving licensing of liquor and gambling and escort establishments, and high powered attorneys from out of state which resulted in court litigation.... From my experience of living in Clark County for over 86 years, I believe that the Board of County Commissioners

at this time [affected by positive Latter-day Saint influence] was one of the most highly respected by the business executives of the community and the electorate. This board of commissioners was in direct contrast to the one which followed, wherein four of them were indicted for taking bribes.[55]

Aside from county commissioners, various Latter-day Saint elected officers also made good contributions. Shari Buck served on the North Las Vegas City Council from 1999 to 2009 and then as mayor of the city from 2009 to 2013. As an elected official, Buck was conscientious about not saturating her fellow workers with her religious beliefs, though she felt strongly about her standards. Buck stated, "I always tried to impart my values, but you couldn't do it in an overt way.... I would quote a scripture or quote a prophet, and I would say, 'A wise man once said.'...You can't really be in a public meeting and say, 'Let me tell you about my [Book of Mormon] prophet.'" Buck added, "I always tried to live the values that I knew were right to represent the Savior.... When I was done with public service, I knew I had not brought any shame to myself, my family, or my God, and that's how I wanted to live in public service."[56]

Harry Reid, who obtained national attention as a powerful senator, described his humble beginnings as a Latter-day Saint southern Nevada boy: "I came over from Searchlight, where I was born and raised, which was a crummy little town...mainly made of prostitutes.... We had no inside toilet. We walked 75 yards to go to the toilet. We had no hot water. So...I wasn't raised in the lap of luxury, but I didn't realize it until later. By then it was too late.... I was already at a point where I didn't worry about it."[57]

A talented competitive athlete in baseball, football, and boxing, Reid became an attorney in the city of Henderson, where he also served as a trustee for the Southern Nevada Memorial Hospital. Historian Leonard J. Arrington proudly described the pathway his former student Reid took as he "was elected a member of the Nevada State Assembly while he was still in his twenties; and in 1970, at age 31, he was elected Lieutenant Governor of Nevada. In 1977 he was appointed to a four-year term as chairman of the Nevada Gaming Board [Gaming Commission]."[58]

Senator Reid recalled that during his early political career, members of the church were serving in powerful positions. For example, Floyd Lamb was the dean of the Nevada state legislature, and Jim I. Gibson was

Senator Harry Reid, 1986. Special
Collections & Archives, University Libraries,
University of Nevada, Las Vegas.

an influential legislator while also serving as a stake president. Richard
Bunker was simultaneously a city manager and chairman of the Gaming
Control Board, while Reid was chairman of the Gaming Commission.[59]

A decade after Reid's appointment as chair, as a retired attorney, he
was elected as a US senator from Nevada and served as the whip leader
for the Democratic Party from 1999 to 2005 and also served as Senate
majority leader, his highest appointment, from 2007 to 2015.[60] Regarding
Reid's influence, Vegas journalist John L. Smith boldly and succinctly
stated, "Harry Reid is the most important political figure in Nevada history, period. The most important. The most influential."[61] Fellow journalist Jon Ralston added, "Reid is the most influential elected official in the
history of the state in terms of what he was able to do, not just legislatively
in Washington...but in the way that he was able to control Nevada politics for decades by being essentially the king maker, and getting people
to run or not run for office."[62]

Yet some Las Vegas citizens have considered Senator Reid to be polar-
izing, even among church members. For example, his stance on pro-life

was a concern to many as well as his charge against Mitt Romney for not paying income taxes, which proved to be without foundation. Yet those not of the Latter-day Saint faith have found Reid's pluck as a Democrat refreshing, especially since most church members in the United States have chosen to adhere to a more conservative stance with the Republican Party.[63] Notwithstanding Senator Reid sometimes appearing to be an enigma, there is real evidence Reid tried to minister faithfully to some fellow Saints in his private life. For example, the only appointments Senator Reid refused to be rescheduled were his home-teaching appointments, a Latter-day Saint calling in which male church members were assigned individuals or families to minister to on a volunteer basis.[64]

Speaking of Reid's adherence to his faith, former US senator, and active Episcopalian, Richard Bryan said:

> I've been with him on hundreds of occasions; in my view, he's absolutely 100% faithful to the tenets of the Church. But he's not a hypocrite; for example, I've gone out with him when we were young guys just elected to state assembly, and we were out some place, and I would have a beer, and he would not have anything like that. But when it was his turn to buy, his credit card was on the table.... He's very tolerant, which I feel is a commendable trait. And sometimes his style irritates people, because he's pretty aggressive and pretty forthright, pretty candid. But he's actually faithful to the tenets of the Church.[65]

Reid was also a devoted family man who considered his family his greatest achievement. In one recent interview, Reid reflected, "I think that as I look back that my number-one accomplishment has been my family. My wife [Landra] and I have been married for more than sixty years. We have five wonderful children. The oldest is a girl, four boys, nineteen grandchildren."[66]

Another influential Latter-day Saint in Las Vegas and southern Nevada is Lloyd D. George. George must have caught the attention of Washington to have been selected as a federal judge. He was appointed district judge for the District of Nevada by President Reagan in 1984 and served as chief district judge for the United States (1992–97).[67] And Judge George has the honor of having the Las Vegas federal courthouse named after him.[68] Known for his integrity and wisdom, George has been awarded several honors, among them the distinction of the Boy Scouts' Silver Beaver Award.[69]

Judge Lloyd D. George, 2020.
Photo by Martin Andersen.

SCOUTING PROGRAM

Another Latter-day Saint who has devoted much public service to Las Vegas is Mark Hutchison, former member of the Nevada Senate and lieutenant governor of Nevada, as noted above. In addition, he spent decades as a leader in the Scouting program. Hutchison observed, "The Scouting program in Southern Nevada has been very, very strong for decades, and probably 70–75 percent of the scouting leadership and the scouting funding, up until recently, came from Latter-day Saints." Hutchison added, "The Scouting program was very influential in my life as a young man, and it was incredibly influential in the lives of my three sons, all of whom were Eagle Scouts. I was an Eagle Scout, my father was a scoutmaster, I've been a scoutmaster three times, and to say that Scouting was a powerful influence for good is an understatement.... Las Vegas has one of the strongest Boy Scout councils in the country, and we have a Scout camp...named after [church president] Spencer W. Kimball."[70]

William "Will" Stoddard, who formerly presided over the Vegas region in his Latter-day Saint church assignment, said, "Frankly the Church has been the backbone of Scouting." He added, "When the Church discontinued being a sponsor of Boy Scout units [in 2019],...it basically decimated the Boy Scout program in Las Vegas.... We don't have the...registration fees that we previously had."[71]

Former US senator Richard Bryan (1989–2001) recalled that when he became involved in Scouting as a boy in 1949, "the LDS Scout troops were very strong,…that's really when I got to appreciate that the LDS church was a major sponsor of youth activities." He recalled that courts of honor in the Las Vegas area were often held at the local Latter-day Saint church building and that the "LDS church troop leaders spent a lot of time at the courts of honor."[72]

Eric Christensen remembered, "My dad, Don Christensen, was a Scouting machine,…and the Church was involved.… Every ward, every stake had massive Scouting programs. It was a wonderful thing in Las Vegas. We used to have pow-wows at the convention center. It would be packed.… My dad and all the leaders back in those days were so active in Scouting."[73]

In fact, Scouting has played a prominent role in southern Nevada for nearly a century. During the early twentieth century, Latter-day Saints provided exemplary Scouting leadership in their local region, via Troop 63, which was mostly made up of Latter-day Saint youth and sponsored by the Church of Jesus Christ of Latter-day Saints.[74] Chauncey C. Riddle, now ninety-four years old and an active Scout in the late 1930s and early 1940s, remembered, "Our scout program was very strong."[75] This was largely the result of local influential Latter-day Saint Scout leaders.

Marion B. Earl recalled, "In 1927, the [Las Vegas] First Ward sponsored the first Scout troop ever organized in Las Vegas, Troop 63. I was privileged to be the first scout master. Many dedicated men have served since then.… At first we belonged [to] the Arrowhead Council with headquarters in San Bernardino.… Troop 63 led all the other troops in our area in

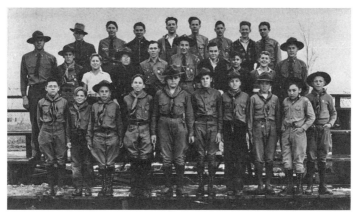

Boy Scout Troop 63, Chauncey C. Riddle (*middle row, fourth from left*), 1939. Special Collections & Archives, University Libraries, University of Nevada, Las Vegas.

advancement and Eagle scouts."[76] Three years after the establishment of Troop 63, in 1930, other Latter-day Saints were appointed to work with the Scouting program: Leslie Edwards, as a Troop 63 Scoutmaster,[77] and Roland H. Wiley, a local Latter-day Saint attorney, as Scout executive for the entire Las Vegas region.[78]

Earl was also interviewed by *Nevadan* journalist Jane Ann Morrison, who reported that when Troop 63 was launched with just eight boys, the population of Las Vegas was only about two thousand. The year after the troop was organized, Earl left for law school in Washington, DC, but upon returning, he assisted the troop again as a committee member. Because the Arrowhead Council was so far away, headquartered in San Bernardino, California, Earl and other Scout leaders successfully secured their own Boulder Dam Council, in 1944. Remarkably, at the time of the interview, Earl, at nearly eighty, could still remember the boys' names and in some instances where they were employed and even their church experience.[79]

Marion's brother Ira Joseph Earl, soon to be a local Scout chairman,[80] fought hard during these early years, albeit unsuccessfully, to keep gambling out of Nevada. In a 1930 article published in the *Las Vegas Age*, Ira Earl passionately made his opinions regarding gambling clear: "I protest with all the vigor of my soul against capital by any such methods. Young people will bet the money they should use to educate themselves to become useful citizens. Any man who will advocate wide open gambling hasn't the best interests of the people in this state at heart. I deny that gambling can be made safe and honorable by any such means."[81]

Two years later, Ira Earl again used the local media, this time to prick the conscience of the community to donate funds to help build boys in the Scouting program. Earl argued that although Scouting in Vegas enjoyed steady growth, he criticized the business and civic leaders for not investing more in supporting these youth. He emphasized the need for more leadership in the Scouting program.[82] As history has evidenced, the community responded to Earl's petition, and the Saints have provided exceptional Scouting leadership ever since Earl's era. In fact, in this same decade (in 1937), Bryan L. Bunker became southern Nevada's first Silver Beaver recipient, and more than two dozen additional Latter-day Saints would receive this prestigious Scouting award in Las Vegas by the end of the twentieth century.[83] Scouting remained an integral organization in the church until the end of 2019, when the church launched its own new activity program for youth.[84]

The Nevada Las Vegas Mission was formed during the summer of 1975, just as membership in the Church of Jesus Christ of Latter-day Saints was at its zenith, constituting about 13 percent of the Las Vegas and surrounding Clark County populace (332,000). Just one month prior to the mission's organization, journalist John Dart noted this high percentage: "It is by far the largest denomination in the Las Vegas area, and more importantly its members are often influential community people. 'The school district is heavily Mormon in administration, the Clark County sheriff is Mormon and the district attorney is Mormon,' a news correspondent pointed out."[85]

The Latter-day Saint standard periodical the *Church News* announced that this newly created proselytizing mission would be presided over by Ronald M. Patterson.[86] Prior to this time, full-time missionaries were sent to Vegas from the California Mission, with the bulk of missionary efforts provided by part-time local Saints for more than a half century.[87] The formal organization of a mission headquartered in Las Vegas provided a greater thrust to this proselytizing work by full-time missionaries, the men serving two years and the women eighteen months. By this time, the area was ripe for harvesting. McClain Bybee, who served in the first three mission presidencies (1975–81), indicated that by the time he was released from the presidency and was serving as the bishop of his local ward (1981–85), his congregation had been divided three times and he had witnessed forty baptisms per month in his ward alone![88]

In 1986, the local press announced that Latter-day Saint missionaries were not only teaching individuals and families in their homes but also inviting the larger public to learn more about the Latter-day Saint faith via discussions and films presented at the local Civic Center and the Latter-day Saint Tonopah church building.[89] Investigators were invited to attend, and the press advertised special events in which general church leaders spoke. For example, at the end of this same year, church apostle Neal A. Maxwell spoke at the "Christmas Family Fireside," where holiday music was performed by 150 members of the Las Vegas East Stake Singers.[90]

Appealing church advertisements later surfaced in local papers, such as an image of a wholesome, happy family, along with the caption, "Don't you wish families could stay together forever?" Offered in the ad was a free audio cassette instructing people about the church and how families could live together after mortality.[91]

By the end of the twentieth century, the Las Vegas Mission was thriving and would become one of the top three proselytizing missions in the United States in terms of baptisms.[92] Currently, there are two Latter-day Saint missions in the area: the Las Vegas Mission and the Las Vegas West Mission (created in 1997), with I-15 the boundary line between east and west.[93]

The current Las Vegas West Mission president, Curtis D. Reese, a native of Las Vegas, said that his mission has between 160 and 180 missionaries serving per year. With the COVID-19 pandemic, the number of missionaries coming from overseas to the United States has increased, swelling numbers to between 230 and 260 since June 2020. One advantage he observed from this influx is the additional international culture that has been woven into the fabric of the mission. Before COVID-19, the Las Vegas West Mission had been averaging 450 to 500 baptisms a year. A major reason for this success, Reese explained, is the "amazing" local church members who help find people to teach. Restrictions from the pandemic have decreased face-to-face interaction, but interested people are reaching out to the mission to learn more about the church.[94]

Missionaries from both the Las Vegas Mission and the Las Vegas West Mission not only offer spiritual messages to church members and investigators but also give hundreds of hours of temporal aid to the local community. For example, during the pandemic year of 2020, Mo Denis, counselor in the Las Vegas Mission presidency and Nevada state senator, wrote, "The missionaries have given a lot of service this past year. Everything from helping to distribute food, helping at vaccination sites, serving at local non-profits to helping individuals. They gave service as companionships and also in much larger groups with many missionaries."[95]

Senator Denis described an initiative introduced by the Las Vegas Mission for the Hispanic community: "[The mission] created a Centro Hispano, which is a Hispanic Center where people can come into one of our chapels that has been designated as a center, learn English, but they can also learn about community resources, they can learn about Family History, they can learn about getting jobs, improving their education, they can get tutoring for schools.... [We teach] English as a second language for those that speak Spanish."[96]

Tom Thomas, currently serving as a counselor in the Las Vegas West Mission presidency, summarized the recent work missionaries are doing within the mission boundaries he serves in and noted their work was restricted in 2020 by COVID-19 as well as "the closure of many non-profits to volunteers." Thomas explained, "Some of the non-profits [which] allowed volunteer help…were: Salvation Army (Food Delivery and Kitchen), Camp Stimson (LDS Girl's Camp), Just One Project (Food Delivery and Preparation), Three Square (Food Bank & Delivery), Deseret Industries (Thrift Store and Food Supplies), Baby's Bounty (Essentials for Infants), Society of St. Stephen (Methodist Church Food Bank), Culinary Academy (Food Assistance and Culinary Training to Reduce Poverty) & Lighthouse Charities (Refugee Assistance)." He further noted, "The total hours recorded by the Mission Office from Aug. 1 to Dec. 31 [2020] was 8,029. The average number of hours per month I expect the missionaries of the Nevada Las Vegas West Mission will provide to non-profits during 2021 is between 1,800 and 2,200."[97]

This type of temporal service resonates well with members of the larger community, many of whom are content with their own religious affiliations or beliefs. They appreciate and at times collaborate in service with their Latter-day Saint neighbors. Thousands of church members have provided assistance in myriad ways to the Vegas community since the church planted roots in southern Nevada.

A stellar example of this community involvement was evidenced at the 1976 bicentennial celebration of America. Before the year dawned, the press informed the public that Latter-day Saint Nevada historian and local educator Elbert B. Edwards had been selected to write a fifty-two-week bicentennial series for this distinctive year.[98] The bicentennial committee was also chaired by a Latter-day Saint, Lila Zona. Lucy Bunker and other church members were immersed in this inspiring commemoration representing the city of Las Vegas and the greater Clark County as a whole. Bunker, a local Vegas musician, led a three-hundred-member-strong interfaith choir and a fifty-piece orchestra. It was reported the choir had collectively rehearsed for thirty thousand hours and drove an estimated one hundred thousand miles of combined travel to prepare for their July 4 performance at the Las Vegas Convention Center. Their program was titled "One Nation Under God," and Bunker noted that it was a tribute to the "universal need for man to worship God."[99] The local press emphasized that the bicentennial-week celebration "should not pass into history without a tribute to the leaders and members of the Clark County Committee and the Church of Jesus Christ of Latter-day Saints, who fostered and presented outstanding patriotic programs."[100]

Another significant service event involving Latter-day Saints was the tremendous clean-up effort following the devastating 1999 summer flood that bombarded Las Vegas on July 8, remembered as "the 100-year storm." The *Church News* reported, "Flood waters filled homes with up to four feet of water.... Latter-day Saints immediately plunged in, helping both Church and community members in the area.... More than 100 people worked July 8, shoveling mud, removing ruined carpet and padding.... The next morning other volunteers brought heavy equipment to scoop up piles of debris."[101]

Church members from the Las Vegas Stake provided a live nativity program for the wider community for nearly two decades (1990–2008), directed by LaPrele George, wife of the honorable Lloyd D. George, who served as a US district federal judge in Vegas.[102] In 1993, the nativity included "70 costumed actors" and was enjoyed by more than ten thousand spectators.[103] Two years later, in 1995, the local news reported that the live reenactment would include "80 actors [and] dozens of sheep, horses, and flying angels." The article also mentioned that the previous year, in 1994, more than eight thousand people had again attended the pageant.[104]

Commenting on the annual event, LaPrele George said, "Every year we have a cast and crew of hundreds of people who contribute their time and talents.... Many just show up and ask what they can do to help. Others loyally come back year after year."[105] Service for the event includes "performing a role, handling the live animals, setting up scenery, sewing costumes, applying makeup, operating technical lighting and sound equipment, providing food, [and] directing traffic."[106]

Jean Cornwall, whose husband, Douglas, built a permanent Bethlehem set for the nativity, recalled that LaPrele "was a stickler for having it be authentic, the costuming and everything. It was fabulous." Cornwall also remembered passing out flyers to the public at the beauty salon she owned. She was most pleased when those who attended the nativity would return to her parlor and say, "Thank you so much for introducing us to this nativity; we're going to make it a yearly event for our family because we want our children to understand the true meaning of Christmas." Every performance was standing room only. This annual Christmas celebration brought both meaning and joy to the Vegas community at large and no doubt helped to firmly establish that Latter-day Saints were in fact Christians.[107] George recalled that she was prepared as a child for this assignment and felt inspiration as she directed the program. During this time, her husband, Judge Lloyd George, provided narration for the pageant and also worked behind the scenes laundering costumes. LaPrele was pleased that people of varied faiths worked to help with the production. She expressed feelings of great satisfaction in knowing that both a Catholic and a Baptist congregation staged their own nativities after observing the tremendous influence the Latter-day Saint program had on the community.[108]

Countless other small community services have been provided by church members during the past few decades. For many years, Cristi Bulloch, president of the American Mothers Nevada Association, has honored mothers in Las Vegas and throughout the state. Bulloch, a local Latter-day Saint, explained that the American Mothers organization has been in the state of Nevada since 1945 and focuses on honoring mothers and providing service and instruction. Bulloch explained that the organization seeks to provide opportunities for mothers and to teach them more about motherhood: "Recently we've had…internet safety classes; we've had…classes on nutrition and working with children with disabilities and challenges."[109]

Bulloch also worked with like-minded organizations and other religions to strengthen families, a central focus among Latter-day Saints. Her group worked with the *Las Vegas Review-Journal* to provide family-focused articles. Bulloch recalled that the Southern Nevada LDS Public Affairs Council—Family Focus Committee had the chance to provide an insert in the *Las Vegas Review-Journal* annual during National Family Week from 1991 to 2009. She explained, "We always had an article from one of our General Authorities focused on a family-life subject. We included articles from many family-oriented service organizations in our community and had writers that submitted stories each year."[110]

These articles included consistent "proclamations from the governor and the senator for family week."[111] The emphasis by Latter-day Saints on the cultivation of strong families was clearly recognized in southern Nevada. Former US senator Richard Bryan stated, "When I think of the LDS church community, a single word comes to mind over and over and over again, and it's family."[112]

Joyce Haldeman, church communications director for the Las Vegas region, has also been involved in finding ways to strengthen the Vegas community. Haldeman highlighted one particular community-service opportunity launched by the Latter-day Saints for one holiday season.

In November 2019, prominent Las Vegas musical performer and church member Donny Osmond unveiled one of the Saints' ten worldwide "Giving Machines."[113] Haldeman recalled, "We were selected as one of ten [global] sites to host a Giving Machine…and over the course of the seven weeks that the Giving Machines were at downtown Summerlin, we brought in $825,000.…As we worked with the representatives of each of the charities, it was such a great experience, and so many things that they said and the feelings that they had about working with members of the Church were so positive and reaffirming, and we worked shoulder to shoulder." Haldeman added, "I think it was interesting because the Giving Machines are not a missionary activity.… They [those involved] walked away with a new respect for the church because here was this new activity designed to help others, not to benefit the church."[114]

Latter-day Saints eagerly look for service needs wherever they live. One such opportunity presented itself in 2011, when Jana Dixon, president of the Highland Hills Stake Relief Society, realized that some local veterans needed help assimilating back into society. Dixon and the women she presided over initiated a program they called "Operation Dignity,"[115] which assisted veterans living in a twenty-unit housing complex. She explained, "As each unit would come [available], we had a day of service." Dixon added that church members "came with paint, they came with furniture, they came with beddings and linens and pots and pans and groceries. And it was such a wonderful experience to partner with them." When Mayor Carolyn Goodman became aware of this extraordinary service, she was most grateful and complimentary of the church leaders and members who had given their time and resources. Dixon recalled that Goodman, in jest, asked, "Will you continue onto the next housing project down the street?"[116]

Opportunity Village is another example of an ongoing Latter-day Saint service initiative. Bob Brown, executive director of Opportunity Village, explained, "This organization is dedicated to helping people with intellectual disabilities and really is the heart of Las Vegas. And one of the things that you see on our board is a lot of leaders in the LDS community.… These are wonderful people that we respect greatly.… I'm an old Catholic and a practicing Catholic, which is a rare thing, but I found these wonderful LDS Mormons…understood that a community is not about buildings, it's about families."[117]

Mark Hutchison added, "Opportunity Village is such a beloved organization, and members of the Church are heavily involved."[118] He noted,

"I can't tell you how many Eagle Scout projects I've been involved in that benefited in some way Opportunity Village."[119]

For decades, Latter-day Saint service missionaries have worked with several local organizations, such as the Three Square Food Bank, dedicated to making sure people are properly fed each day. In addition, Hutchison noted, "We work with Catholic charities very, very closely. There's a great homeless shelter in downtown Las Vegas that many, many Church members volunteer at throughout the year."[120] The press also reported under the headline "Crocheted Comforts" that Latter-day Saint women from the Las Vegas Redrock Stake had gathered to crochet hats for chemotherapy patients. The ladies also made pillowcases and blankets for newborns and estimated that from 2000 to 2014, they had made more than eighteen thousand items for both children and adults.[121]

Keith Thomas, Latter-day Saint interfaith specialist for the Greater Las Vegas Communication Council, described another long-term service project that began the 1990s at the Blind Center of Nevada. Thomas explained that through diligent service led by Latter-day Saints, "the BCON has been transformed from a rundown set of buildings with very little to offer the blind community into an award-winning day center offering daily transportation, hot meals, employment opportunities, learning opportunities and much more."[122]

The Church of Jesus Christ of Latter-day Saints also has a total of thirty-four family history centers to serve Las Vegas and communities spread throughout the state of Nevada.[123] In these centers, groups and individuals of any culture or faith receive genealogical instruction and assistance. Furthermore, the worldwide church humanitarian project "Helping Hands"[124] is also active in this region to provide public service and disaster relief, as is "Just Serve," the community-service program initiated by Latter-day Saints.[125]

Apart from the formal service forums, hundreds of everyday Latter-day Saints quietly and consistently practice the tenets of their religion by meeting whatever community needs they become aware of. A letter submitted to the local press described the multitudinous small acts of kindness Latter-day Saints perform in their neighborhood communities. The author informed the editor, in an article titled "High Praise," "I am not a Mormon, but I am impressed with their love and concern for mankind." The writer then listed three reasons: first, his experience using a local Latter-day Saint church building for a relative free of charge; second, the compassionate help he received when a flood washed away his house and belongings; and third, the assistance he observed church members pro-viding to an elderly Latter-day Saint man by trimming his lawn, painting his house, and providing transportation for him.[126]

Ruth Johnson, an active local Latter-day Saint, summarized the com-munity service she observed by her fellow church members: "I saw them step up in so many capacities. At the state legislature, those who sought positions of judges, the police force... Just in every section, in every cross-section, every economic section, every part of the city was influenced so positively by members of the Church who were willing to step out and do something besides take care of their family, besides take care of their calling. They went above and beyond." Johnson continued, "They served at every level, and they did it, not because they were asked to do it, they did it because they saw a need."[127]

6

Ecclesiastical Community Service to a Local Congregation in Need

Whether your color is dark, light...it doesn't matter!
—Deacon Adolph Huddleston

A unique community project deserving special recognition occurred in a West Las Vegas neighborhood at a time when there was deep racial tension where Blacks were marginalized. Flames soaring more than eighty feet high engulfed a local house of worship. Nine fire trucks and thirty-five firefighters futilely battled the burning church still in the late stages of construction on Lexington Street near Highland Drive and Wyatt Avenue.[1]

Latter-day Saint president of the Las Vegas Stake, Charles Johnson (1931–2011),[2] picked up the *Las Vegas Review-Journal* and gawked at the image of charred remains.[3] "Come and look at this!" he called to his wife, Ellie.[4] The destroyed African American Baptist church was within the boundaries of his stake, a large congregation numbering several thousand members.[5] Johnson recognized a crisis and responded immediately to a piercing cry for help, notwithstanding the unfamiliar cultural and religious divide. He would be crossing a racial boundary not commonly traversed by most white inhabitants of the Las Vegas region. Further, though African Americans could be baptized into the Church of Jesus Christ of Latter-day Saints, men were denied priesthood ordination until June 1978, when the church issued an official declaration permitting all worthy males to receive the priesthood.[6]

This area, derogatorily referred to at the time as "Westside," is located in West Las Vegas, northwest of downtown. It takes in a three-and-a-half-square-mile radius from the north of Bonanza Road to the south of Lake Mead Boulevard, lying between I-15 and Rancho Drive. From 1960 to 1990, it had a rather stagnant population of about fifteen thousand, even as Clark County quadrupled in size. At the time of the 1990 census, 78 percent of the West Las Vegas population was Black, which was the highest

Greater Evergreen Missionary Baptist Church on fire, 1983.
Courtesy of the Greater Evergreen Missionary Baptist Church.

concentration of African Americans in either the city of Las Vegas or all of Clark County.[7]

At this time, the neighborhood was commonly avoided by taxicab drivers because of its reputation for kidnappings, rapes, and even murders. Yet one local who ran the largest shopping center in the area said, "You never hear of any of that stuff going on here."[8] Despite the stigma, historically, West Las Vegas was also known for its vibrant Black entertainment at the Moulin Rouge Hotel, which opened in 1955, though it closed that same year. West Las Vegas possessed a strong spiritual element in the latter part of the twentieth century. West Las Vegas was described by one journalist as having "a church on every corner," and one author reported that there were more than forty-five different congregations in a square mile. It was a place where "black civic leaders often become ministers of local churches."[9]

Segregation was still a serious issue during this decade of the 1950s. Therefore, the African American press reprimanded the city that never sleeps because of their "lily-white policies in their swank resorts and gambling spots." Due to its backward racial attitudes, it was known as the "Mississippi of the West."[10] During this period, regardless of their income, local Black citizens were nearly all confined to West Las Vegas.[11]

One of the vibrant Westside churches was the ill-fated Evergreen Missionary Baptist Church.[12] Parishioners had outgrown their smaller church less than a mile away at 1011 H Street. The new larger building, which would be known as the Greater Evergreen Missionary Baptist Church, had been under construction for eighteen months and was scheduled to be completed by the end of 1983. Sadly, the fire claimed about 60 percent of the building. Although no injuries were reported, the disaster was emotionally devastating to this Christian congregation of three hundred.

Pastor Nathaniel Whitney, who had served the congregation since 1965, said that the "people were stunned" by the inferno that took their church building, "but they regrouped and were able to go forward." He added, "This is a beautiful congregation to work with. It has the love and spirit of Christ." Church clerk Retha Hawkins said, "We cried but we stayed together.... God just kept us together." Church officer Eugene Robertson remarked, "If it is determined to be arson we don't know why anyone would do it." Eyewitness to the blaze and neighbor Mary Howard reported, "I didn't see anyone in the area when the fire broke out. I feel sorry for anyone who would deliberately set a church on fire.... Lord help them."[13] Little time was necessary to wonder. The day following the fire, a thirteen-year-old boy was arrested, and the police searched for four additional juveniles wanted for questioning in what appeared to be the work of young arsonists.[14]

Bernard Hawkins III, 2020.
Photo by Martin Andersen.

Bernard Hawkins III recollected at the time of the burning, "I was…
listening to the radio and…over the airwaves it came about that a church
under construction had been set on fire and it's on the west side, and
at that point there was no other church being constructed at the time,
and my heart just sank. I said, 'Oh my God, someone has set the church
on fire.'" Hawkins felt overwhelmed because the congregation lacked
the money to rebuild. At this time of devastation, he remembered, "Our
hearts just sank, and all we could do was say, 'God help us.' And God did;
God did help us. He sent the Latter-day Saints to our aid, and they helped
us in every way they could."[15]

COMPASSION IN ACTION

Stake president Charles Johnson rang Pastor Whitney and initiated meetings with him and Johnson's counselors Dwayne Ence and Frank Bingham. Ence remembered that each Sunday they met as a stake presidency
with Pastor Whitney and other leaders from his congregation to plan
reconstruction and the procurement of necessary equipment.[16] They
learned that the church's fire insurance did not cover all the loss, and
Whitney estimated the cost for the new edifice at $850,000 for his grow-
ing congregation of 450 members.

Latter-day Saint volunteers heading up the project included Gary
Halverson (1934–2018),[17] owner of Southwest Air Conditioning, and especially Douglas Cornwall (1940–91), a general contractor who supervised
the project.[18] It was said Cornwall could work around the clock and was
always willing to assist with service projects when asked. He donated his
time and equipment for this enterprise, which inspired many, including
the Latter-day Saint youth.[19] Cornwall's charitable labor was also augmented by many others from the Las Vegas stake who were willing to go
to work. Stake funds covered all the materials because of generous donations from church members.[20]

Local Saints provided aid leveling the old structure and erecting
the new one. Frank Bingham, second counselor in the stake presidency,
recollected, "We as a stake presidency wanted to help them. We got some
of the members of the Church who were contractors with dump trucks
to help with the cleanup. After that, we helped them to put up the walls
and the roof and helped them to finish the inside. It was a big job."[21]

One local Latter-day Saint journalist wanted to write up the story
about his congregation helping the Baptists rebuild, but Charles Johnson
and his counselors refused to cooperate because they wished to serve in

(*Left to right*) Dwayne Ence, Charles Johnson, and Frank Bingham.
Courtesy of Eleanor Johnson.

anonymity.[22] Ellie Johnson, wife of Charles Johnson, described her husband's deportment and position:

> He was a quiet individual, never bringing attention to himself. So, I truly feel like he was inspired that day when he read the paper, that there was an impression that came over him that he needed to do something about this congregation, and that he wanted to help them any way he could.... When someone had mentioned it would be good to get the newspapers in on this or get some publication to show what the Church was doing for other congregations, he said, "No, we just want to do it because it's in our hearts to help these people because we love God's children."[23]

Authentic compassion, not publicity, motivated Johnson and his counselors as well as the other Saints assisting with the work. As a testament to the genuine mutual friendships being forged as the new building rose from the ashes, various members of the Baptist congregation occasionally attended Latter-day Saint church services and social activities with their newfound friends. This forging of authentic friendship was refreshing inasmuch as there had been some tension originating from the church policy noted above that did not allow Blacks to receive ordination to the priesthood until 1978.[24] With the change of official church policy, tensions were reduced, and the service that Johnson and his stake provided not only strengthened the relationship of local neighbors in this area but also sent a message to church members beyond the reef.

INDISTINGUISHABLE

Baptists and Latter-day Saints worked hand in hand, setting aside any differences. Ence stated, "In the beginning it was very dirty work because of all the soot and burnt wood that had to be removed.... That black congregation were very Christian in their approach and in their response.... They were very...open in their appreciation for what we had done."[25] Bernard Hawkins III, a member of the Baptist congregation, remembered, "They came over, and...everybody was black from the ashes, and so that was one thing that we held in common, that we was all brothers. We would check our arms and I put my arm beside another LDS brother, and we would all look the same. And that was so heartwarming that they didn't mind getting dirty in the ashes and helping us, and we thanked God for the help that we received from them and their expertise that they allowed themselves to come over and give us a helping hand."[26]

Loretta Whitney, another member of the Baptist congregation, married Pastor Whitney two years after the devastating fire. She reminisced about the cleanup of the burned church building and remembered the

Pastor Welton T. Smith III, 2020.
Photo by Martin Andersen.

Latter-day Saints and her fellow church members covered in soot. "You could not tell one from the other, and the joy they shared I can [still] hear it in my heart," she recalled. "Everybody was doing what they needed to do with joy. Nobody was grumpy.... The many times they came over to help. It was just a great time."[27] She also reflected, "It was amazing to see it and hear the laughter, yet the love and the fellowship that were going on, you would just stand and be in amazement to see it, because it was just such togetherness. Now you talking about one body, that was one body. It was wonderful,...nobody discriminating."[28]

Current pastor Welton T. Smith III was touched that Latter-day Saints came out to assist the Baptist congregation, the women cooking meals and the men working hand in hand to clean up the rubbish. He noted, "the beauty about the story is that [in] the beginning, you had black and white. But at the end of the day, because of all the soot and ash, you couldn't tell a black man from a white man."[29]

THE MARCH

On February 9, 1986, at 8:00 A.M.,[30] a march was held, beginning at the old church and moving to the newly completed one. Latter-day Saints joined their Black Christian friends to celebrate. Ellie Johnson remembered people singing "Amazing Grace" that day and recalled that "everybody was so happy."[31] She recorded in her journal: "We took the children down to the Greater Evergreen Missionary Baptist Church today for the march from the old church building to the new. It was a humbling experience to see Charles cry. He had worked with these humble people and seen their faith and diligence for such a long time. We have learned from them and they from us about Christian love and caring. The walk of over one mile was bitter cold but our hearts were warm."[32]

Loretta Whitney still remembers what happened at the time of the march: "It was a beautiful day. Even the police were out in front of the Church, and we marched from the old to the new building.... It was just amazing.... The joy, the tears that were shed.... Satan tried to stop it, but he couldn't stop it.... We had a glorious time that day."[33] Following the march, Pastor Whitney dedicated their new church building just before they entered the door.[34] The *Las Vegas Review-Journal* reported, "The new Church was built with an eye toward the future. The sanctuary seats more than 600 people in pews upholstered in a bold evergreen shade. The balcony has space for 150 people. There's room in the choir section for 100 people." With a broad smile, Bernard Hawkins Jr., who chaired the

Loretta Whitney, 2020. Photo by Martin Andersen.

church's deacon board, remarked, "You can never build a choir (section) big enough. People love to sing."[35] Referring to the completion of the new church, Pastor Whitney said, "This is a blessing from God that we have been able to accomplish this."[36]

After the march, Latter-day Saints joined with their Baptist brothers and sisters to celebrate in a joyful meeting.[37] According to Ellie Johnson, wife of stake president Charles Johnson, those in attendance included the Las Vegas stake presidency and their wives. She remembered that local political leaders were also at the dedication and recorded their names in her journal: "Harry Reid, [James] Seastrand, Governor Richard and Bonnie Bryan." Ellie mentioned that her children were not accustomed to the lively worship style of their Baptist friends: "It was a long meeting with a couple of sisters getting the spirit. Mark's mouth dropped open, and he wanted to know what in the world they were doing. I guess it's their way of expressing themselves when they feel emotional. The experience was overwhelming for the children."[38]

Other Saints likewise appreciated the diversity between their own reverent, more reserved mode of worship and that of their energetic Baptist friends. Dwayne Ence stated that "their music is traditional black music, you know, a lot of hand clapping and interaction with the congregation."[39] Ellie was in a quandary when Pastor Whitney asked those assembled to stand up if they had been saved. She hesitated only because Latter-day Saints don't utilize this terminology, but she knew Jesus Christ was her savior and that by grace she had been redeemed from death to enjoy immortality. Therefore, Ellie sat quietly, although she felt united in faith with her Baptist Black brothers and sisters.[40]

IMPACT ON THE YOUTH

These mutual friendships and feelings of acceptance were not limited to the adults. Latter-day Saint youth participating in the cleanup and erection of this new church also enjoyed a new appreciation for their Baptist neighbors. From the ages of thirteen to sixteen, Justin Roberts helped with the cleanup and construction under the direction of Doug Cornwall, who supervised the work. Roberts recollected the "distinct vision" of Black and white merging as one: "We got together with shovels and brooms and rakes and dump trucks and garbage bins [to clean] up.... We all had a gray tone to us because of the ash and the soot.... I remember...going down there as a young man that feeling of 'do we belong? Are we in the right place?' And how that eventually melted away, how we were accepted for who we are, they were accepted for who they were, and we had a common goal to clean up and build this building."[41]

A decade after the completion of the church building, Roberts became a police officer in North Las Vegas, which borders the Greater Evergreen Missionary Baptist Church location. Roberts said, "I remember several conversations as...a young white police officer in an otherwise Black neighborhood, using that as a common denominator, expressing to them the memories that I had of going over there after the fire and helping clean up and the friendships we forged then, and I was able to forge new ones because I think it gave me some credibility." Later in his career, when he had become the North Las Vegas assistant chief of police, Roberts was invited by Pastor Smith, who succeeded Pastor Whitney, to speak at the Evergreen Baptist Church. As he walked down the church hall, he recognized people in a picture of the cleanup effort after the old building had burned. He then shared with the congregation his warm memories of being a part of the building of their house of worship and told them, "We are all sons and daughters of our Heavenly Father, which makes us all brothers and sisters."[42]

Another young man involved with the Evergreen church project was Lynn Hughes. He remembered that between 100 and 150 Latter-day Saint youth helped with the cleanup process. In retrospect, Hughes felt

Derek Ence, 2020. Photo by Martin Andersen.

that working with youth from these two different denominations for a common cause was a deeply meaningful experience from which he reaped benefits later in his life. Currently a Las Vegas attorney, Hughes remarked, "I do think that [experience] has affected my life in having respect for people of other cultures, the diversity, etc. I have many clients that I have dealt with that I feel comfortable dealing with, Black, Hispanic, Filipino, just many. I learned that there are many different varieties of life."[43]

The Ence family, parents Dwayne and Bonnie as well as their sons, Derek and David, were also transformed by this unique service opportunity. As a sixth grader, Derek Ence experienced segregation in his neighborhood and helplessly absorbed the negative cultural prejudices inherent in American society at that time. Derek recalls once riding his bike "beyond the border" of what was then referred to as the "Westside." Instantly, he felt a sickening feeling that he had trespassed and was not welcome there.

When school integration programs were introduced, tensions sometimes ran high among the children because of old fears and misconceptions. It was not until Derek began cleanup work on the charred African American church a half-dozen years later that his paradigm completely shifted. With tears in his eyes, Derek shared the joy he felt working shoulder to shoulder with his Black brothers cleaning up the sooty remains of the church. Through this experience, Derek gained a clear understanding that there is no inferior color in God's eyes; all are alike unto him.[44]

Derek's younger brother, David, organized an Eagle Scout program at age sixteen to assist with the cleanup of the construction portion of the project. Like his brother, David also remembered the reality of segregation in his boyhood and experienced a shift in his perception and attitudes through the service he rendered.[45] David recounted, "Some of the goals of that project were not only to render service, but also to bring together the two religious communities,…the two races."[46]

Derek's mother, Bonnie Ence, remembered how she felt when she observed a group of generous Baptist women serving unexpectedly when Bonnie was providing refreshments for those involved in the cleanup project:

> I was laying out the paper plates and utensils…getting things ready for the luncheon. I looked over and here are four of the ladies behind the Missionary Baptist Church with big platters of chicken…. We visited a little bit, and…it was a really sweet experience because the youth were involved and then also the fact that those ladies or sisters brought that chicken. It was a very successful day…. I was deeply touched by their graciousness…because that was certainly a big project for them.[47]

Jean Cornwall, wife of Douglas Cornwall, who had overseen construction on the new church building, recalled that members of the Evergreen Baptist Church graciously arranged for a special program one evening after their new house of worship was completed to thank their Latter-day Saint friends for their generous assistance. She recounted, "They did a dinner for the Las Vegas Stake, invited everyone to come to the[ir] church…. And then, the Baptist choirs, the Black Baptist people, they rock. When they sing, they rock the rafters, and it was wonderful. They sang and shouted for joy."[48]

Ned Day, *Review-Journal* columnist, having heard of this celebratory interfaith event, wrote, "You may remember when the Evergreen facility burned down…leaving the Baptists with nowhere to attend services. What you probably didn't know is this: LDS Church members have quietly been raising money that has been earmarked to help rebuild the Westside Baptist Church. Last night, the Mormons and good Baptists all got together at the new church and toasted a little punch to celebrate the interfaith effort."[49]

FELLOWSHIP

Goodwill between the Las Vegas Saints and members of the Greater Evergreen Missionary Baptist Church has endured. Long after the flames subsided and a new Baptist church building rose, current pastor Welton T. Smith III and his Latter-day Saint friend Lamar Noorda became acquainted. At Noorda's invitation, Pastor Smith's choir joined the Latter-day Saint college-age chorus along with other church choirs in a festive Christmas-season music performance. Noorda recalled, "We just kind of became fast friends. They accepted our invitation and came to our first night of choirs. And since then we've done it fourteen years." Noorda added, "They're so different than us, and yet, zealous in their faith."[50]

Later, at a New Year's Eve event, the two friends again joined forces, this time to celebrate the African American tradition known as Watch-night. Noorda explained, "[Watchnight] commemorates when churches all through the South were wondering if Abraham Lincoln would sign the [Emancipation] Proclamation or let it lapse. And so, they were waiting and waiting and then of course got the word just a few minutes before midnight that he had signed it and that they were free. So, they celebrate that in a huge way, and it's really moving to see." Noorda added that after his dear friend Pastor Smith had addressed the audience like it was "an athletic event," with "pouring sweat, singing, and he's preaching, and he's yelling, and he's moving, imagine that after all that he said, 'Pastor Noorda is gonna say a few words and then give us a benediction.' So, yeah, that was interesting enough."[51]

Noorda's wife, Elise, reported that she and Lamar have been dear friends with Pastor Smith and his wife, Deborah, over the past fifteen years. She confirmed the reciprocal appreciation and respect between their local stake and the Greater Evergreen Missionary Baptist Church. Elise Noorda admires their spirited choir and enjoys participating in their worship services. Elise said that although "the music is so different than what we're used to…it's a great experience to…be part of that and just again rub shoulders, and see how much we have in common along with the things that are so different."[52]

Though the tenor of their worship differs, the tender feelings are reciprocal between the Noordas and the Smiths as well as among their congregations. With decades long passed and the flames but a smoky memory, this singular event continues to pay residual dividends in the souls of these people. In what is known as the "Hall of History"[53] inside the Greater Evergreen Missionary Baptist Church, a faded photograph

Left to right: Charles Johnson, Pastor Nathaniel
Whitney, and Terry Rogers. Courtesy of Greater
Evergreen Missionary Baptist Church.

of Charles Johnson standing beside his friend Pastor Nathaniel Whitney
hangs in a simple wooden frame.[54] Congregants can look at the picture
and reminisce about a most extraordinary time. Both men wear ear-to-ear
grins, with mutual affection emanating from their eyes. For them, they are
color-blind. The only color they see is the color of brotherhood.

Pastor Smith reflected, "When I walk by that picture, it reminds me
of what God designed our world to be and what our world should and
still can be. With all the hurt that we see, that picture reminds me of the
promise that comes with *agape*,"[55] a Greek word referring to the highest form of pure love. Fellow church leader Deacon Adolph Huddleston
contributed his reflections on this inspiring story: "For me, significantly,
was the bridge that came out of the tragedy of the burning down and the

Adolf Huddleston, 2020.
Photo by Martin Andersen.

total devastation of the church. And those relationships that were bridged
and forged out of people that were cultivated out of something that was
totally separate from the church.... That's the most powerful thing that
came out of it,...men of God that come together. And I think that is
the most significant, the...fellowship. It is something that both churches
cherish." Huddleston continued, "That's something that just needs to be
highlighted today.... And whether your color is dark, light,...it doesn't
matter...we're all the same."[56]

Pastor Whitney's wife, Loretta, added, "My mother taught me that
love must be extended to everybody.... Our job is to obey God. Jesus said
love one another, and he did not say just love the black or the white, and
I have to follow him. Sometimes it's hard,...but I've got to love. At that
burning church, they [the Latter-day Saints] showed love."[57]

RECIPROCITY

A welcomed opportunity for payback presented itself when the Latter-
day Saints sought approval for their own sacred edifice, a temple in Las
Vegas. Charles Johnson was then serving as president of the Las Vegas
Stake and also as a spokesman for the Las Vegas Temple committee.[58]
No doubt he apprised his friend Pastor Whitney of an upcoming Clark
County Commission zoning meeting to be held in late December 1984.

Pastor Nathaniel Whitney and some of his Baptist congregants attended to show their firm support and love for their Latter-day Saint friends.[59]

After the zoning meeting, Loretta Whitney asked her future husband what had happened. He replied, "They want to build their church [temple], and…we just have to pray for them, so they can get it done…cause they're some nice people…. I really want them to get their church [temple] because that's what they need."[60]

Bonnie Ence said, "I remember Dwayne coming back from that… planning meeting, and he was so elated because of the support that had been given by Brother Whitney and those that were involved with the church. And it was his feeling [that it was] their influence and their speaking up that really helped with the zoning, and the planning commission kind of put it over the top…. Their support was really quite valuable because of the opposition."[61]

7

The Story of the Las Vegas Temple

Never has there been so beautiful a day in Las Vegas as we dedicate the House of the Lord, the crowning jewel overlooking the city.

—President Gordon B. Hinckley

A DESERVING NEED

Church president Gordon B. Hinckley was once asked by the local southern Nevada press why Las Vegas was selected as the place for a temple. President Hinckley's honest response: "I don't know of any place in all the world that needs one more. I don't know of a place in the world where you see more clearly the contrast between evil and good, than you do in this city. This place needs a temple."[1]

The need for a temple had been recognized decades earlier. Old-time Boulder City church member Don Atkin told of a conversation he once had with church apostle Harold B. Lee while Lee was visiting the Las Vegas region. Elder Lee invited Atkin to come to the side of one of the Henderson church buildings, where together they could view both the Las Vegas and the Henderson Valleys below. Lee then turned to Atkin and said, "'I think the people in this area are the most righteous people in the church.' 'You think so?' I asked. Lee responded, 'Their attendance at their meetings is the highest in the church, their payment of tithes is the highest, and the temple attendance is the highest (though they had to drive to St. George), and all this within the shadow of the wickedness and sin that is in this city.'"[2]

PROPHECY OF CHURCH GROWTH, BUILDINGS, AND A TEMPLE

About a decade before Lee's visit, church patriarch Robert Olson Gibson had a sacred experience as he spiritually prepared to offer a dedicatory prayer for a local church farm, a prayer requested by Bryan L. Bunker, president of the Moapa Stake. President Edwin Wells, a member of the stake presidency, described Patriarch Gibson's preparation before the land was dedicated: Patriarch Gibson worried about giving a dedicatory prayer

140

because of the division among some of the Saints at the time regarding the purchase of the church farm. Yet after concerted meditation and fervent prayer, Gibson had a dream that brought him peace. In his dream, he envisioned the Las Vegas Valley and saw many Latter-day Saint meetinghouses and one at the base of Sunrise Mountain.

Church member Denzel Aiken remembered Patriarch Gibson saying, "I was standing on a high mountain where I could see the whole valley. I could see the LDS activities all around the valley…chapels and other buildings and other things that would come to pass. I could see church buildings and that houses just covered the valley in every direction." Aiken also remembered Gibson stating, "Eventually you will have a temple here."

Bishop Tom Adams remembered, "It was a prophetic prayer. He said one day the valley would be dotted with chapels and a temple. I thought it would come true because of the righteous man he was. I was not sure about seeing it myself." Patriarch Gibson's son R. Owen Gibson recalled his father saw many church buildings in the valley and also "looked down to see a temple at the base of the mountain upon which he was standing."[3]

After Gibson's experience, and approximately three decades before the temple was announced, another Latter-day Saint had a special experience regarding the future location of the temple following a serious accident. Scott Seastrand recounted, Vern Frehner had told his father, James Seastrand, the night the Las Vegas Temple was announced that thirty years earlier he had seen where the temple was to be located. Frehner said "he saw in his mind…it was up on Sunrise Mountain, just up Bonanza Hill.… And he said, 'I came to tell you because I wanted you to know that I've seen where the temple is supposed to go.' And so, that was a spiritual experience confirmation to my father that this man came out of nowhere, came to share something that had happened thirty years prior."[4]

DESIRE, DISCUSSIONS, AND SELECTION

Las Vegas Temple committee historian Elbert B. Edwards wrote of observing what he referred to as a "temple awareness" among the Saints of southern Nevada. Edwards discerned that the local growth of the church brought an increase in various church programs and a surge of faith and spirituality. In addition, he perceived that new technology brought greater opportunities for genealogical and family history research. Edwards stated, "Members in the region also became increasingly aware of the conveniences a temple in their own area would provide if freed from the time and expenses of transportation and lodging in order to attend the temples

Elbert Edwards, ca. mid-twentieth   James K. Seastrand.
century. Special Collections &   Courtesy of Scott Seastrand.
Archives, University Libraries,
University of Nevada, Las Vegas.

elsewhere.... It was also mentioned repeatedly in informal discussions at meetings of...[church leaders] throughout the area."[5]

Sometime during the 1970s, Apostles James E. Faust and David B. Haight also expressed their feelings to local church leader James I. Gibson that Las Vegas should have a temple. Gibson said, "They encouraged me as the Regional Representative at the time to initiate inquiry as to how to proceed. Some land was offered for a site, but the time was not yet right."[6]

Elder James K. Seastrand, who followed Gibson as a regional representative in 1980, remembered, "The first time I heard of the firm possibility that a temple would be built in Southern Nevada was during an Area Council Meeting on February 20, 1981, presided over by Elder John Groberg...a member of the First Quorum of the Seventy.... In this meeting, besides Elder Groberg, were the three Regional Representatives for the state of Nevada, Elder Lenard D. Robison, Elder Samuel M. Davis, and Elder James K. Seastrand." Seastrand explained, "A comment was made about the desirability of a temple in Southern Nevada. Elder Groberg mentioned that he could not state when it would happen but that on a list he had seen of the first one hundred temples to be built, Las Vegas was listed within that projected one hundred. He suggested it would be a good idea for the Regional Representatives to begin looking for prospective land which would be suitable upon which to build a temple."[7]

Historian Edwards recorded, "The information was electrifying. It fell on ready, eager and willing ears. The enthusiasm was contagious and spread rapidly among all church leaders, and into the congregations. It provided relief and expression for years of pent-up hopes and dreams."[8] A year later, Seastrand related that during a Church Area Council meeting with Elder Vaughn J. Featherstone, the possibility of a Las Vegas Temple was again considered. Seastrand wrote, "We had a glorious time in being together in discussing the kingdom of God in our area."[9]

Six months later, Elder Seastrand presided at a ten-stake welfare meeting in which local stake presidents made recommendations for temple sites. Seastrand explained:

> [As a result of the meeting,] Elder Donald C. Whitney (the other Regional Representative) and I set up an unofficial committee of three stake presidents to visit all potential sites and give us their feelings. President William Calvert was asked to take the lead, assisted by Presidents Theron L. Swainston and Neil "C." Twitchell. Between August 29, 1982 and December 10, 1982, the three stake Presidents visited various potential sites throughout the Las Vegas Valley.
>
> December 20, 1982, I joined with Brothers Boyd Bulloch, Donald Whitney, William Calvert, Theron Swainston, and Neil Twitchell at the North Las Vegas airport from where we flew over the Las Vegas Valley and looked at prospective temple sites. The one on Sunrise Mountain foothills…(turned out to not be the site, but only a short distance away)…. I was asked if I would present this information to our new Executive Administrator, Elder Hartman Rector, Jr. as he was expected to be in Las Vegas in a few weeks.
>
> A short time thereafter…Elder Rector telephoned me. In a kindly way, he informed me that he had been instructed to tell me the Brethren had heard we had formed a committee to recommend a temple site for Las Vegas and that only the First Presidency could form a temple site selection committee. "There is no temple committee," he said. "Yes, Sir," I said, "as of this moment there is no committee!"[10]

Yet the following month, Seastrand was pleasantly surprised to receive a phone call from church headquarters informing him that the First Presidency would like him to confidentially search for a prospective temple site. Seastrand was told that Claire Bankhead of the Church Real Estate Division would be in touch with him to locate "investment property" of five acres. Soon thereafter, on March 10, 1983, Bankhead came to Vegas, and, following some preliminary discussion, Bankhead felt that they should go to the proposed site on Sunrise Mountain.

On March 17, Elder Hartman Rector Jr. visited one of the local stakes, and Seastrand drove him to the proposed site.[11] Six months later, Bankhead phoned Seastrand to let him know the land had been approved. Several days later (October 28, 1983), Lee Earl, counselor in the Central Stake presidency (of which the temple land selected was a part), and Seastrand took Bankhead back to the temple site for final confirmation.[12] Bankhead told Seastrand, "There is nothing more for you to do.... Nothing should be said.... The next event will be an announcement of the temple when the First Presidency is ready."[13] Seastrand, struck by the spiritual grandeur of the occasion, said:

> As I stood on that gently sloping desert ground, I imagined the temple, surrounded with luxurious lawns, shrubbery, and colorful flowers—like Zion's most beautiful garments! A warm feeling settled over me as I contemplated and imagined our people coming out of the temple at night, buoyed with having just partaken of the sacred ordinances of the Lord's House, looking over the sparkling Las Vegas Valley. Here where our pioneer forefathers settled many years ago; now fulfilling their dreams of firmly establishing the Kingdom of God. I could imagine lighted white spires, impelling the eyes of those in the valley upward to their God.[14]

TEMPLE ANNOUNCEMENT

On April 7, 1984, President Gordon B. Hinckley announced in the semi-annual church general conference that a temple would be erected in Las Vegas.[15] It would become the forty-third operating temple of the church. At this time, the Latter-day Saints in the Las Vegas region numbered about fifty thousand in twelve stakes.[16] Church member Elaine Kennedy said, "When a temple was announced in Las Vegas, we jumped for joy because we never figured that we would ever get a temple in Las Vegas. We were known as Sin City."[17]

Local journalist and church member Charlie Zobell remarked, "When the temple was announced, there was a gasp in the tabernacle. A temple in Las Vegas? I mean, an audible gasp. Now, we were quite thrilled of course,...kind of like a crowning moment for Southern Nevada to be able to have an LDS temple up on the hillside up here. It meant, I guess, that we had arrived as a group."[18] For Robin Dixon, a local Latter-day Saint, the announcement was "thrilling." Dixon commented that although her family "would gladly sacrifice" by driving two hours to the St. George, Utah, Temple each way, having the temple in Las Vegas was a great blessing.[19]

President Hinckley explained, "We regard it as a significant thing that we take the temple to the people, rather than asking the people to travel so far to come to the temples of the church." The nearest temple to Las Vegas at that time was the St. George Temple, which required two hours of travel each way. A temple in Las Vegas would be a tremendous advantage, as Las Vegas stake president Charles Johnson estimated that the Vegas Saints made twenty thousand trips annually to attend the St. George Temple.[20]

The temple announcement was met with elation from the Saints, and many from the general community responded positively. Tom Thomas, son of famed Las Vegas banker E. Parry Thomas, observed:

> When the announcement came out, what I remember was a great deal of support from all the other faiths, and I believe that the building of a temple in Las Vegas, to members of other faiths,…was a bookmark that this is a good place, this is a community, there are families that are here, and now The Church of Jesus Christ of Latter-day Saints is going to build a temple here. And that's a seal of good housekeeping for the entire community, for all the religions in the valley.…I remember, actually for members of other faiths, their own excitement that this was going to happen here, and they were curious, they wanted to know, what's the difference? I've got a ward house that's down the street from where I live, but what is this? So, it opened up a lot of opportunities for discussion.[21]

TEMPLE COMMITTEE

Just weeks after the Las Vegas Nevada Temple was announced, a local church temple committee was formed. Historian Elbert B. Edwards wrote, "The first Las Vegas Temple Committee meeting was held on Tuesday, April 24, 1984, in the…North Las Vegas Stake Center. Elder James K. Seastrand presided and conducted the meeting." Seastrand had been called by the church's First Presidency as committee chairman and was assigned to work under the direction of general authority Hartman Rector Jr., who was appointed as the executive administrator.[22]

Others in attendance were "Helen[e] Amos, Administrative Aide, Grant Bowler, Vice Chairman, Judie Brailsford, Assistant P.C. [Public Communications] Director, Boyd Bulloch, P.C. Director, Samuel Davis, James I. Gibson, W. Brent Hardy, President Robert H. Parker, Ace Robison, Assistant P.C. Director, and Reed Whipple." Edwards recorded, "It subsequently occurred to Elder Seastrand that each of the twelve stake presidents should also be members of the committee…thus providing a close liaison for all members of each stake."[23]

The climax of the meeting occurred when Grant Bowler suggested that those assembled share their testimonies of the blessings that would come from having a local temple. Brailsford-Marcucci stated, "There were those in the testimony meeting that knew a temple would be built here. It had literally been revealed to them. They just didn't known when, and so they were not shocked. But these were men who had helped establish the community and helped it grow and had the vision;…they were visionaries."[24] Elbert B. Edwards recorded that heartfelt testimonies were shared regarding the hand of God in the settling of the Saints in Las Vegas and the inspired leadership that has presided over the region to the current time. The full support of establishing a temple was also noted as well as the blessings that come to those who diligently serve and strive to overcome opposition by their faith and good works.[25]

About nine months after this inspiring meeting, Seastrand wrote, "It is a great joy to serve as chairman of the Las Vegas Temple Committee…. Challenging often, but always spiritually exhilarating." He described that his role "evolved around planning, organizing, calling individuals to the Temple Committee…and trying to listen to what the Lord has in mind at each step along the way. This is one of the best 'teams' I have ever been associated with."[26]

His son Scott provided an intimate sketch of his father, who was highly respected and loved by fellow church members, as well as by the broader community, because he had served as mayor of North Las Vegas for sixteen years and as a city councilman for another six years:[27]

> He was just a very positive person striving to find how to uplift people and how to build in his community service. I recall one story he shared with just our family that they had organized for a cleanup [for] the city day, and he was there, as the mayor, on his knees picking up litter next to some citizens that didn't know him, obviously, and somebody started talking to him and saying, "Well I'd like to thank that mayor, whoever he is, because you know this is a great

thing to do," and he didn't really quite know how to say, "Well I'm the mayor."

And it just demonstrates he never asked people to do anything he wouldn't do himself, and he tried to lead by doing, and he was just very approachable. From a son's perspective, [he was] a humble man…they could have a connection with…and that he could have influence [on]. I still, to this day, almost can't go anywhere that somebody doesn't recall some influence that he had on them by just his mannerisms and how he treated them, whether it be in the community as far as the government end or through the church.[28]

Las Vegas Review-Journal reporter Charlie Zobell stated, "I think you'd be hard-pressed to ever find anything that Jim Seastrand did…that was questionable in any way. I mean he was just totally honest."[29] Boyd Bulloch, public communication director for the temple committee, said, "Jim Seastrand was just one of the unique guys on the planet, and… everybody pretty much loved him, and he had some relationships that were just beyond belief. And if he decided he had a project he wanted to get going…he could pick up the phone and before he could hang the phone up, whatever he needed would be at his front door."[30]

Others later joined the original temple committee to assist Seastrand. For example, Gwen Ferrell penned, "On December 1, 1984, I was given the assignment of having the radio talk shows and television news monitored" for information regarding the temple. A week later she was asked in a committee meeting to "assist in the gathering of 'Declarations of Support' for the temple." She reported, "Many phone calls were made to the stake and ward Relief Society presidents"[31] in an effort to extend responsibility for soliciting affirmative responses from neighborhoods.

Another enlisted was Maxine Taylor, president of the Las Vegas East Stake Relief Society. Taylor wrote, "I was given several assignments by Elder Seastrand. I was asked…to distribute the Declarations of Temple support to each Relief Society President in the Henderson Region.… The purpose of the Declaration was to obtain signatures of members and non-members to confirm their support for the Temple." In addition, she described, "I was asked to attend the Sunrise Manor Township Advisory Board; the Clark County Planning Commission, and Clark County Board of Commissioner meetings to help show respect for the Temple."[32]

Charles L. Brailsford, husband of original temple-committee member Judie Brailsford, lent his support to the temple committee by collecting Las Vegas news clippings that contained any mention of the temple. He observed, "I must admit the overwhelming opposition at first to this project was not only deafening but very annoying. Since last October [1984] and into the new year, most of this ridiculous opposition seems to be dying out completely. Most of the news from outside the membership of the church is now optimistic in favor of our Temple construction."[33]

Just one group was seemingly unrelenting. This "anti-Mormon" contingent was led by a former Latter-day Saint named Ed Decker. He became a vindictive enemy of the church and founded the organization Ex-Mormons for Jesus. Decker and his cohorts spread lies about the Latter-day Saint doctrines via a venomous movie titled *The God Makers* and toxic literature.[34] Judie Brailsford-Marcucci recounted that the group's purpose was "to raise havoc in the community." As soon as the temple was announced, Decker and his crew took their film "to every church and denomination they could.... and we [local church members] had a lot of backlash."

Brailsford-Marcucci further remarked, "As the temple progressed, I think the neighborhood became less antagonistic. They began to see the beauty. They began to see that we were real careful not to bother them on their streets and...they actually became friendly, but the 'God Makers' did not, and they picketed."[35]

Some were critical of Decker and his methods. One letter written to the *Review-Journal* editor by local citizen Cheryl Hymer expressed, "The thing that really bothers me about anti-Mormon films and literature...is do they really think they are building their [own] religion up? Why aren't these 'Christians' using in their sermons things that enhance their religion?"[36]

Charles W. Johnson, stake president of the Las Vegas Nevada Stake and temple-committee member assigned to public communications, recalled that reaching out to the neighbors in the temple-site area really paid off. Johnson remembered a meeting held December 8, 1984, with about forty neighbors in attendance at the home of Barry and Sandy Pardo, who were not members of the church. Johnson stated, "We expressed appreciation for their taking time during the busy holiday season to attend the meeting. We acknowledged the fact that there was some opposition among the neighbors [due to] zoning rather than upon religious bias. We explained how important a Temple is to members of the church and how we spare no expense making the Temple and the temple grounds as beautiful as possible."

Johnson further noted, "We acknowledged that one of the reasons the church chose to locate a Temple in this area was because of the nice homes and well-kept yards of the neighbors…and we were sure that the Temple would compliment [*sic*] the neighborhood and make it even more attractive and beautiful than it is now." Johnson added, "We then addressed some of the concerns…such as traffic, flood control, property values, etc. The short video tape, entitled 'Temples of the Church of Jesus Christ of Latter-day Saints,' was shown and was well received…. The meeting at the Pardo home was very successful, we had a unanimous expression of support by everyone there."[37]

Johnson also told of another event occurring the following week at the Sunridge Homeowners Association, which again resulted in a marginal degree of success. He wrote, "We probably didn't change anybody's mind. However, we do feel that perhaps a few hearts were softened and we were able to communicate with the people in a calm, friendly way. I came away from the experience with a conviction that it never hurts to talk with our enemies."[38] One spoonful of sugar softening the negativity may have been the increase in neighborhood home values near this sacred edifice. In fact, just one month after the temple's announcement, real-estate ads touted property "near new proposed Mormon Temple."[39]

ARCHITECT AND PLANS

In his dedicatory prayer for the Las Vegas Temple, President Gordon B. Hinckley said, "We thank thee for the faith and skills of all who have contributed to make it possible."[40] One of those key players with conviction as well as skills and gifts was the temple architect, George G. Tate. Tate had been spiritually prepared for this sacred work as a church member in his youth, though he did not fully recognize it until decades later. Tate noted that when he was only sixteen years old, he received an inspired priesthood blessing in which "mention was made several times of my future involvement in temples and temple building…. None of this sank in very deeply until at age fifty two, I sat in my living room watching general conference on television."[41]

Regarding the announcement by President Hinckley of a temple to be constructed in Las Vegas, Tate recounted: "Suddenly the specific wording of my patriarchal blessing concerning this important subject came to mind. After several days of serious thought on this matter, I wrote a letter to our Area Representative at that time, Hartman Rector, requesting that my firm be considered for the architectural assignment for the Las Vegas Nevada Temple." A few weeks later Tate was notified his firm, Tate & Snyder Architects, had been selected to design the Las Vegas Temple.[42]

The reason the firm's role soon expanded, Tate explained, was that Clark County had no zoning category for churches or religious buildings. Therefore, the firm moved into unchartered territory, needing to produce plans without clear zoning parameters. Furthermore, Tate recalled, "When the deadline for submittal of our drawings to the Clark County Planning Commission was almost upon us, I received a call from Evan Nelson [a church architect assigned to assist Tate] who was likewise anxious about meeting the timeline and looking for directions from the First Presidency. His last words to me before the submittal deadline were, 'If you haven't heard from us in time, go with the best thing you've got.'"[43] Tate added:

> Based on that, at the last minute we submitted our own preliminary site plan, a rendering sketch of the building as we envisioned it at the time, and the legal documents for a 65,000 square foot building with a 125 ft. high steeple—these numbers being purely a guess on my part. In their first meeting after receiving our submittal, the planning commission approved the application by a five to zero vote...[on] condition that construction must be commenced on the site not later than one year from the date of approval...January 1985.[44]

Initially, church leaders were pleased with the Clark County approval but did not seem to take seriously the deadline for commencing construction. Tate was invited to attend a Las Vegas Temple committee meeting to grapple with this issue. During the meeting in which this issue was

George G. Tate, Las Vegas Temple architect,
2020. Photo by Martin Andersen.

Las Vegas Temple groundbreaking, 1985. *Left to right*: Elder Boyd K. Packer, Grant Bowler, President Gordon B. Hinckley, and Senators Richard Bryan and Harry Reid. Courtesy of Boyd Bulloch.

discussed, the presiding church official at the gathering, Elder Harvey A. Dahl, the regional representative, stepped out of the room and made a direct call to church president Ezra Taft Benson. Dahl was well acquainted with President Benson, as he had previously served as undersecretary of agriculture when Benson was the US secretary of agriculture (1953–61). Elder Dahl returned to the meeting and announced, "Brethren, the First Presidency has instructed us to proceed immediately with the design using our locally selected architect, [George Tate,] and to be under construction within the one year as required by the county."[45] Tate moved forward and mentioned that in the ensuing year, "there were many occasions when [they] had worked together with other firms and other people who were not church members." He felt fortunate that individuals and organizations functioned well as a team to get things done in a timely fashion.[46]

SOME OPPOSITION AND EVENTUAL CLEARANCE

George Tate recalled, "Ever since the temple had been publicly announced, there was generally quite strong community acceptance and support—with the exception of a small group of anti-L.D.S. individuals who managed to draw the interest of the local press, making it a somewhat controversial issue."[47]

Church member Ashley Hall, then serving as city manager of Las Vegas,[48] remembered that one individual belonging to this antitemple faction even went to the extreme of wiretapping the home of the local chair of the temple committee, Jim Seastrand:

> One day someone said in the [temple] committee, the…town board committees and others, it appears, are aware of what we have talked about. [The question was then asked] "Is there anyone on the committee that's going and talking about what we're talking about here?" and the answer was "No no no," and so Jim Seastrand asked an active duty metro police guy, Don Helm, to bring in a sweeping device [to his home],…and, lo and behold, they found a bug on the phone, they found a bug on the light shade, on the easy chair where he sat to conduct the meetings, and so there had been some people who had formed a committee against the temple.[49]

Tate also explained how this group attempted to capitalize on a legal technicality to prevent the temple construction. The state legislature had recently passed a law increasing the number of county commissioners in Clark County, and a majority of Latter-day Saints on the commission could pose a problem. He recounted:

> Prior to January 1, 1985, there were five county commissioners, two of whom were L.D.S. By the new law the board of county commissioners would be increased from five to seven members [with two additional LDS]. This would make the board consist of a majority of L.D.S. members [to be elected in 1985] and thereby create the grounds for a legal challenge from the dissenters to the temple project. To avoid the potential problem, the five member board voted to hear the application for the temple on the 28th of December, 1984 while there was not yet an L.D.S. majority.[50]

Judie Brailsford-Marcucci, an original member of the committee who worked with public communications, explained how she learned of the group's intentions: "While I was always grateful for my calling, I often wondered exactly why I was on the committee and what it was I could do to serve more fully. My answer came during the last week of November [1984] when I received a call from a good Catholic friend I worked with on campaign consulting.[51] Knowing how deeply I cared about the Temple, he called to pass along some information he had picked up in a bar the night before as he sat with some newspaper reporters." She passed on knowledge of the conspiracy to Seastrand, and plans were quickly put in place to avert the scheme.[52]

Mahlon Edwards recounted, "There was some opposition from the neighborhood. They weren't sure about the lights, and they didn't want all the traffic,...the really bright lights, and they couldn't have a visitors center up there because they didn't want people traveling up there."[53] Jody Walker, whose family were not church members, had moved to the temple-site location sixteen years before the temple was built. She experienced the resistance firsthand. Walker's mother, LoRena Hiatt, was concerned about lights and traffic. But Walker, who lived near her mother and the site, was primarily concerned about the potential depreciation of her home value if the temple was established.[54]

Both sides of the issue were presented in a three-and-a-half-hour Clark County Commission planning meeting. Church members presented 5,000 signatures that they had collected from Sunrise Manor residents in favor of the temple, while the opposition announced they had gathered 750 signatures against the Latter-day Saint edifice being constructed in the Sunrise Manor temple-site neighborhood.[55]

Wendell Waite recalled that one man living within the temple-site neighborhood reversed his opinion after observing the Saints. At the hearing, this man told the assembly, "I went to St. George where there's a temple, and I talked to people around the temple, and they're all good people." He said, "I was opposed at first;...[now] I'm in favor." Waite added, "These are good people; there's not going to be any problem."[56]

Commissioner Manny Cortez lightened the tension in the meeting when he asked, "I am disappointed with the committee that chose this site...because I wish they would have selected a site in the west end of town in my area."[57] Another author mentioned that on this occasion, Commissioner Cortez remarked, "It is an honor to have the Mormon Church build a temple in our community. And where are temples built? They are built on a hill where all can look to it as a symbol of God's love. That's where it should be and will be built." In the end, "all three planning boards approved the project."[58]

A few Latter-day Saints were present at this planning meeting to contribute to the discussion. Gwen Ferrell, Las Vegas Stake Relief Society president and an additional temple-committee member, said, "I was so excited to be privileged to be a part of it. I only spoke for three minutes, briefly telling what an L.D.S. Temple is and how having the Church choose to build a temple in Las Vegas was a declaration that Las Vegas is a quality community and that the temple would enhance the image of Las Vegas and what it will do for the membership of the Church." Ferrell added, "The excitement at the unanimous vote of approval brought tears, clapping, smiles, handshakes, hugs, sighs of relief and an excitement unequalled. I didn't even need a car to get me home. I was so excited I could have flown home."[59]

Under the headline "The Right Decision on Mormon Temple," the *Review-Journal* reported, "In the end, the commissioners made the right decision: they approved construction of the temple.... Everyone can empathize and sympathize with the neighbors who objected to the temple.... For the greater good of the community, however, a Mormon temple is a welcome addition."[60]

Moving from approval of the temple to completion took several years. Temple architect George Tate explained why:

> The county required that once they approved the use permit and the variance that there was a condition of one year that you had to be under construction. That was because there were so much people who would rezone and so forth, and they didn't want to have any of that, but it created the problem for us because we just didn't have the plans that were coming from Salt Lake we thought we were going to adapt from. Instead, it turned out we designed it.
>
> So, the way that we dealt with that was by issuing the construction contracts in three different groups. The first one was site preparation; then the second one was structural steel, the framework for the building; then the third one was the total contract. And we just simply folded those subcontracts into the bid for the next one. I guess a little bit to my surprise, it worked out so smoothly. It was kind of a risk to do it like that, but it just went great.[61]

Tate also mentioned a unique symbol his team added to the Las Vegas Temple. Of all the worldwide temples, the white lily had been used only on the Logan Temple doorknobs. Tate visualized the Las Vegas Temple to be like this "beautiful white flower."[62]

Bruce Woodbury, who served as a Clark County commissioner for many years, felt that his Latter-day Saint affiliation eventually helped the commission decide to allow the Las Vegas Temple to be built, though there was initial controversy. Woodbury recounted:

A lot of the surrounding neighborhoods had…good, well-meaning people. This was part of my commission district, so they focused on me. They were very much opposed; they felt it would be a big intrusion on their semi-rural neighborhood lifestyle. Traffic and lights and so on. So, there were a lot of public meetings. There were a lot of protests, and the matter eventually came to us on the Clark County commission to make that decision, and there were even calls that the LDS members of the commission should abstain from voting…. But we ended up with a unanimous vote in favor of it.

We listened to the neighbors, and…the church agreed to various revisions and modifications to make it as compatible as possible in the neighborhood. The nonmembers of the commission took the lead in…making the motion for approval and making the arguments in favor, and many good members of the community came forward to support it. And after it was built, I never had one constituent then tell me that they regretted it…. Many came forward to say it actually benefitted the neighborhood in many ways, so that was a good experience for all of us, and I think it helped with the LDS standing in the community quite a bit.[63]

Scott Seastrand recalled, "I know that there was a great deal of personal effort in organization to go out and speak individually with all the neighbors…. I think that the local officials understood who members of the Church were because of the individuals who were serving right beside them and recognize[d] that it was a blessing that they in fact thought it would be a wonderful thing to bring to the community."[64]

An editorial published three days after the commission's approval of the temple project read, "Everyone can empathize and sympathize with the neighbors who objected to the temple. But when any major project…is planned for an area, there invariably are those who will feel they were adversely affected. For the greater good of the community, however, a Mormon temple is a welcome addition."[65]

Following the completion of the temple, its architect, George Tate, reminisced:

I can't think of anything but positive responses and reactions. And the people who had been neighbors in that area,…who were fighting the temple,…were concerned because they had horses and things like this. They turned out to be some of the most wonderful support that we could have imagined. And while at the beginning they didn't want bright lights in their neighborhood and so forth, they're the very people who said, "This is a wonderful thing to have in our neighborhood." Everything that I heard, at least, was very supportive in that regard.[66]

Less than two weeks after the temple announcement, Reed Whipple received a letter from Jim Seastrand indicating that he had been called by church general authority Elder Hartman Rector Jr. to be a member of the Las Vegas Temple Executive Committee. Whipple wrote, "On May 22, 1984, I was notified I was chairman of the [temple] Finance Committee. My duty would be to help the wards raise the money to build the temple. I asked that a committee be organized, a member from each of the twelve stakes to assist me."[67]

Bruce Woodbury reported that soon after news of a Las Vegas Temple broke, fund-raising efforts began: "There immediately started a fund-raising drive so that the local members could participate in building the temple through their donations. Various goals were set, and we exceeded those goals by a huge amount. I remember we all felt so good about being able to make those donations and to participate in it leading up to the construction and then the dedication."[68]

At the time of the announcement, Shari Buck recollected that there was "excitement." Though she was a young mother with two children and pregnant with a third, Buck recalled, "My husband [Keith] and I...took all of our savings and donated it toward the temple fund.... It was a sacrifice because we were a young family,...but we felt like it was the right thing to do, and it was.... We had sacrificed everything that we could."[69] Ed Smith, then a bishop seeking temple funds from his ward members, remembered:

> The members of the church were so excited.... I remember...there was a family in our ward,...and I went to their house to ask them for $1,000.... He said, "You sit right here, and my wife and I will go and discuss it in our bedroom." And he came back, and he said, "We decided that we will give you the $1,000." Well, I knew what kind of tithe payer he was because I was the bishop, and I knew that it would have been a sacrifice to give the $1,000, and they were a frugal people

and really didn't have much of an income of any kind. But they gave the money. It was amazing.

And the same way with the open house, I mean, I'd ask for $1,000 by letter, [and]…most everyone gave it. It was hardly anybody that didn't give it, and most of them were not active in the church…. They responded in just amazing ways. And I really appreciated that. It tells you a lot about what happened here in Las Vegas with the Latter-day Saints because of that temple.[70]

The youth also contributed their widow's mite, which included holding many car washes. Little children even participated by making homemade items to sell.[71] It was reported that the Redrock Twenty-First Ward in the Redrock Stake raised more than $1,200 via a Cub Scout Carnival,[72] and the Henderson Fifth Ward in the West Henderson Stake raised funds from an "Old-Fashioned Country Fair." Children from the Las Vegas Fourteenth Ward in the Redrock Stake donated via a "pennies for the temple" program, and the members of the Henderson Third Ward in the Henderson Stake offered their talents and time by auctioning services such as "yard work and babysitting hours, upholstering, dental work, air conditioning service, and homecooked dinners."[73] Mahlon Edwards gleefully recalled that eventually President Gordon B. Hinckley had to tell the stake presidents in the Vegas region, "Brethren, you've got to stop raising money."[74]

GROUNDBREAKING

At a meeting held by the temple committee on September 25, 1985, the date of November 30, 1985, was set for the groundbreaking ceremony. Grant Bowler was selected as chairman for the groundbreaking event and facilitated committee discussion. At this gathering, Charles Johnson expressed his concerns about having large numbers of church members at the temple site in deference to the sensitivities of neighbors in the area. It was later decided that only a small group of church leaders and city officials would be invited to the temple site for the groundbreaking, and church members and other interested parties would assemble at the Las Vegas Convention Center Rotunda to view a tape recording of the event.[75] Three days before the event, the *Beehive Sentinel* published an article headlined "Is It Secret? What Goes on in LDS Temples?" which contained a Q&A with then St. George Temple president John Russon, hoping to better educate the Saints as well as the public.[76]

During the week prior to the groundbreaking, church area president Charles Didier expressed his hope of "the new temple becoming a new symbol for Las Vegas—a beacon of righteousness that will outshine the lure of the Strip and enhance the community's image as something more than a gambling mecca." Didier added, "The rest of the city [outside of the Strip] is made up of homes, of churches, of businesses, and the temple will be a part of that community. It will enhance it, become another emblem of Las Vegas. You can see the emblem of faith, of eternal values in front of the emblem of worldly values."[77]

Concerning the impending groundbreaking, journalist Ned Day hinted at the church's desire to generate more light than heat: "Cautious church officials are treading lightly in an effort to avoid more unseemly controversy. In any event, the big Mormon Temple is coming to Las Vegas. And it seems like something we can all be proud of and from which we can all benefit in one way or another."[78] One of the government officials invited to this historic event was Richard Bryan, who served as governor of Nevada from 1983 to 1989.[79] Looking back, Bryan explained from an outsider's perspective the significance of this event:

> The groundbreaking for the temple was a big event in the community, obviously for the church members…. [But] for the community at large it was a little bigger than that in the sense that…Las Vegas still suffered from this reputation that, you know, the gangsters run the place, or did. That this is the incarnation of sin and having the church make the decision to place [a temple here] was, if not a good housekeeping seal of approval, it was a recognition that there are a lot of good, wonderful people in the community who are really no different than people living in other parts of the country but whose principal industry is tourism, and obviously gaming is a big part of that…. Certainly the groundbreaking and the establishment of the temple, I think, sent a message.[80]

Local surgeon and church spokesman Dr. Don Christensen said that the forthcoming temple "shows a great deal of confidence in the Las Vegas area—faith in the members here and confidence…the church will grow. It is also a factor in improving the image of Las Vegas as a community. Tourists who come here rarely see this as a place to raise a family, but it is."[81]

Christensen was held in high esteem in the Vegas community. During temple construction, UNLV president Robert C. Maxson wrote to a local newspaper editor in praise of Christensen: "Dr. Christensen is surely one of our community's most distinguished citizens.... Christensen is not only a leader in the Mormon church, but in the wider community as well. His presence here has added to the quality of life for all Nevadans. His good influence spreads far beyond the confines of his church."[82] Such exemplary behavior by a church member no doubt helped pave the way for the acceptance of the forthcoming temple.

On November 30, 1985, the groundbreaking ceremony proceeded as planned. Elder Seastrand recalled some of the highlights of these memorable festivities. After several general authorities were picked up at the airport, the official groundbreaking party of about one hundred assembled at the base of Sunrise Mountain, where President Gordon B. Hinckley, counselor in the First Presidency, presided and offered a prayer to dedicate the site. In his supplication, President Hinckley prayed that "the work may go forward without...hindrance or trouble, and that those who have felt unkindly toward Thy people concerning this holy house, may be touched by Thy spirit and that their attitude may change, and that they may come to realize that this house will be a great blessing to this community."[83]

After President Hinckley concluded his dedicatory prayer upon this piece of ground, Governor Richard Bryan, Congressman Harry Reid, and church apostles Elder Hartman Rector Jr. and Elder Boyd K. Packer were invited to make comments. Following their remarks, select leaders were invited to pick up shovels and symbolically "break ground" along with President Hinckley.

The official news of the church reported on the speeches general authorities offered at the event. President Gordon B. Hinckley told those gathered at the groundbreaking ceremony, "The spirit of the temple will be a blessing to all in the community, not only to those who enter." He added that a temple "speaks of our eternal values" and is "a visible testimony...of the everlasting nature of family." Elder Packer suggested that Las Vegas might be considered an unusual place to build a temple, "unless you know Las Vegas and the number of worthy and faithful Saints who live here." The temple will be an indicator, he said, that church members can live within the world without being a part of it. Elder Rector commented that the temple would "add moral tone" to the city of Las Vegas.[84]

In addition to these general authorities, the church's *Ensign* magazine reported that former Nevada governor Mike O'Callaghan was also in attendance and that Nevada governor Richard Bryan and Clark County

Commission chairwoman Thalia Dondero gave remarks.[85] The local *Bee-hive Sentinel* reported that the groundbreaking for the Las Vegas Temple was the largest temple groundbreaking the church had ever had. On this singular occasion, Commissioner Dondero stated, "This is an event we can all be proud of. It stands as a compliment to all those who have taken part.… The temple will add beauty, strength and solace in our community affairs." Bryan said, "The decision to build a temple in Las Vegas shows the wholesome values and feelings for families that we have in this community."[86] Bryan added, "By the construction of this marvelous religious edifice, the word goes out…to friend and to critic alike about the wholesome values that we cherish in this community."[87]

Following a luncheon, the small group drove to the Convention Center to join the thousands there assembled. Seastrand recalled, "I conducted and also gave some opening remarks. This assembly set a new experience for the church in temple groundbreaking, a small gathering with its proceedings videotaped; a large indoor assembly with the video tape shown as part of the program. The assembly program was a beautiful experience." He added, "In all, some 8,000 to 9,000 were in attendance of which some 600 hundred were non-members."[88]

After the program at the Convention Center concluded, employees from the Latter-day Saint local newspaper, the *Beehive Sentinel,* asked a number of those attending the event, "Why are you so happy that there is going to be a temple in Las Vegas?" Several respondents mentioned the closer proximity, which would save them a two-hour drive each way to and from the St. George Temple in Utah. Others believed the local temple would enhance missionary work, resulting in church growth in the metro region. Church member Chris Turek said, "I think on a national basis it will help get rid of the ideas of Las Vegas as 'Sin City.'" Another Latter-day Saint, Rose Smith, added, "I think it shows a good moral environment for Las Vegas. We're not all bad."[89]

North Las Vegas Stake mission leader Rick Bailey and his wife, Laura, capitalized on the groundbreaking to initiate a new approach to proselytizing. At the Convention Center, they distributed almost five thousand bumper stickers with the message: "Don't Rent Your Family. Keep Them Forever." Also on the sticker was the phone number of the Las Vegas Mission. The idea was that when interested people called the mission office as a result of the bumper sticker, they would be offered a presentation emphasizing the eternal nature of the family.[90]

CONSTRUCTION, CONTRACT, AND OVERVIEW

Just two days following the groundbreaking ceremonies, on Monday, December 2, 1985, the contractors for the site development, Williams and Sons, moved their equipment to the temple grounds to commence work. One of the major concerns voiced by the local residents was their fear of flooding below the temple site due to the heavy rainstorms that occasionally ran off the mountain. Therefore, plans for a head wall were incorporated into the design to channel the floodwaters away from the neighboring homes. In additional, a thirty-six-inch conduit was made to channel water under the temple parking lot for proper drainage. Although these precautions exceeded a half-million dollars, they eventually proved successful.[91]

The church delayed revealing the detailed plans of the temple for more than two and a half years after the temple was announced, most likely due to a variety of clearance issues. Don L. Christensen, the church spokesman for the Southern Nevada Multiregion, issued an official news release on November 6, 1986. Among other things, the letter announced that temple construction had been awarded to Hogan and Tingey, a company from Centerville, Utah. The total cost of the temple was estimated at $15.1 million, which included costs for landscaping the surrounding grounds. The letter estimated that the sixty-thousand-square-foot temple would take about two years to complete.

Christensen further noted, "An impressive copper roof with a steep slope and six gracefully tapered spires, each rising approximately 110 feet above the first floor, will be the main features of the structure. A 13-foot high, gold-leafed statue of the Angel Moroni holding a trumpet will rise at 125 feet atop the east cross-axis spire."[92] Impressively, the temple was completed on time with the features promised. From the temple announcement to its completion, the hand of the Lord was observed and recorded. Jim Seastrand recalled one significant example he interpreted as divine intervention:

> I had many spiritual experiences in connection with securing the property for the Temple, as well as its construction. Shortly before the dedication…the Los Angeles earthquake occurred. One of the cut glass windows for the Celestial room had been cut and was ready to be shipped. The artisan felt impressed the night before the earthquake to put it in a sling, which preserved it through the quake.

Nearly everything in his shop was destroyed except for that window! Since it had taken four months to do the cutting to make another one, [it] would have postponed the dedication by that long.[93]

A temple open house can have a tremendous impact on individuals as well as communities. Such was the case for Loran Amadore. She lived near the Las Vegas Temple site and had apprehensions about the proposed edifice until she visited a Latter-day Saint temple in another city just two months before the decision would be made whether to permit the Las Vegas Temple to be built at the base of Sunrise Mountain. In an article she sent to the *Las Vegas Sun,* published under the heading "Big Asset," Amadore shared, "I was a little concerned when the Mormon Church announced it would build a temple near my home a few months ago.... But my opinion has changed drastically. I visited a Mormon temple open house last week while in Dallas, Texas. I wanted to see what this was all about before they started building near my home. It was one of the most beautiful buildings and grounds I've ever seen.... I witnessed a tour of a building that left me breathless!"[94]

This catalytic article may have affected some residents in Amadore's neighborhood, and five years later the Saints of Las Vegas hosted a temple open house of their own. Much preparation went into paving the way for the open house. Church members Cristi Bulloch and Jeanette Clark served on a special subcommittee to select and arrange for about twenty speakers to explain what a temple is and to encourage community members to visit the upcoming temple open house. Bulloch recollected that her assignment was to contact various associations, such as the Rotary Club, Kiwanis Club, senior homes, and so on, and set up appointments for speakers to make presentations.

Bulloch remembered, "We went out to any number of organizations, and these men would drop everything, sometimes they wouldn't have much notice, and go out and do this presentation.... We had a lot of those people come that heard the presentation and then were interested in coming to the temple open house.... It just felt like there was a light on that hill."[95] When eight-year-old Ryan Dixon attended the temple open house, he described the glow of this sacred edifice as "like a great big flashlight going up to heaven!"[96]

Las Vegas Temple, 2020. Photo by Martin Andersen.

Local church member Ed Smith remembered that some members of the Las Vegas Temple committee flew to Portland, Oregon, to glean ideas for the Las Vegas Temple open house. The result was that the Las Vegas Temple committee arranged a very successful event. Smith recalled, "The members came out in droves, and the nonmembers came out in droves, and it was a wonderful open house, and it was well organized, and… everyone was happy." He added that neighbors living near the temple "were specially invited to the temple open house." Smith also remarked, "There was a lot of press…. One of the editors of the [Review-] Journal was a member of the church, and so there was some good press from that."[97]

One advertisement in the Las Vegas Sun, titled "Temple Open House," simply stated, "You are invited to the Las Vegas Nevada Temple…. No tickets are required for free tour."[98] This unpretentious invitation reaped a tremendous response. In fact, the general Latter-day Saint periodical, the Church News, reported, "Nearly 300,000 visitors toured the new Las Vegas Nevada Temple during its 23-day open house [November 16–December 9], which introduced them to the purpose of temples and established the temple as an important part of the city. A total of 297,480 attended, reported James K. Seastrand, temple committee chairman." This participation went beyond the expectations of Seastrand and his committee, who would have considered 200,000 visitors a success. Hal Parker, chairman

of the temple open house, stated, "This is the greatest thing that has happened in Las Vegas." Parker calculated that the daily total of volunteers
was 1,100 and that their accumulated service hours totaled 122,000.[99]

Eyewitness volunteer Shari Buck remembered that the community
had some apprehension about what goes on in a Latter-day Saint temple.
She said there was "a lot of interest from nonmembers to come through
the temple. Once there was the open house, that really changed opinions
and views, and it was…such a positive experience, I think, in the southern
Nevada valley." Both she and her husband, Keith, took visitors on temple
tours, and Keith gave tours to the blind. Buck recollected that on these
special occasions, Keith would describe the furniture, particularly an intri-
cate inlaid wooden table, noting, "That was an amazing experience."[100]

Jody Walker, a nonmember neighbor who lived in close proximity
to the temple property, questioned why she was asked to wear coverings
on her shoes during the temple tour, wondering whether it was to keep
the carpets clean or perhaps to keep her "non-Mormon cooties" out of
this sacred edifice. At the time, Walker didn't know that all visitors (both
church members and nonmembers) were asked to wear the coverings to
protect the carpets. It was just this kind of misunderstanding that needed
clarifying during the tours.[101]

Another example of needed clarification occurred during one temple
tour when a group observed the Latter-day Saint temple baptismal font.
Ashley Hall, then serving as the Las Vegas city manager, recalled, "[I told]
all of the city council who wanted to go to the temple open house that
I'd be glad to work out a tour of the temple with them so they would
have a chance to see what went on in the temple." He said, "I took them
initially to the baptismal font, and…they looked at that font, they looked
at the twelve oxen, and they…would always wonder what in the world
that was for. [They] didn't know if it was for cooking, boiling or whatever it was."[102]

Hall also recounted that there was time allotted at the conclusion of
the temple tours for questions.[103] Las Vegas institute director Bruce W.
Hansen observed that whereas visitors at other temple open houses might
question why Latter-day Saint temples carry such high costs, visitors to
the Las Vegas Temple didn't raise the issue during the time he fielded
questions from various groups. He reasoned that part of the explanation
may lie in the comparison between the exorbitant cost of the new Vegas
hotel the Mirage and the exquisite temple dedicated to the Lord, which
was constructed for significantly less.[104]

Church member Tom Thomas recalled:

I went to the open house of the temple,...and it was a big deal. And what I remember is seeing so many of my friends who weren't in the church going, driving all the way across town, because we all lived on the far west side of town, so it's a good 25-minute drive. But, there was such an interest in the community because so many of my friends had grown up having good friends who were members of The Church of Jesus Christ of Latter-day Saints, and they had no idea what a temple was. They just knew it was very special to us.... We had thousands and thousands of citizens in Las Vegas that flocked to go through during the open house.[105]

At the conclusion of the temple tours, Parker, chairman of the temple open-house committee, wrote a letter to each of the committee members letting them know that the Temple Department housed at church headquarters had informed him, "This is the smoothest Open House we have ever seen." Parker also pointed out that many of the visitors had said, "It is not just the beauty of the Temple that we admired, but it was the beauty of the people that were working there, so happy and delightful." One non-Latter-day Saint guest stated, "I saw the Lord in the eyes and the faces of the Hosts."[106]

COMMENTS FROM TEMPLE OPEN-HOUSE VISITORS

Following the inspiring open-house tour, scores of expressions of awe and gratitude were written on comment cards from people of various faiths living locally in the Vegas region as well as in other cities, states, and countries. Rosette Wirtz from Boulder City wrote, "I better appreciate the Mormon faith as a viable religion." Pat Schreiber of Henderson penned, "Thank you for letting me learn about your faith." Connie Crabb from Spring Branch, Texas, wrote, "Thank you for sharing. As a Baptist Christian, I feel uplifted in your joy." Another visitor wrote, "During the tour I felt I was with friends; people smiled at me and met my eyes. I felt humanity had a real value.... I am not a Mormon."

Kenneth James of Glendale, Arizona, observed, "I was able to spend two days in Las Vegas. The first night we toured 'the strip.' The second night, the Temple. It was comforting to find the temple surpassed in spirituality the strip's worldliness." Barbara Dempsey, a Vegas local, penned, "The temple was beautiful.... Although I am not a Mormon, I feel your temple helps Las Vegas shed its tarnished image."

Mrs. Harold Mueller, also of Las Vegas, wrote, "I have many Mormon friends…. The beauty of the temple is equally matched by the beauty of the people!" Christina Manteris from Boulder City commented, "Inspiring experience; however, the thing that touches me most was the happy peaceful and loving looks on *all* the men and women…. Something on their faces that cannot be described."

Las Vegas local P. Wolfsohn wrote, "You have confirmed in my very Jewish mind that The Church of Jesus Christ of Latter-day Saints has a kinship to our faith in that you expound on the highest principles of human existence." Mrs. Sidney H. Copeland, also of Vegas, observed, "As a Jew, I found the links between Judaism and the Mormon Church very interesting."

An unnamed visitor simply put, "Absolutely Fantastic—a joy to behold! From a Catholic." R. Johnston wrote, "I am a Buddhist, what a magnificent temple. Your hosts are so friendly." Reverend Troy D. Perry said, "Well worth my one day trip from L.A." William Rieman from Minneapolis recorded, "One of the most beautiful houses of worship I've had the pleasure of visiting. The highlight of our visit to Nevada."

Harley Nosker, a Las Vegas local, mentioned, "I am a Christian and of a different denomination. I think this temple's awesome, and I felt the presence of the Lord everywhere. *Thank you. Thank you* for letting me see this." Bette Shortridge from Henderson commented, "Beautiful church. Ushers very pleasant. Tour well organized. This is a wonderful experience. I am delighted to learn more of the Mormon religion."

Many others responded that they would like to learn more about the Latter-day Saint faith. For example, Julie Gonzales stated, "Breath taking! Made me feel like I did not want to leave…. I would like to know more about this Church." Pamela J. Gomez wrote, "This visit was very special to me. I would like to join with the Mormons." Patricia Monroe said, "I was extremely surprised at the beauty of the temple. I am interested in learning more about the inner peace of the Mormon religion." Barry Klassoff wrote, "I've never seen anything so beautiful. I enjoyed coming to see your church. I am also interested in becoming Mormon. Can you please get back with me?" Several visitors who were inactive church members also expressed interest in getting their lives in order and returning to full activity.[107]

This collage of praise and interest no doubt brought the open-house committee much joy, as they, along with many volunteers, had worked so hard to provide the best experience they could for the Vegas Valley community. Missionaries were soon busy with the fourteen hundred referrals generated by the open house, and two hundred of those who attended the open house either were being taught by the missionaries or had made commitments to receive additional instruction about the church.[108] But for church members, the temple dedication ceremony was the climactic event.

DEDICATION

Less than a month before the temple dedication, Steve Wynn's luxurious Mirage Hotel was completed and opened for business. At the time, the Mirage was the largest hotel in the world, with more than three thousand rooms, but the resort, with the combined hotel and casino, carried an exorbitant cost of $630 million![109] Historian Hal Rothman noted, "This exorbitant cost was $500 million more than any previous casino, and needed to clear $1 million, a day, to meet its overhead."[110] Another author wrote, "The 3,000-room Mirage ushered in an era of lavishly themed resorts on the Strip. Erupting volcanoes, exotic white tigers, playful dolphins and lush jungle foliage created a destination, and an escape, for tourists…and sparked an unprecedented construction boom along the Strip."[111] Though the endeavor was risky, Wynn was willing again to throw the dice, persuaded that gamers would soon compensate for the expense and deliver him a handsome profit.

Unlike the opening of the Mirage, the Latter-day Saint Las Vegas Temple dedication and official opening was focused on the reality of the afterlife and the eternal purposes of this life. Cristi Bulloch, in comparing the two buildings, remarked, "I remember when the temple was announced, and it was right about the same time they announced that Mirage hotel,…and the difference between The Mirage…and our temple, there was such a different feel there. And when the temple was done…it just felt like it was the right thing, that finally our pioneer heritage had this edifice that would represent really what Las Vegas was started to be: a family community."[112]

John Ryan, columnist for the *Las Vegas Sun*, also noticed the stark contrast. After a touring the temple during the open house, he wrote, "There are two new structures in Las Vegas. One, The Mirage, is indeed an impressive building. But for graceful beauty with its six narrow spires seemingly almost touching the sky, there is the Church of Jesus Christ of Latter-day Saints' magnificent Las Vegas Nevada Temple…. The aura of holiness pervades you…. You are transported to another world apart from the frenzied

Las Vegas life."[113] Local campaign strategist Lisa Mayo-DeRiso toured the Las Vegas Temple during the open house and a week later attended the opening of the Mirage. In contrasting her two experiences, she observed, "There is no comparison to the feeling at the temple.... You feel this sense of calm, serenity and safety. When you walk into The Mirage it is chaos."[114] The contrast between confusion and order was readily apparent.

Just prior to the dedicatory service, President Thomas S. Monson, first counselor in the church First Presidency, and a former navy man, checked every inch of the sacred edifice like a general inspecting troops, ensuring there was orderliness and that all was "pristine and perfect."[115] With the holy dedication event of the temple held on December 16, 1989, patrons were officially authorized under the direction of newly appointed temple president Boyad Tanner[116] to participate in sacred ordinances for both the living and in proxy for deceased ancestors. This was a priceless opportunity for patrons, and the dedication was viewed as a sacred occasion. President Ezra Taft Benson presided over the cornerstone[117] ceremony and expressed his love to about ten thousand church members. President Gordon B. Hinckley, first counselor in the church First Presidency, told the assembled Saints, "Never has there been so beautiful a day in Las Vegas as we dedicate the House of the Lord, the crowning jewel overlooking the city."[118]

In total, more than thirty thousand Saints attended the temple dedicatory sessions. In one later session, President Hinckley commended church members for their faithfulness and noted their total monetary temple contribution was $11 million, 428 percent of the temple building–fund assessment. He stated, "I don't know of more faithful Latter-day Saints than in this temple district.... I believe the Lord has accepted your sacrifice. I want to make you a promise that you will never miss that which you have contributed; the windows of heaven will be opened."[119] On this special dedicatory day, it was noticed that "a deep red sunset colored the sky. It was as though a divine stamp of approval had been placed upon the efforts of that temple."[120] The inspiring dedicatory prayer pronounced by President Hinckley stated:

> We thank thee for the faith and skills of all who have contributed to make [the temple] possible. It stands in this community which has become an oasis in the desert. As men have brought water to the dry earth of this region it has become fruitful, and now as a crowning jewel stands thy holy house with its surrounding lawns of green, its beds of colorful flowers, and the trees and shrubs which enhance

its beauty. Within its walls are to be tasted the refreshing waters of living and eternal truth. For all who enter the portals of thy house may this be an oasis of peace and life and light, in contrast with the clamor and evil and darkness of the world.[121]

Less than a decade later, President James E. Faust, counselor in the church's First Presidency, told the Las Vegas Saints, "While in the early days the fort marked the Church's presence in Las Vegas, the Las Vegas Temple symbolizes the rise of the Church in present-day Nevada."[122]

IMPACT OF TEMPLE AFTER DEDICATION

Just two years following the dedication of the temple, the press reported that fifty new wards had sprung up and that the Latter-day Saint population in the Las Vegas region had swelled to 9 percent. An additional one hundred wards were expected to be organized over the following decade. It was thought that the establishment of the Las Vegas Temple had "fueled the LDS increase."[123]

Architect George Tate, who won a local award for architectural merit for the temple design,[124] stated, "It is with some emotion that I often study the beautiful workmanship and feel an overwhelming appreciation not only for the opportunity to have participated in its design, but also for the marvelous craftsmanship and labor of so many who carried it out. At this time, I am just happy to be in the temple doing important work, and am grateful to have been permitted to have a part in its creation."[125]

Church member Robin Dixon commented on the spiritual protection the temple offers her and also added, "Now that I work there as a temple worker, it's just manna to my soul. It feeds my spirit. It just fills me with love and gratitude that we have a temple in this valley."[126] Former North Las Vegas mayor Shari Buck pointed out that one of the strengths of Las Vegas is that it is an international city that hosts more than forty million visitors annually. Buck said that many of the Latter-day Saint visitors "will come and do sessions at the temple, and that's exciting too to meet and share testimony with people from all over the world that happen to come into Las Vegas for a conference or for a visit,…so that strengthens us as members."[127]

The profound beauty of the temple's exterior has also attracted those not of the Latter-day Saint faith. While serving at the front desk of the temple, Ashley Hall recounted, "I've had people come in that front door of the temple, nonmembers, who would say 'Why does this temple shine? I mean, I live down the hill a little way, and I find myself on my back patio, and I look up at this glow around the temple. It hasn't got lights on it, it does at night, but not in the daytime,' and so we would have those conversations."[128] Cristi Bulloch surmised, "I think that there's a security about having a temple here in Las Vegas to even people who aren't members of the church.... Having a temple here locally has been a wonderful thing in that it feels like it brings peace to our community."[129]

CONCLUSION

Both the Las Vegas Saints and many local citizens appreciate the stunning temple illuminating the eastern horizon, a stark contrast to the remnants of their original fort. In their concerted effort to assimilate into this great desert community, Latter-day Saints have improved neighborhoods; inspired educational institutions; brought integrity to the marketplace; provided wholesome entertainment, cultural refinement, and family stability; and amply served in their communities.

The Latter-day Saint Las Vegas Temple now stands as a beacon in this desert oasis and is a source of light and spiritual nourishment for church members, numbering more than 105,000 in this metropolitan region at the time of writing. Though currently representing only about 6 percent of the local population and Nevada as a whole, members of the Church of Jesus Christ of Latter-day Saints are among the most influential body of citizens in an ever-expanding Vegas metro community numbering more than 2 million people. In addition, their influence is sprinkled throughout the entire state. The Saints worship north to south and east to west in 345 scattered congregations statewide.[130]

Oscar Goodman, former three-time mayor of Las Vegas (1999–2011), summarized the influence the Saints have had in his metropolitan city:

> They have paid special attention to the infrastructure. They have placed themselves in places of responsibility, not necessarily elected but more so appointed, in order to shepherd what makes an area successful, roads, streets, schools, that kind of thing. Their presence was always felt, they were always well-respected.... Most of them devoted their time, their energy, and their rectitude to a position, and because of the respect they inherently deserved, they were able to get things done. And a lot of projects that are named after that. I think when they look into themselves, they'll say, at the end of the day, that they did the right thing as far as the community was concerned.[131]

Brian Greenspun, 2021. Photo by Martin Andersen.

Brian Greenspun, editor, chief executive officer, and owner of the *Las Vegas Sun,* observed that although the Latter-day Saint population of Las Vegas and Clark County was only a small percentage of the total population, it seemed to him more like 30 or 40 percent, not in terms of size but in influence. He enumerated, "The commitment to governance. The commitment to civic engagement. The commitment to charitable endeavors always outsized as compared to the rest of the community.... The LDS community was vibrant across every facet, politically, public service, charitable.... No other group of people came close."[132]

From their editorial perspectives, well-known Las Vegas journalists Jon Ralston and John L. Smith also described the Latter-day Saint influence on their local communities. Ralston believed that the "influence has been pervasive because it's been so broad and so deep.... They were known for standing up, men of moral rectitude."[133] Smith added:

> You cannot say that Las Vegas would be anywhere near what it is today without that tremendous influence of some very dedicated people who happen to be Mormon in faith and practice.... I don't think there's an area of Las Vegas life that has not been touched by the LDS faith,... participating and organizing in the community,... focusing on public education,... values that are so important to a community if you're going to put down roots.... I think the[ir] greatest contribution is stability.... To have members of the community that are stabilizing influencers, can't be overstated; it's so important.[134]

Perhaps Senator Richard Bryan encapsulated the Saints' influence best:

> The LDS community has had a profound impact on southern
> Nevada, dating back to the early founding of the mission in 1855
> here in Las Vegas and the growth of the community largely in the
> early days.... They brought with them strong family values. They
> brought with them the virtue of hard work, discipline, all of which
> is part of a value system that even those who were not members of
> the church, but always it was family. Family was first, not second, not
> third, and the family structure impresses all. We don't understand
> necessarily the theological roots to the belief, but the family values,
> the civic responsibility. In effect they're good people who helped to
> make Las Vegas a good city for all of us to live in.[135]

Yet the Latter-day Saints have been and continue to be reciprocally
influenced and blessed by good people like Senator Bryan and countless
others. Current Latter-day Saint Clark County commissioner Jim Gibson
stated:

> One thing that I feel has to be said is we would not be where we are
> today without our nonmember friends. The credibility we achieve,
> and have achieved over time, is not because we go around telling
> people we're incredible. Rather it's because our friends have called
> upon us, or interact with us, and we do our part. We're helping with
> the heavy lifting; we're not doing it all. We're helping with fram-
> ing the policies that will drive us forward and make us a success-
> ful economy, make us a successful neighborhood, or whatever it is
> we're focusing on. And we have never, as a people, never been afraid
> to reach out and to have as our colleagues people not of our faith.
> And we have gained so much.... I would say we are where we are in
> some part, no small part, because of our nonmember friends who
> worked with us, helped us, and then bore witness of the experience
> they had with us.[136]

Latter-day Saint contributions to the Las Vegas milieu demonstrate
the symbiotic relationship forged between a conservative sect and a
vibrant community. Along with many other faith-based peoples of various cultures and denominations, members of the Church of Jesus Christ
of Latter-day Saints have been bright lights in this vast desert metropolis
as they illuminate family values, morality, community service, and wholesome stability.

Nevada Mothers of the Year

1945	Una Reilly Dickerson	Carson City/Reno
1946	Daisy Burke	Reno
1947	Mrs. Joseph Collins (Dorothy)	Ely
1948	Bertha Ronzone	Las Vegas
1949	Mrs. James Jensen	Las Vegas
1950	Mary Fulstone	Smith Valley/Yerington
1951	Agnes Gregory	Elko
1952	No recognition	
1953	Julia Ann Walther	Las Vegas
1954	No recognition	
1955	Harriet Arentz	Smith Valley
1956	Arville Packham	unknown
1957	Catherine Gianella	Reno
1958	Mrs. C. C. Taylor	Reno
1959	No recognition	
1960	No recognition	
1961	No recognition	
1962	No recognition	
1963	Amy Gulline	unknown
1964	Emma Calvert*	Caliente
1965	Gladys Dula	Caliente
1966	No recognition	
1967	Theresa A. Laxalt	Carson City
1968	No recognition	
1969	Jesse Lamb Stewart*	Alamo
1970	Mary Lowman	Las Vegas
1971	Vilda Bulloch Ronnow*	Reno
1972	Merle Jones*	Las Vegas
1973	Virginia Zobrist*	Las Vegas
1974	Harriet Lenz	Reno
1975	Helen Early	Las Vegas
1976	Katherine Ernst	Panaca
1977	Laura Bell Kelch	Las Vegas
1978	Genevieve A. Smith*	Las Vegas
1979	Ruth McGroarty	Las Vegas
1980	Lila Zona*	Las Vegas
1981	Darlene Wagner*	Las Vegas
1982	Lucy Bluth Bunker*	Las Vegas

1983	Josephine Scofield Stewart*	Las Vegas
1984	Marva Bunker Davis*	Las Vegas
1985	Shirley Holst	Las Vegas
1986	Doree Dickerson	Las Vegas
1987	Patricia Bagley	unknown
1988	Bernice Martin	Reno
1989	Mary Edwards*	Boulder City
1990	Lois Tarkanian	Las Vegas
1991	Noreen Bishop*	Overton
1992	Margaret LaRue Worthen*	Las Vegas
1993	Ethelyn Peterson*	Las Vegas
1994	Margaret Lou (Peggy) Draper*	Pioche
1995	Lora Dee Christensen*	Las Vegas
1996	Rosel Seastrand*	North Las Vegas
1997	Patricia Bulloch*	North Las Vegas
1998	No recognition	
1999	Merian Murphy*	Las Vegas
2000	No recognition	
2001	Sandra Louise Taylor*	Las Vegas
2002	No recognition	
2003	Elaine Hardy*	Las Vegas
2004	Susan Leavitt*	Henderson
2005	Carole Ann Davis*	Henderson
2006	Laurie Anne Richardson*	Henderson
2007	Vicki VanMeetren	Henderson
2008	Colleen Haycock*	Las Vegas
2009	Mary Beth Scow*	Henderson
2010	Patrice Tew*	Las Vegas
2011	Rose Woodbury*	Boulder City
2012	Mary Holcombe	Las Vegas
2013	Zan Hyer*	Las Vegas
2014	Robin Van Kempen	Las Vegas
2015	Candy Krausman*	Las Vegas
2016	Amy Ellsworth*	Henderson
2017	No recognition	
2018	Jana Dixon North*	Las Vegas
2019	Susan Brager	Las Vegas
2020	Dara Marias	Las Vegas
2021	Truvella (Trudy) Reese	North Las Vegas

*Member of the Church of Jesus Christ of Latter-day Saints. Thanks is expressed to Cristi Bulloch, the current president of the American Mothers Nevada Association, who compiled this list.

APPENDIX B

Clark County Schools Named
After Latter-day Saints

Bowler, Grant	ES	Kesterson, Lorna	ES
Bowler, Joseph L., Sr.	ES	Leavitt, Justice Myron E.	MS
Brinley, J. Harold	MS	Long, Walter V.	ES
Brown, B. Mahlon	JHS	Lyon, Mack	MS
Bryan, Roger	ES	Mannion, Jack and Terry	MS
Bunker, Berkeley L.	ES	O'Roarke, Thomas J.	ES
Christensen, M. J.	ES	Reid, Harry	ES
Cram, Brian and Teri	MS	Ronnow, C. C.	ES
Earl, Ira J.	ES	Roundy, Dr. C. Owen	ES
Earl, Marion B.	ES	Rowe, Lewis E.	ES
Edwards, Elbert	ES	Schofield, Jack Lund	MS
Gibson, James	ES	Swainston, Theron L.	MS
Gibson, Robert O.	MS	Thiriot, Joseph	ES
Givens, Linda Rankin	ES	Twitchell, Neil C.	ES
Hayes, Keith C. and Karen W.	ES	Walker, J. Marlan	IS
Hollingsworth, Howard E.	ES	Woodbury, C. W.	MS
Iverson, Mervin	ES	Woolley, Gwendolyn	ES
Johnston, Carroll M.	MS		

Note: ES = elementary school; IS = intermediate school; JHS = junior high school; MS = middle school.

Select List of Elected or Appointed Officials in the Las Vegas Metropolitan Area

Jay Bingham	Clark County commissioner
Berkeley Bunker	US senator
Mo Denis	Nevada state senator
Lloyd D. George	US District Court judge, federal courthouse namesake
Jim C. Gibson	mayor of Henderson (served three terms) and Clark County commissioner
Jim Gibson (son)	mayor of Henderson (served three terms) and Clark County commissioner
Andy Hafen	mayor of Henderson
Ashley Hall	city manager of Las Vegas
Keith Hayes	Clark County district judge (presided over the Howard Hughes will trial)
Mark Hutchison	lieutenant governor of Nevada
Karen Hayes King	assemblywoman and Clark County commissioner
Ralph Lamb	sheriff of Las Vegas
John Jay Lee	mayor of North Las Vegas
Ray Rawson	Nevada state senator
Harry Reid	US Senate majority leader
Mary Beth Scow	Clark County commissioner and Clark County school board
James K. Seastrand	mayor of North Las Vegas (served four terms); twenty years on the city council
Bruce L. Woodbury	Clark County commissioner (longest serving ever); beltway named for him

Las Vegas Temple Dedicatory Prayer, Given December 16, 1989

O God our Eternal Father, Almighty Judge of the nations, we thy thankful children solemnly bow before thee in a prayer of dedication. We are gathered in thy holy house to present it unto thee and unto thy Beloved Son, our Redeemer.

We lift our voices in gratitude for thy manifold blessings. Thou hast favored us with life in this glorious dispensation of time. Thou hast granted us citizenship in this good land. Above all, thou hast blessed us with the truths of thine everlasting gospel and the authority of thine eternal priesthood.

We thank thee for the Prophet Joseph Smith, an instrument in thy hand in bringing to pass this great work of restoration in preparation for the time when thy Son shall come to reign as King of kings and Lord of lords.

We thank thee for this beautiful temple, this house of worship, of learning, of covenants and everlasting promises. We thank thee for the faith and skills of all who have contributed to make it possible. It stands in this community which has become an oasis in the desert. As men have brought water to the dry earth of this region it has become fruitful, and now as a crowning jewel stands thy holy house with its surrounding lawns of green, its beds of colorful flowers, and the trees and shrubs which enhance its beauty.

Within its walls are to be tasted the refreshing waters of living and eternal truth. For all who enter the portals of thy house may this be an oasis of peace and life and light, in contrast with the clamor and evil and darkness of the world.

It stands where it will be seen by multitudes of the generations of men. May all who look upon it regard it reverently as the house of the Lord. May the hand of the destroyer be kept from it by thy power.

We are mindful of thy promise given in the early days of the Church that "inasmuch as my people build a house unto me in the name of the Lord, and do not suffer any unclean thing to come into it, that it be not defiled, my glory shall rest upon it;

"Yea, and my presence shall be there, for I will come into it, and all the pure in heart that shall come into it shall see God" (D&C 97:15–16).

We plead for forgiveness and strength to overcome our weaknesses. We long for the day when we may be worthy to look upon thy face. Keep us from the decay and servitude which come from sin. Bless us with the light and freedom which come of righteousness.

Thy house is now complete. It is beautiful, and we present it as the gift of thy thankful children.

And now, acting in the authority of the holy priesthood which comes from thee, and in the name of Jesus Christ thy Son, we dedicate unto thee and our Savior this, the Las Vegas Nevada Temple of The Church of Jesus Christ of Latter-day Saints. We dedicate it as thy holy house. We pray that thy Spirit may fill this sacred structure and that thy influence may hover over it by day and by night. We pray that thou might hallow it by thy presence.

We dedicate unto thee the grounds on which it stands with their vegetation and all of the ancillary construction associated therewith. We dedicate the sacred rooms, each one, with its associated fittings and furnishings. We dedicate the baptistry, the endowment rooms where thy people will enter into covenant with thee, the sacred altars and the sealing rooms where eternal promises will be made and accepted, and every other facility within this beautiful structure. May it be hallowed to all who enter. May their thoughts be lifted to thee and thy Beloved Son. May a spirit of peace and reconciliation be in their hearts. In the great work that will be performed here, everlasting in its consequences, may thy people find satisfaction and gladness.

O Father, look with favor upon thy sons and daughters wherever they may be. When they err, and come unto thee in repentance, wilt thou forgive and remember their sins no more. Give them grateful hearts for the blessings which thou hast showered upon them. Grant unto them strength to walk the straight and narrow way that leads to life eternal. May the people of thy Church across the world become a great and singular community, united by the bonds of the everlasting gospel, with love and respect one for another, with faith and knowledge of thee and thine eternal purposes, with obedience to thy commandments and that happiness which thou hast promised to those who walk acceptably before thee.

We pray for thy prophet of this day, even President Ezra Taft Benson. Give him strength of body and mind according to his need. Give him joy in his heart concerning thy work and thy people. Bless those associated with him among the General Authorities and officers of the Church. Bless all who hold responsibility of any kind in thy Church and kingdom wherever it may be organized. Pour out thy spirit upon thy faithful saints everywhere.

Touch the hearts of the people of the nations that they may receive the testimony of thy servants the missionaries. And bless these, thy dedicated servants, that they may be powerful in their teaching of divine truth and in their testimony of thy Beloved Son.

Bless the homes of thy people. May there be peace and harmony and love. May thy people look to thee and live.

Father dear, we remember before thee the suffering and needful of the earth. There are so many who struggle and yearn. There are so many in the depths of sorrow and pain, of hunger and want, of darkness and sin. Let thy spirit brood over the earth and lead thy sons and daughters of all lands that they may drink of the waters of divine truth.

We so invoke thy blessing, dear Father, with grateful hearts and in humility before thee, in the name of thy Beloved Son Jesus Christ. Amen.

Source: "Dedicatory Prayer: Las Vegas Nevada Temple, 16 December 1989," https://www.churchofjesuschrist.org/temples/details/las-vegas-nevada-temple/prayer/1989-12-16?lang=eng.

Latter-day Saint Las Vegas Regional Timeline

1855   Latter-day Saint pioneers build and occupy the old Las Vegas Mormon Fort.

1857   Pioneers abandoned fort due to problems with each other and US government.

1861   Albert and William Knapp run a general store at the Mormon Fort.

1864   Brigham Young sends Thomas S. Smith to settle the Muddy River Valley.

1879   The Bunkerville Ward is organized as part of the St. George Stake.

1884   The Overton Ward is organized.

1901   The Mesquite Ward is organized.

1905   Railroad is built, linking Los Angeles and Salt Lake City via Las Vegas; town sites are sold.

1909   Clark County is established, with Las Vegas as an incorporated city.

1912   The Moapa Stake is organized from the St. George, Utah, Stake.

1915   The First Las Vegas Branch is created (Charles C. Ronnow, first presiding elder).

1924   The First Las Vegas Ward is created.

1925   Las Vegas receives its first chapel at the corner of Sixth and Carson Streets.

1927   The Las Vegas First Ward establishes Boy Scouts of America Troop 63; Marion B. Earl is the first Scoutmaster.

1930   Latter-day Saint population increases to 410; President Heber J. Grant visits Las Vegas.

1931   Gambling is legalized in the state of Nevada, and divorce laws are relaxed.

1932   The second chapel built at Ninth and Clark Streets at a cost of $38,000. (Presidents H. J. Grant and D. O. McKay attend the quarterly conference. Members are upset because of ward location.)

1935   The Mormon Tabernacle Choir performs on the steps of the Las Vegas courthouse.

1936   The Hoover Dam is completed, and the Mormon Tabernacle Choir performs there in 1935.

1940   The second ward in the city of Las Vegas is created (by this time, eighty-four hundred citizens make up Las Vegas).

1941   Berkeley L. Bunker, former bishop of the Las Vegas Ward, is appointed a US senator from Nevada.

1945   The population of Las Vegas reaches about thirty thousand, with Latter-day Saints totaling three thousand of that amount (10 percent of the city).

1948   The seminary program begins in Las Vegas. President J. Harold Brinley is the first seminary teacher.

1954   The Las Vegas Stake is created from the Moapa Stake.

1960   The North Las Vegas Stake is created. On November 6, 1960, the meeting for its creation is held in the convention center due to the large number of members in attendance.

1966   Howard Hughes comes to Las Vegas. Bill Gay and five other Latter-day Saints (Howard Eckersley, Roy Crawford, John Holmes, Lavar Myler, and George Francom) worked closely with Hughes.

1975   The Las Vegas Mission is created.

1979   The Latter-day Saint population in Las Vegas reaches about thirty-five thousand.

1984   The Las Vegas Nevada Temple is announced.

1989   The Las Vegas Nevada Temple is dedicated; three hundred thousand attend an open house prior to the temple's dedication.

1997   The Nevada Las Vegas West Mission is created.

2000   Las Vegas reaches eighteen stakes.

2001   The Latter-day Saint population in Las Vegas rises to eighty thousand.

2008–19 Latter-day Saints Donny and Marie Osmond perform for hundreds of thousands in Las Vegas.

2020   The Latter-day Saint population of the Las Vegas metropolitan region makes up roughly 6 percent of the area's two million people.

Notes

PREFACE

1. The Old Las Vegas Mormon Fort is the official title used by the state of Nevada, which maintains a national park at this historic site. See http://parks.nv.gov/parks/old-las-vegas-mormon-fort, accessed May 12, 2020.

2. A stake is an ecclesiastical term that describes a Latter-day Saint church unit and is usually made up of several thousand people, like a Catholic diocese. It is based on biblical imagery of an expanding tent on which stakes continue to be placed, as evidenced in this scriptural passage: "Enlarge the place of thy tent...lengthen thy cords, and strengthen thy stakes" (Isa. 54:2).

3. "Facts and Statistics, Nevada," Church of Jesus Christ of Latter-day Saints Newsroom, https://newsroom.churchofjesuschrist.org/facts-and-statistics/state/nevada, accessed May 1, 2020.

CHAPTER ONE. THE LATTER-DAY SAINT CORRIDOR
AND THE OLD LAS VEGAS MORMON FORT

1. This chapter is a distillation and updated modification of content culled from Fred E. Woods, *A Gamble in the Desert: The Mormon Mission in Las Vegas, 1855–1857*.

2. Milton R. Hunter, "The Mormon Corridor," explains the establishment of the Mormon Corridor as "the founding of a contiguous line of Mormon settlements from a good seaport to Salt Lake City and also the connecting of those towns by a highway over which immigrants could be conveyed with ease and safety" (181).

3. Brigham Young, "Fifth General Epistle," 213.

4. Military historian Sherman L. Fleek, *History May Be Searched in Vain: A Military History of the Mormon Battalion*, noted, "The Mormon Battalion was the only religious unit in American military history in federal service, having been recruited solely from one religious body and having a religious title as the unit of designation" (27). The battalion served in the US military from July 1846 to July 1847 during the Mexican-American War of 1846–48.

5. On the exploration of the Las Vegas region prior to the entrance of the Latter-day Saint missionaries in 1855, see Stanley W. Paher, *Las Vegas as It Began—as It Grew*, 11–18.

6. Leonard J. Arrington, "The Harvest of '49," 88. Edward Leo Lyman, *San Bernardino: The Rise and Fall of a California Community*, 296, lists three Hawaiian women who gathered to San Bernardino in the mid-nineteenth century with their *haole* husbands.

7. See Marjorie Newton, *Southern Cross Saints: The Mormons in Australia*, 223–26, for a list of Australian Latter-day Saints and the vessels that transported them to California in the 1850s.

8. "Letter from Elders A. Lyman and C. C. Rich," 75–76.

9. Brigham Young, "Sixth General Epistle," 24.

10. Arrington, "The Harvest of '49," 86.

11. Arrington, "The Harvest of '49," 89.

12. Elbert Edwards, "Early Mormon Settlements in Southern Nevada," 27.

13. "Diary of John Steele," spring 1855, L. Tom Perry Special Collections, Harold B. Lee Library, Brigham Young University, 35, hereafter cited as PSC. The "Record of the Los [sic] Vegas Mission," hereafter cited as RLVM, April 22, 1855, 1–2, Church History Library, the Church of Jesus Christ of Latter-day Saints, Salt Lake City, hereafter cited as CHL. The RLVM lists the following men who served under mission president William Bringhurst: Edward Cuthbert; Thomas E. Ricks; Ira S. Miles; Albert Knapp; James T. S. Allred; Benjamin Cluff; George W. Bean; William Hamblin; James A. Bean; Richard James; Aroet L. Hale; William P. Jones, 2nd; William C. A. Smoot; William Foster; George G. Snyder; William Vance; Joseph Milam; Stephen C. Perry; Amasa E. Mereiam [Miriam]; Sidney Carter; William Nixon; William Maxwell; John Steele; William C. Mitchell; Benjamin R. Hulse; William R. Burston; and Joseph C. Clowes. William Hamblin and Richard James ended up going to the Elk Mountain Mission instead of the Las Vegas Mission.

14. Jonathan Foster, *Stigma Cities: The Reputation and History of Birmingham, San Francisco, and Las Vegas,* 126.

15. RLVM, April 22, 1855, 1. Leonard J. Arrington notes that at the same time men were called to settle the Las Vegas Mission, Apostle Orson Hyde had been appointed as the probate judge of Carson Valley. Along with conducting court business, Hyde was assigned to "prepare the establishment of a mission among the Indians, and provide a way station for Mormon emigration headed from Oregon and California to Salt Lake Valley." Thus, the Carson Valley Mission was established at the same time as the Las Vegas Mission with the same purpose to minister among the Native Americans and to be a way station for emigration. See Leonard J. Arrington, *The Mormons in Nevada,* with a foreword by Mike O'Callaghan, governor of Nevada, 1971–78. Originally published in twelve parts by the *Las Vegas Sun* (1979), 13.

16. Susan Easton Black, comp., *Membership of the Church of Jesus Christ of Latter-day Saints, 1830–1848,* 41:317–21.

17. "Diary of John Steele," spring 1855, 35. Those who had previously served in the Mormon Battalion were James T. S. Allred, William A. Follett, Sylvester Hulet, Albert A. Knapp, William B. Maxwell, and John Steele.

18. John Steele Las Vegas Mission setting apart (May 23, 1855) by George A. Smith and Wilford Woodruff, vault MS 528, series 7, box 3, folder item 3, PSC. The term *Lamanites* refers to a people mentioned in the Book of Mormon. Latter-day Saints believe that many Native Americans are descendants of Lamanite people who left Jerusalem in about 600 BC to settle in the promised land of the American nation.

19. Frank Esshom, *Pioneers and Prominent Men of Utah,* 769.

20. RLVM, April 22, 1855, 1.

21. Kate B. Carter, *The Las Vegas Fort,* 14; Black, *Membership of the Church,* 12:2–6.

22. *Deseret Weekly News,* August 14, 1878, 448.

23. RLVM, May 15, 1855, 3. RLVM, July 1, 1855, 14–15, notes that George G. Snyder later

replaced Ira S. Miles as second counselor in the mission and that George W. Bean replaced Miles in his additional responsibility of serving as the clerk of the mission.

24. Andrew Jenson, *Latter-day Saint Biographical Encyclopedia*, 4:611.

25. Arrington, *The Mormons in Nevada*, 23–24. The word *ward* is an ecclesiastical term to refer to a Latter-day Saint congregation generally consisting of several hundred people.

26. Flora Diana Bean Horne, comp., *Autobiography of George W. Bean: A Utah Pioneer of 1847, and His Family Records*, 115. Arrington, *The Mormons in Nevada*, 11, notes that Steptoe had been assigned by US president Franklin Pierce "to investigate the possibility of constructing a road from Salt Lake City to California." Another called to assist Bean as an interpreter was James T. S. Allred, who wrote, "At the spring conference [1855] I was called to go on a mission to Los Vegas to preach to the Piute Indians as Brigham Young knew that I was a good Indian interpreter. I was also a peace maker among the Indians and always had many Indian friends." Diary of James T. S. Allred, 4, PSC.

27. Horne, *Autobiography of George W. Bean*, 117.

28. Paher, *Las Vegas as It Began*, 16–17; Michael S. Green, *Nevada: A History of the Silver State*, 71.

29. Ray M. Reeder, "The Mormon Trail: A History of the Salt Lake to Los Angeles Route to 1869," 215–16.

30. *Deseret News*, July 25, 1855, 158.

31. RLVM, June 16, 1855.

32. Carson Fehner, interview by Fred E. Woods and Martin Andersen, February 7, 2020, at the Old Las Vegas Mormon Fort State Historic Park where Fehner is the interpreter, typescript in possession of the author.

33. RLVM, June 18, 1855.

34. "Day Book of James Tillman Sanford Allred," typescript, June 19–29, 1855, PSC. The drawing of lots was also later used for work division on the fort. "The Journal of George W. Bean," September 3, 1855, typescript, Utah State Historical Society, notes, "Drew lots for building in the fort. Mine is 29 by the gate."

35. "Diary of John Steele," June 19, 21, 29, 1855.

36. RLVM, July 1, 1855, notes that Bean replaced Ira S. Miles as clerk of the mission. Miles had been released from this assignment as well as from his calling as second counselor to President Bringhurst because of inappropriate behavior. Therefore, Miles returned home. Bean recorded in his journal for this day, "July 1st…At meeting today was unanimously voted to be clerk and Recorder of the mission." He must have anticipated his official assignment, as evidenced from his journal, which states, three days prior to his nomination, "[June] 28th Spent the day in copying the record from Ira Miles Scrap of Journal." See "Journal of George W. Bean," June 28, July 1, 1855.

37. For an excellent treatment of Native Americans residing in the Las Vegas region at the time of the Latter-day Saint entrance and beyond, see Martha C. Knack, "Southern Paiutes, the Native Americans," in *The Peoples of Las Vegas: One City, Many Faces*, ed. Jerry L. Simich and Thomas L. Wright, 37–56. For an overview of Native Americans in Las Vegas and Nevada in general, see https://americanindian coc.org/category/native-americans-in-nevada/.

38. "Journal of George W. Bean," July 21, 1855.

39. Thomas E. Ricks to his wife, Tabitha, July 20, 1855, in *Thomas E. Ricks, Colonizer and Founder,* by Wanda Ricks Wyler, 33. Yet raising peas was not impossible, as evidenced from the RLVM, July 25, 1855, entry previously mentioned, which states for this week, "Bro. Hulse had a mess of green peas that he has raised in his garden at this place."

40. William Bringhurst to Brigham Young, August 6, 1855, Brigham Young Correspondence, CHL.

41. "Day Book of James Tillman Sanford Allred," July 27, 1855.

42. "Journal of George W. Bean," December 24–25, 1855. The term *ball* used herein may be an early version of baseball. For information on the evolution of baseball, see Warren Goldstein, *Playing for Keeps: A History of Early Baseball;* and Harold Seymour, *Baseball: The Early Years.* The author expresses appreciation to Dr. Richard I. Kimball for bringing these sources to his attention.

43. "Journal of George W. Bean," December 28, 1855.

44. "Journal of George W. Bean," January 1, 1856.

45. "Journal of George W. Bean," November 11, 24, December 1, 8, 1855.

46. Young to Bringhurst, August 23, 1855, recorded in RLVM, September 15, 1855.

47. Young to Bringhurst, December 29, 1855, Young Correspondence, CHL.

48. RLVM, November 4, 1855.

49. Apparently, Miles Anderson learned of his call from the *Deseret News* and departed immediately for Las Vegas without receiving counsel before his departure. In a letter to Brigham Young dated six months after the call, he wrote of his situation and his need for reassurance and encouragement: "I found my name last Spring in the paper as a missionary for Vagus I emediatly went not being Instructed what to do.... I would like to recive aline of Incoragement from you as I retain the same good feelings to you that I ever did and the same resulution to percevere In truth & righ[t]eousness." See Miles Anderson to Young, August 23, 1856, Young Correspondence, CHL.

50. "Missionaries," *Deseret News,* February 27, 1856, 405.

51. Mariah Burston Wheeler [Mariah Walker], "History of My Life," typescript, 31, Maria Burston Wheeler Collection, MS-00062, folder 1, Lied Library Special Collections, University of Nevada, Las Vegas, hereafter cited as Lied Library Special Collections.

52. "Journal of George W. Bean," July 8, 11, 1855.

53. "Diary of John Steele," July 5, 1855.

54. RLVM, February 10, 1856.

55. "Journal of George W. Bean," August 19, 1855.

56. RLVM, September 2, 1855.

57. RLVM, February 10, 1855. Nine days earlier, "Journal of George W. Bean," February 1, 1856, notes that Chief Joshua was taught to pray privately by Bean: "I told Pat Sar-ump [Patsearump] how to pray & he made his first trial which was well done." Following an entry for the date of July 12, 1856, the RLVM also inserts a list of the Native Americans baptized from each tribe. The second one on the list mentioned is Patsearump, who was also known by his English name, Joshua. This record reveals that he was baptized by President Bringhurst on November 4, 1855.

58. RLVM, November 4, 1855. John Steele wrote on another occasion, "I stood in the water at one time until I Baptized 55 Indians." See "John Steele Church Assignments," vault, MS 528, series 7, box 3, folder 3, item 3, PSC. Following an entry for the date of July 12, 1856, the RLVM also lists each of the Native Americans baptized on this date and includes their tribe, their Native name, an English name "given by the Elders at the time of baptism," and who baptized and confirmed them. It also includes several others who were baptized on other days. Interestingly, the RLVM mentions only four Native Americans from the Quoeech (Diggers) tribe and only three from the Iatt (Iat) nation who were baptized. Furthermore, these different tribes were not baptized on November 4, but rather all those baptized on that date were from the Paiute tribe.

59. "Day Book of James Tillman Sanford Allred," November 4, 1855. Allred also notes on this date that the number baptized was sixty-six. However, this appears to be an error, inasmuch as the official mission record puts the number at fifty-six baptisms.

60. Andrew Jenson, "History of the Las Vegas Mission," December 2, 1855, 184.

61. RLVM, January 27, 1856.

62. Young to the Piedes at Los [sic] Vegas, October 8, 1856, vault, MS 792, series 3, subseries 7, box 15, folder 9, item 10, PSC.

63. "Third Book or Journal of the Life and Travels of Aroet L. Hale," March 23, 27, 1856, CHL.

64. "Third Book or Journal," January 27, 1856, CHL.

65. Bringhurst to Young, October 15, 1856, Young Correspondence, CHL. In a letter written by William W. Riley to Young, December 17, 1856, Riley explained to Young the reason for the school: "Concluded that we ought to have a school as we have Children enuff." Riley also wrote that he and Edward Cuthbert had been appointed to be school trustees, and they proceeded to hire a teacher for their children "as well [as] for the Lamanites." The RLVM, December 17, 1856, indicates that the trustees assessed a poll tax of $38 on each of the men. It also notes that the house or school was to "be built in the center of the Fort to be 18 by 26 feet 2 stories high cost $2000.00 or more." It further reveals, "The upper part of the house was assigned as a pray[e]r circle Room, spiritual instructions, and as they said, to give the natives Endowments &c."

66. Milton R. Hunter, Brigham Young the Colonizer, 349. According to his wife, Rebecca M. Jones, "Extracts from the Life Sketch of Nathaniel V. Jones," 1–6, Nathaniel was born October 13, 1822, in the town of Brighton, Monroe County, New York. At the age of seventeen, he moved to Potosi, Wisconsin, and in 1842 became a Latter-day Saint. Three years later, he married Rebecca M. Burton, and the following year Nathaniel served in the Mormon Battalion. In 1850 he gathered with his family to the Salt Lake Valley. In 1852 Jones was called on a mission to Hindustan (India) and was therefore separated from his family for three years. Following his lead mission to Las Vegas (1856–57), Nathaniel served two more missions, one to England (1859–61) and the other to southern Utah, where he helped make iron. Jones died in his Salt Lake City home of inflammation of the lungs and brain on February 8, 1863.

67. Young to Bringhurst, March 3, 1856, Young Correspondence, CHL.

68. RLVM, April 5, 1856, indicates that Steele had just returned to the Las Vegas Mission and had brought with him "Bros Miles Anderson Beason Lewis and John Lowder." The following day the mission record notes that Steele was voted unanimously as the temporary president of the mission, while the presidency was away. See RLVM, April 6, 1856. According to RLVM, June 15, 1856, and "Diary of John Steele," June 15, 1856, Steele served in this capacity until June 15, when William Covert, a counselor in the mission presidency, returned to the mission.

69. "Diary of John Steele," April 21, 1856, notes that the guide was named Koonah-Kibals and further reveals that Steele took along with him Sylvester Hulet, John Lowder, and Beeson Lewis Jr.

70. "Diary of John Steele," April 22, 1856.

71. John Steele to Young, April 23, 1856, Young Correspondence, CHL.

72. Young to Steele, May 30, 1856, Young Correspondence, CHL.

73. Steele to Catherine Campbell Steele in Parowan, Utah, April 23, 1856, PSC.

74. "Diary of John Steele," May 6, 1856.

75. RLVM, May 6, 1856.

76. RLVM, May 16, 1856, indicates the temperature was 120 degrees Fahrenheit. Four days later, the RLVM, May 20, 1856, entry states, "This morning Bro Jones returned and…reported that he did not suceed in finding the Silver mountain."

77. "Diary of John Steele," May 11, 1856; RLVM, May 22, 1856. According to Hunter, *Brigham Young the Colonizer,* 350–51, Jones returned to Salt Lake City on June 13, whereupon he "immediately visited Brigham Young and made a full report of the prospects of lead and other matters related to his trip. The Church officials considered the report favorable and notified Jones a few days later that he was to take a company and proceed immediately to the working of the mines. Jones, with three companions…and supplies, left Salt Lake City, July 9, 1856."

78. Entries in the RLVM reveal that Bringhurst left the mission for a visit home to Salt Lake City on February 28, 1856, and returned to Vegas on July 7, 1856.

79. Young to Bringhurst, August 4, 1856, Young Correspondence, CHL.

80. This letter was dated July 7, 1856, and is included in the RLVM, August 10, 1856. A bishop is an ecclesiastical office in the Church of Jesus Christ of Latter-day Saints that presides over a ward. Latter-day Saint bishops worldwide serve on a volunteer basis without any monetary compensation.

81. RLVM, August 10, 1856.

82. RLVM, August 10, 1856.

83. RLVM, August 10, 1856.

84. RLVM, August 12, 1856, Journal History of the Church (hereafter cited as JH), April 16, 1857, CHL, indicates that Jones left Vegas for Salt Lake on September 15, 1856, having spent just over a month on this mining expedition.

85. Bringhurst to Young, August 12, 1856, Young Correspondence, CHL.

86. Young to Bringhurst, September 3, 1856, Young Correspondence, CHL.

87. Bringhurst to Young, September 23, 1856, Young Correspondence, CHL.

88. Edson Barney to N. V. Jones, September 21, 1856, Young Correspondence, CHL. Amasa M. Lyman, who passed by the Las Vegas Mission two weeks later, also wrote a letter to Young, explaining, "In reference to the feelings Existing between Brothers

B[ringhurst] and J[ones], with whom and their associates I have done all I could in the limited time I had to put down every thing like a partizan spirt and encourage them to labor for the interests of the common cause, whether in one place or another, feeling that the cause was one and its interest one also." See Amasa M. Lyman to Young, October 7, 1856, Young Correspondence, CHL.

89. Young to Bringhurst, October 13, 1856, Young Correspondence, CHL. Although Bringhurst was disfellowshipped, meaning full church services were temporarily suspended for a time, he returned to full fellowship and died in Springville, Utah, where he had been serving faithfully as a bishop in his later years of service. See Woods, *Gamble in the Desert,* 186.

90. Young to Samuel Thompson, October 13, 1856, Young Correspondence, CHL.

91. Young to Thompson, January 7, 1857, Young Correspondence, CHL.

92. Thompson to Young, January 13, 1857, Young Correspondence, CHL. In a letter from Samuel Thompson to Brigham Young, February 16, 1857, Thompson suggested that other men be called to Vegas to spare the mission: "I have often thought if I could see you I would suggest the idea to you of calling us all away, and if you wish the missions continued to send an entire new set of missionaries to carry on the work on a better policy than has been carried out heretofore, which I do not think can be done under present circumstances. There are few here who do not wish to leave at present." However, by this time, Brigham Young had decided to release the missionaries. Thompson had not yet received Young's letter written two weeks earlier telling of the release of all the Vegas missionaries. See Young to Samuel Thompson, February 4, 1857, Young Correspondence, CHL.

93. Young to Thompson, February 4, 1857, Young Correspondence, CHL.

94. Nathaniel V. Jones to Young, February 17, 1857, Young Correspondence, CHL.

95. Young to Jones, February 4, 1857.

96. RLVM, February 4, 1857.

97. Young to Los [*sic*] Vegas Lead Mines, February 21, 1857.

98. "The Diary and Autobiography of Lorenzo Brown," October 19, 1856, PSC, describes the furnace used for smelting as well as the fuel gathered: "The furnace is built on the side hill & is a wall built up in front with 2 places for the fire each 3 1/2 feet square & 6 high with the back open with each a small hole in front for the lead to run out The back is open into which we roll logs as large as we can get On those logs we put the ore about 2000 lds [lbs] in each space & cover with wood & set it on fire."

99. JH, April 16, 1857.

100. In addition to some of the men Jones drew upon from the Vegas fort, others were called specifically to assist him in the lead mission. On June 22, 1856, Brigham Young called other men to assist Jones. JH, June 22, 1856, reports, "The following missionaries were called for the lead mines: Nathaniel V. Jones, Peter Maughan, Jacob Peart, Milo Andrus, Harrison Burgess, Geo. Grown, Philander Colton, James Davis, James Hall, Oliver B. Huntington, Wilson Lund, Darvin Richardson, Thos. Sanders, Charles Woodard, Wm. T. Van Noy, Benjamin M. Roberts, and Geo. Woodward."

101. JH, April 16, 1857.

102. *John Woodhouse: His Pioneer Journal, 1830–1916*, 26–27.

103. Thompson to Young, March 20, 1857, Young Correspondence, CHL.

104. Diary of Alexander Abraham Lemon, March 23, 1857, CHL.

105. Autobiography of George Mayer, 49, PSC. Jenson, "History of the Las Vegas Mission," 277, notes, "With the departure of the brethren mentioned in the fore-going, the Latter-day Saint mission on Las Vegas was practically broken up, but a few of the missionaries, determined not to leave the place until they were released in a more formal way, remained and endeavored to do the Indians all the good they could." However, it is evident in the previously mentioned statement that President Thompson insisted that all must leave. That all did leave is supported by a state-ment made by William W. Wall to the Church Historian's Office at the close of this same year: "We traveled on, nothing of importance occurred until we reached Las Vegas, we found a few Indians there." But no mention is made of any Mormons being at the fort. See JH, December 12, 1857, for Wall's statement. Jenson, drawing upon a letter written by an Andrew Gibbons to George A. Smith, further states in his history (279) that in June 1858, Benjamin R. Hulse, president of the Las Vegas Mission, subdued a party of hostile Indians bent on killing a mail party. Finally, Jenson also notes, "At a special conference held by the missionaries at Santa Clara on Sunday, Sept. 26th, 1858, it was decided that the Las Vegas and Muddy Mis-sion should be dropped for the time being. The missionaries were called in from the Muddy and Las Vegas Missions on account of the thieving disposition of the Indians at those places" (281). However, it appears that at this time, there was no longer an official Las Vegas Mission. Rather, any missionaries (including Benja-min R. Hulse) who passed through the Vegas territory were part of the Muddy Mission. Edward Leo Lyman, *The Overland Journey from Utah to California: Wagon Travel from the City of the Saints to the City of Angels*, 82, drawing upon the diary of Caroline Crosby, indicates that when Crosby's small company came upon the Las Vegas fort on February 1, 1858, they found it to be in a "dilapidated state having been partly destroyed by the Indians." Lyman further notes that Benjamin Hulse was then the only Latter-day Saint missionary at the fort. Hulse "had been assigned to reside among the local Paiutes and help pacify them until the last of the evacuees from the California [San Bernardino] Mormon colony passed through the vicinity." Furthermore, the last entry of the official Las Vegas Mission record ends on March 19, 1857.

106. Jenson, "History of the Las Vegas Mission," 277.

107. "Journal of Amasa Lyman," typescript, May 9, 1857, 4, Utah State Historical Society.

108. The ecclesiastical term of bishop in the Church of Jesus Christ of Latter-day Saints has reference to a man who serves without pay in presiding over a local con-gregation (known as a ward). A bishop has similar responsibilities of leadership that may be assigned to a rabbi, a priest, or a pastor. https://newsroom.churchofjesus christ.org/article/bishop, accessed August 14, 2021.

109. See Woods, *Gamble in the Desert*, Appendix A, 183–97, for a biographical sketch of Bringhurst and the other missionaries who pioneered the Las Vegas Mission in 1855.

110. "First Vegas White Child Born at Mormon Fort," *Las Vegas Review-Journal,* June 28, 1964, 118, notes that the name of this child was Zelpha Deadeura Fuller, daughter of Mr. and Mrs. Elijah Knapp Fuller, born August 20, 1856.

111. "First Post Office Marker to Be Dedicated by DUP," *Las Vegas Review-Journal,* February 1952, 12, notes that a local unit of the Daughters of the Utah Pioneers demonstrated through their research that the first post office in Las Vegas was named after William Bringhurst, the leader of the Mormon pioneer settlers who came to the region in 1855. The DUP also arranged for this post office site to be dedicated, which was the second memorial plaque erected in the Las Vegas region at the old ranch property, which was part of the settlement of the first Latter-day Saint pioneer settlers in 1855. The first DUP plaque erected here was in honor of those pioneers who built the old Las Vegas Mormon Fort.

112. RLVM, November 17, 1856.

Chapter 2. Post–Old Mormon Fort Early Settlement to Las Vegas Stakes (1857–1960)

1. Woods, *Gamble in the Desert,* Appendix A; "Albert Knapp," 191, notes, "Born July 10, 1825, in Antwerp, Jefferson County, New York. Son of Silas and Lydia Mann Knapp. Baptized March 1846. Member of the Mormon Battalion. Came to Utah, 1847. Settled in Farmington. Married Rozina Shepard, 1849. Farm laborer. Married Judith Oviatt. Joined miners in Utah who were searching for gold. Died 1864 in California. Buried at the Village Church Yard in Centerville, Alameda County, California." Mary Bryant and Karla K. Oswald are currently working on a history of Albert Knapp. Mary Bryant, email to the author, January 22, 2020 (Bryant is a great-great-granddaughter of Albert Knapp).

2. Barbara Land and Myrick Land, *A Short History of Las Vegas,* 26. Paher, *Las Vegas as It Began—as It Grew,* 34–36, provides an overview of Fort Baker and Carlson's strategy for deception. Herein, Paher explains, "Fort Baker fulfilled a mission for Carleton by diverting attention from his march through southern Arizona during a critical time early in the Civil War. The abandoned Mormon fort buildings, garrisoned no troops; there were no bugle calls, no fighting, no improvements made. It is incorrect to refer to the remaining buildings of the Mormon fort as 'Fort Baker'" (36).

3. Nevada State Parks, "History of Old Las Vegas Mormon Fort State Historic Park," http://parks.nv.gov/learn/park-histories/old-las-vegas-mormon-fort-history, accessed April 3, 2020, provides a concise overview of the "Old Las Vegas Mormon Fort" history. For a detailed account of the history and its ranch development from the time of the Gass purchase until Helen Stewart sold the property to William Clark, see Paher, *Las Vegas as It Began,* 37–65. See also James Schoenwetter and John W. Hohmann, "Land Use Reconstruction at the Founding Settlement of Las Vegas, Nevada," for an archaeological survey and land-use study of the Las Vegas Old Mormon Fort land up until 1905. For a study of Clark and his relationship to Las Vegas, see James W. Hulse, "W. A. Clark and the Las Vegas Connection."

4. Mark R. Davis, "Saints in Sin City: Religion and Community Building in Twentieth Century Las Vegas," 58.

5. T. S. Kenderdine, *A California Tramp and Later Footprints; or, Life on the Plains in the Golden State Thirty Years Ago, with Miscellaneous Sketches in Prose and Verse,* 161–63.

6. Andrew Jenson, "Las Vegas Ward," 415.

7. Francis H. Leavitt, "The Influence of Mormon People in the Settlement of Clark County," 64.

8. Elbert E. Edwards, "History of the City of Las Vegas, Las Vegas High School Tales of Las Vegas Collection," folder 21, MS-00030, Elbert Edwards Papers, Lied Library Special Collections, University of Nevada, Las Vegas, hereafter cited as Lied Library Special Collections.

9. Don Ashbaugh, "Ed Von Tobel Recalls Arrival Here on City's 56th Anniversary," *Las Vegas Review-Journal,* May 21, 1961, 77.

10. *Elbert B. Edwards, Memories of a Southern Nevada Educator, Scion of an Early Mormon Pioneer Family,* published oral history conducted by Mary Ellen Glass, Oral History Program, University of Nevada, Reno, 1968, 143.

11. J. Harold Brinley, "The C. C. Ronnow [Elementary School] Dedication," December 15, 1966, 2, Charles C. Ronnow & Family, biographical file, Lied Library Special Collections.

12. "E. W. Clark Forwarding Co.," *Las Vegas Times,* August 19, 1905, 1, is the first attestation of advertisement for this business in this local newspaper. Weekly front-page advertisements continued throughout the year. In each advertisement, the same information was presented: "E. W. Clark Forwarding Co. General Merchandise and Forwarding Wholesale Dealers in Anheuser Busch and Salt Lake Co.'s Beer Las Vegas—Caliente." This is evidence that Clark Forwarding Company sold beer, which Latter-day Saint employees did not purchase for personal use but instead distributed. There are no advertisements listed for the Clark Forwarding Company in another local newspaper, the *Las Vegas Age,* for 1905. However, one article contains information about the company under the title "Slight Improvement," *Las Vegas Age,* September 16, 1905, 1, noting, "Forwarding Business Shows Substantial Increase."

13. Ralph J. Roske, *Las Vegas: A Desert Paradise,* n.p. Herein is an image showing the Ronnow home to the left of the Clark Forwarding Company. See also biographical information on Charles Christian Ronnow, including his mission to Scandinavia, "Charles Christian Ronnow," Missionary Database, Church of Jesus Christ of Latter-day Saints, https://history.churchofjesuschrist.org/missionary /individual/charles-christian-ronnow-1865?lang=eng, accessed April 4, 2020. "Mr. and Mrs. Charles C. Ronnow Celebrate Fiftieth Anniversary," *Las Vegas Age,* June 20, 1941, 2, further states that following a lifetime of civic service in southern Nevada, which included his influence as a teacher in the local schools, Charles, his wife, and their three children were "held in the highest esteem and affectionate regard of all who know them." "Pioneer Vegans Observe Golden Wedding Date," *Las Vegas Evening Review-Journal,* June 17, 1941, 5, provides a detailed overview of Ronnow's life, including the facts that he became the bishop of the Panaca Ward in 1884 [1894], served a mission to Denmark in 1899, and "was interested in civic affairs and served as chairman of Clark county commission for six years."

14. Sharrell D. Williams, "A Historical Study of the Growth of the L.D.S. Church

in Clark County, Nevada," 58. For an early history of the Church of Jesus Christ of Latter-day Saints in Clark County (1855–1912), see 42–58. For an overview of Latter-day Saints in Nevada from 1855 to the late 1970s, see Arrington, *The Mormons in Nevada.*

15. Elbert Edwards, "Mormon Influences in Southern Nevada," box 1, folder 18, 6, MS-00031, Edwards Papers.

16. Arrington, *The Mormons in Nevada,* 57.

17. Marion B. Earl, "The History of the Las Vegas First Ward," 1, unpublished history, 1977, CHL.

18. "Newel K. Leavitt," Church of Jesus Christ of Latter-day Saints, https://history .churchofjesuschrist.org/missionary/individual/newel-k-leavitt-1888?lang=eng, accessed April 3, 2020.

19. Lisa Leavitt Messenger, interview by Fred E. Woods and Martin Andersen, March 7, 2020, Las Vegas, typescript in the possession of the author. Messenger is the great-granddaughter of Newel K. Leavitt.

20. Earl, "History of the Las Vegas First Ward," 1. Unfortunately, Earl further notes (2) that just seven years later, Leavitt died at the young age of thirty-three, leaving his wife, Nettie, a widow, with four boys to provide for.

21. Earl, "History of the Las Vegas First Ward," 1.

22. Leavitt Messenger, interview, March 7, 2020. Messenger further stated that in 1917, Leavitt moved back to his home in Bunkerville to assist his sick father, who soon passed away. He then moved to Delta, Utah, to work in a sugar-beet factory, as he had heard about employment there. However, Newel became sick and passed away in 1921.

23. "L.D.S. Meeting," *Las Vegas Age,* July 5, 1913, 1.

24. "Latter Day Saints," *Las Vegas Age,* April 4, 1914, 1. Eugene P. Moehring and Michael S. Green, *Las Vegas: A Centennial History,* note that the "Block & Botkin's store between First and Second Street was the first large men's shop in the summer of 1905" (21). This is the first-known public meeting place where the Saints met. Apparently, word got out, because the following year, although church meeting times were advertised, their meeting place was not mentioned. See "Church Notices" under the category "Latter-day Saints," *Las Vegas Age,* February 6, 1915, 2.

25. Williams, "Historical Study," 59, notes that the Moapa Stake, established in 1912, was an outgrowth of the St. George Stake.

26. Earl, "History of the Las Vegas First Ward," 2. A short announcement in the *Las Vegas Age,* May 13, 1914, 1, notes that even before the branch was officially organized, a wedding ceremony "was performed in the Overland Hotel by Charles C. Ronnow, Elder of the Church of Jesus Christ of Latter Day Saints."

27. Moapa Stake confidential minutes (LR 5636 10, folder 1), CHL, cited as "Historical Record Book A" and Moapa Stake "Historical Record from 1912 to 1929, Book B," in Lloyd K. Long, "The Establishment of the Church of Jesus Christ of Latter-day Saints," unpublished paper, 1977, 5, Lied Library Special Collections. The author thanks Jeff Thompson, CHL archivist, for checking this primary source.

28. *Las Vegas Age,* June 12, 1915, 4. Wendell Waite and Bonita "Bonnie" Waite, "Reflections: History of the North Las Vegas Stake," unpublished manuscript, 2000,

202, note that on June 30, 1912, William A. Whitehead was called as the bishop of
the Overton Ward, one of the wards of the Moapa Stake, and served in that position for three years. (The author thanks Wendell and Bonnie for giving him a copy
of their manuscript, which they were commissioned to write by their stake president, Harold H. Tanner.) Williams, "Historical Study," 103, seems to incorrectly note
that the Las Vegas Branch was "organized as part of the Bunkerville Ward," but this
appears to be incorrect, as Whitehead is the bishop listed in the advertisement for
the Las Vegas Branch. The ecclesiastical terms *branch* and *ward* are designations for
the size of Latter-day Saint Church units. A branch is a smaller unit made up of
usually a hundred or so members and a ward of several hundred members.

29. "To Assist Members," *Las Vegas Age*, January 23, 1915, 1.

30. Earl, "History of the Las Vegas First Ward," 2. Ira Joseph Earl was born at Bunkerville, December 16, 1884, and died April 28, 1957. See https://www.findagrave.com
/memorial/18786555/ira-joseph-earl, accessed May 14, 2020. He lived in Las Vegas
from 1920 until his death. Earl worked at a wood and coal business and owned several properties. He helped build the first Latter-day Saint chapel in Nevada. See
"Ira J. Earl Dies in Clark," *Reno Evening Gazette*, April 29, 1857, 1. Ira's father, Joseph I.
Earl, was a prominent church leader in southern Nevada, and Ira's paternal grandfather, Sylvester Henry Earl, was a member of Brigham Young's vanguard company
who entered the Salt Lake Valley in 1947. See "Family Honor Bishop Earl," *Las Vegas
Age*, September 1, 1932, 4.

31. "Mormon Church Officials Visit Las Vegas Stake [Branch]," *Las Vegas Age*,
May 6, 1922, 2, gives evidence that church leaders were visiting the prosperous Las
Vegas Branch at this time. The article notes, "President W. L. Jones and Bishop J. I.
Earl of Overton arrived in our city Saturday and assisted in the services of the Latter
Day Saints Sunday morning. The services were very well attended."

32. Earl, "History of the Las Vegas First Ward," 2.

33. "l.d.s. Bazaar an Unqualified Success," *Las Vegas Age*, December 8, 1923, 1,
notes, "The ladies of the Latter Day Saints Church held a bazaar in Beckley's hall
Friday which was a success in every way. The room was lined with booths in which
were displayed various kinds of very beautiful fancy and useful articles, most of
which were sold during the day. Apetizing [*sic*] refreshments were also dispensed
through the day. The combined…netted a sum which repays the loyal women for
their years' work." "The Church World," under the subheading "To Hold Bazaar," *Las
Vegas Age*, October 26, 1934, 13, announced, "The Relief Society ladies of the church
of the Latter Day Saints are holding their annual bazaar. Among the various features there will be a fish pond for children and very lovely fancy work for sale." This
reveals that the Relief Society had been holding an annual bazaar for more than a
decade. Further, another activity open to the public is mentioned right above this
article: "m.i.a. to Entertain with Dance," noting that the Latter-day Saints would be
sponsoring a Halloween dance at their church recreation hall.

34. These dances may have been used to raise funds for a much-needed church
building. "Mother's Day, May 12, a National Holiday," *Las Vegas Age*, April 28, 1923, 1,
advertised that the Latter-day Saints would be sponsoring a Mother's Day program
and dance, noting that tickets for the event were a dollar, although ladies were free
of charge. The following year, another Mother's Day program was sponsored by

the church, but no fees were listed in the advertisement. See "Latter Day Saints to Observe 'Mothers' Day," *Las Vegas Age*, April 12, 1924, 4.

35. Earl, "History of the Las Vegas First Ward," 3. "L.D.S. Held Service in Fine New Church," *Las Vegas Age*, June 30, 1923, 1, suggests that Earl, decades later, may have referenced the wrong year the Latter-day Saint church building was finished, as it notes, "The church is completed with the exception of a little painting and the placing of the new seats. Our Mormon friends are to be congratulated on their new church home."

36. "Churches Unite in Service of Thanks," *Las Vegas Age*, November 19, 1927, 1.

37. "Boulder Churches in Outdoor Rites," *Las Vegas Review-Journal*, August 25, 1934, 3.

38. "Daily Vacation Bible School," *Las Vegas Age*, June 11, 1927, 6. Mahlon Edwards remembered, "Growing up in Boulder City in the 1940s was a wonderful experience. During the summer the Churches organized and held a two-week Bible Class.... We met in the Grace Community and LDS chapels and were taught by members of both churches, in additional to having craft projects" (S. Mahlon Edwards, email to the author, April 27, 2020).

39. "Pioneer Day Celebration," *Las Vegas Age*, August 1, 1925, 6. The Latter-day Saint Pioneer Day celebration was also mentioned several times years later in the Vegas region. See, for example, "Picnic Planned for Pioneer Day," *Las Vegas Age*, July 15, 1930, 1; and "Pioneer Day Will Be Observed Here," *Las Vegas Age*, July 23, 1933, 3. A. E. Cahlan, "From Where I Sit," wrote, "Whether you are a member of the Mormon faith or not, you can't help thrilling to the significance of the annual Pioneer Day which is celebrated annually wherever there are Latter-day Saints." *Las Vegas Evening Review-Journal*, July 26, 1938, 6. Nearly two decades later, "LDS Fete Saturday Big Affair," July 24, 1956, 10, notes that thousands of local Vegans joined in the celebration. The following year, another editorial commented about the impressive Pioneer Day program. "It seems to us," the *Las Vegas Review-Journal*, July 26, 1957, 4, penned, "members of the Church of Jesus Christ of Latter Day Saints are to be highly congratulated for their annual observance of Pioneer Day on July 24.... It is a shame that all American churches do not tell the story of their foundation in America.... Not only would it instill more religious fervor,...but it also would give the entire story of the founding of America."

40. Earl, "History of the Las Vegas First Ward," 3.

41. "L.D.S. Meet Put Off Because of Smallpox," *Las Vegas Age*, March 9, 1929, 3.

42. "20-30 Club Adds to Library Fund," *Las Vegas Evening Review-Journal*, September 12, 1929, 1, notes, "A touching farewell was said to Paris Stewart, charter member of the organization who is leaving next week for the east on a Mormon mission."

43. Earl, "History of the Las Vegas First Ward," 3. Jenson, "Las Vegas Ward," notes, "The total population of the Las Vegas Precinct was 5,922 in 1930, of which 5,165 were residents of Las Vegas City" (416).

44. "L.D.S. Officers Hold Meeting," *Las Vegas Age*, October 7, 1930, 1.

45. Earl, "History of the Las Vegas First Ward," 3.

46. An advertisement titled "Reduced Fares via Union Pacific" announced, "On account of Annual Conference of the Mormon Church and 100th Anniversary celebration," *Las Vegas Review-Journal*, March 7, 1930, 6; and "Reduced Fares to Salt Lake

City on Account of Semi-annual Conference Mormon Church," *Las Vegas Review-Journal,* September 22, 1930, 4.

47. "Between the Wave Lengths," *Las Vegas Review-Journal,* January 10, 1931, 2.

48. "Archaeology Lecture L.D.S. Church Tonight," *Las Vegas Review-Journal,* February 28, 1933, 3.

49. "B.C. Legion," *Las Vegas Review-Journal,* September 21, 1933, 3; "B.C. Legion," *Las Vegas Review-Journal,* December 8, 1933, 4.

50. "Las Vegas Church Services," under the category "Church of Jesus Christ of Latter Day Saints," *Las Vegas Age,* January 24, 1931, 4, as well as the same advertisement, February 21, 1931, 5, which was quite large, more than three by three inches, while most others were much smaller during the decades of the twenties, thirties, and forties.

51. "Latter Day Saint Services," *Las Vegas Age,* September 6, 1931, 8. In addition, under the heading "Las Vegas Church Services" and the subheading "Church of Jesus Christ of Latter-day Saints," *Las Vegas Age,* January 3, 1931, an entire musical program was outlined to be performed the following evening. See also the minute details laid out for church meetings found in "Church Directory," under the segment titled "L.D.S. Church," *Las Vegas Review-Journal,* December 31, 1932, 2.

52. "L.D.S. Work on Church Plans," *Las Vegas Age,* April 20, 1929, 4.

53. "A New Church," *Las Vegas Review-Journal,* August 5, 1929, 2.

54. Earl, "History of the Las Vegas First Ward," 4.

55. Earl, "History of the Las Vegas First Ward," 5.

56. "L.D.S. Confernce [*sic*] Convenes in L.V.," *Las Vegas Age,* March 13, 1932, 1.

57. "L.D.S. President to Address Two Meetings Sunday," *Las Vegas Age,* January 18, 1930, 1. According to Bryan L. Bunker, the meeting was to be held in the local high school auditorium, and this was the first visit President Grant had made to Las Vegas. See also "A Welcome Visit," *Las Vegas Review-Journal,* January 16, 1930, 2.

58. "Caliente Now Church Ward," *Las Vegas Age,* March 15, 1932, 1.

59. "Moapa Stake 20 Years Old," *Las Vegas Age,* May 29, 1932, 1.

60. Earl, "History of the Las Vegas First Ward," 5.

61. "Mormon Church Is Dedicated," *Las Vegas Age,* December 13, 1935, 1.

62. "L.D.S. Church Presents Program," *Las Vegas Age,* March 11, 1930, 1. See also "L.D.S. Dinner," *Las Vegas Evening Review-Journal,* May 13, 1932, 8, which was put on for the community by the Latter-day Saint women of the Church Relief Society organization to help raise funds for their local chapel.

63. Chauncey C. Riddle, telephone interview by the author, February 21, 2020, transcript in possession of the author. Joseph Harold Brinley was born in Greenwich, Utah, February 11, 1899. He married Vera Lee in 1923, registered for the military draft in 1942, and passed away July 2, 1968. See https://www.familysearch.org/tree/person/details/KWZ3-RS4?icid=amp_hdr_signin, accessed April 4, 2020.

64. "Plan Dance at Mormon Church," *Las Vegas Age,* December 13, 1935, 1. A third front-page article highlighting Latter-day Saints was published in the same issue, "Testimonial to Bishop Bunker," *Las Vegas Age,* December 13, 1935, 1, which expressed appreciation for Bunker's service as a bishop. Earl, "History of Las Vegas First Ward," 5, notes that Bunker was replaced by J. Harold Brinley at the time of the dedication of the chapel, which was also the quarterly conference of the Moapa Stake.

65. The Mormon Tabernacle Choir's name was changed to the Tabernacle Choir at Temple Square due to a request issued in 2018 by church president Russell M. Nelson to drop the use of the word *Mormon* and emphasize the full name of the Church of Jesus Christ of Latter-day Saints, which is the sponsoring organization of the choir. See "World-Renowned Mormon Tabernacle Choir Changes Its Name," October 5, 2018, https://newsroom.churchofjesuschrist.org/article/world-renowned -mormon-tabernacle-choir-changes-name, accessed May 12, 2020.

66. "LDS Choir Is a Decided Hit," *Las Vegas Review-Journal,* July 29, 1935, 1.

67. Earl, "History of Las Vegas First Ward," 4. "L.D.S. Choir Is Urged to Stop over in Vegas," *Las Vegas Age,* June 7, 1935, 9, reveals that Arthur Goerman, secretary of the Las Vegas Chamber of Commerce, announced, "Great efforts are being made to have the great choir of L.D.S. Tabernacle in Salt Lake City, stop in Las Vegas on their way to the San Diego Exposition" rather than on their return to Salt Lake City. The article also suggests there was already an unofficial plan in place to have the choir visit the Hoover Dam, as the article further states, "It has been suggested that, in addition to the trip to the dam, it might be possible to induce the choir to give a concert while here." The next Tabernacle Choir visit in Las Vegas occurred the last week of December 1953. Arlene Dutch, "Famous LDS Vocal Group to Sing Here," *Las Vegas Review-Journal,* December 20, 1953, 22, wrote, "The 381-voice Mormon Taber-nacle choir…will appear in Las Vegas December 28–29." Dutch added, "Church and city officials hope to gain about $90,000 from the choir's two appearances to apply to a $500,000 Las Vegas youth center building fund." About 375 choir members ended up singing at the Las Vegas High School auditorium in three performances. See Frank C. Davis, "Tabernacle Choir Sings in Las Vegas," *Church News,* January 2, 1954, 45. The choir did not perform in Las Vegas until a decade later, when they sang at the Las Vegas Convention Center for the Clark County centennial commemora-tion. See "Centennial Concert," *Las Vegas Review-Journal,* October 17, 1964, 3. "Taber-nacle Choir Wows Las Vegas," *Las Vegas Review-Journal,* October 18, 1964, 1, gave a strong review, stating, "The group is everything we ever heard it is. It is marvelous, unbelievably good.… It filled the gigantic Rotunda of the Convention Center.… They stayed because they heard a swell concert." The choir would again perform in the Las Vegas Valley forty years later at the Orleans Arena on Tropicana Boule-vard to a crowd of more than five thousand, who gave the choir a standing ovation. Their delightful music included "a varied repertoire from Broadway tunes to classi-cal selections, as well as some popular hymns, folks songs and a surprise or two." See Julia Osborne, "Choir's Secular Music Surprising," *Las Vegas Review-Journal,* April 22, 2004, 60.

68. "Cars Are Sought for Use of Choir," *Las Vegas Review-Journal,* July 25, 1935, 1.

69. The date of July 29, 1935, was given to an image showing the Tabernacle Choir at Hoover Dam. See PH 10099, CHL.

70. Bureau of Reclamation, "Hoover Dam," https://www.usbr.gov/lc/hooverdam /faqs/damfaqs.html, accessed April 4, 2020. For additional information on the Hoover Dam, see Joseph E. Stevens, *Hoover Dam: An American Adventure;* and Andrew J. Dunbar and Dennis McBride, *Building Hoover Dam: An Oral History of the Great Depression.* It is noteworthy that the Bureau of Reclamation used the old Las Vegas Mormon Fort site as a laboratory for testing concrete used in the dam

(1929–31). Nevada State Parks, "History of Old Las Vegas Mormon Fort State Historic Park."

71. Earl, "History of the Las Vegas First Ward," 5–6.

72. "Society," under the section titled "A Group of Home Missionaries...," *Las Vegas Review-Journal*, February 24, 1936, 2. Home missionaries were still functioning in the mid-twentieth century and gave reports to local congregations of their work within their own vicinity. See "L.D.S. Churches to Hear Reports," *Las Vegas Morning Review-Journal*, February 22, 1952, 4.

73. "Mormons Care for Their Own," *Las Vegas Age*, February 5, 1937, 12.

74. Williams, "Historical Study," 61. For a biographical sketch of President Bunker written a decade after he took office as the president of the Moapa Stake, see "A Stalwart in Community Life," *Church News*, September 4, 1949, 7c. The extended Latter-day Saint Bunker families have had a tremendous influence on Las Vegas and southern Nevada. For an overview of the historical roots of the Bunkers, see Josephine B. Walker, ed., *Bunker Family History*.

75. "A Splendid Choice," *Las Vegas Evening Review-Journal*, September 11, 1939, 8.

76. Earl, "History of the Las Vegas First Ward," 6. "High Tribute Is Paid to Senator Bunker by Church," *Las Vegas Review-Journal*, December 5, 1940, 1, notes that in a farewell party in which more than five hundred church members attended to pay tribute to Bunker, he told the assembled gathering, "As long as I stay in Washington, I shall hold it most sacred that I was a Mormon bishop. First, I shall represent the people of the church. I shall always be a Mormon."

77. At the same time, although Bunker's seat on the US Senate seems to have boosted recognition of the church in southern Nevada and perhaps even nationally, the local community generally knew that the first white settlers in the Vegas region were church members and were reminded of it in historical articles from time to time. For example, see "Missionaries Reach Las Vegas; Make First Settlement, 1855," *Las Vegas Age*, December 20, 1940, 1, written about the same time as Bunker's senatorial appointment. An earlier historical piece on this topic was published in the *Age* four days earlier, as noted in this article.

78. Las Vegas Second Ward general minutes, vol. 1, 1940–45, March 19, 1940, 1, Church History Library, the Church of Jesus Christ of Latter-day Saints, Salt Lake City, hereafter cited as CHL. Herein, it is mentioned that Johnson Everett White was designated bishop, with Joseph O. Christenson serving as first counselor, Thomas L. Adams as second counselor, and William Dee Whipple as ward clerk. Further, "The new bishopric was given to May 1st before the membership would be transfered [*sic*] and the ward completed." See Eugene Moehring, *Resort City in the Sun Belt, 1930–2000*, 38–39, for a succinct overview of the growth and development of North Las Vegas.

79. Las Vegas Second Ward general minutes, vol. 2, 1954–59, handwritten note appearing just after the minutes of the North Las Vegas Ward, "Second Ward Conference," June 27, 1954. However, the date of the creation of the North Las Vegas/Second Ward is not correct, but it is assumed the division line is.

80. "LDS Conference Set for Sunday in Bunkerville," *Las Vegas Age*, March 16, 1940, 1.

81. See, for example, Sunday meeting times posted for the Latter-day Saint Las Vegas Ward and North Las Vegas Ward, *Las Vegas Age*, January 31, 1941, 6. Among Latter-day Saints, these two wards were also referred to as the Las Vegas First and Second Wards. See, for example, Waite and Waite, "Reflections," 204–5. Even the CHL refers to it as the Las Vegas Second Ward, as previously indicated.

82. Las Vegas Second Ward general minutes, vol. 1, 1940–45, August 7, 1940, 30, CHL.

83. "Terrible Tragedy Takes Seven," *Las Vegas Age*, August 9, 1940, 1. Herein, those listed as dead were Thomas H. Myers; his wife; their oldest daughter, Linda Myers, age nineteen, wife of Gerald Leavitt; Kathleen Myers, age sixteen; Teddy Myers, age nine; Doreen Myers, infant daughter; and Elvira Negrete, a neighborhood friend and daughter of Mr. and Mrs. Negrete. A week later, "The 'Tank Gas' Tragedy," *Las Vegas Age*, August 16, 1940, 6, called for an investigation of the explosion so that this kind of accident could be avoided. Eighty years later, Chauncey C. Riddle, a local Saint, still remembered this tragic event and remarked that the Myers family was in the propane business. Chauncey C. Riddle, phone interview by the author, February 21, 2020.

84. Earl, "History of the Las Vegas First Ward," 6–7. Marion B. Earl remembered, "That was one of the saddest funerals I have ever attended. That funeral was the last joint meeting of the two wards. The Las Vegas Ward conducted the funeral service, and the North Las Vegas Ward the gravesite service."

85. "1,000 Pay Last Honor to Victims of Gas Explosion," *Las Vegas Review-Journal*, August 12, 1940, 1.

86. "Reed Whipple New Church Bishop," *Las Vegas Age*, January 24, 1941, 1. Arrington, *The Mormons in Nevada*, 62, notes that Whipple "began work for the First National Bank of Nevada as a vault teller, and in 45 years with the concern worked up to vice president."

87. Earl, "History of the Las Vegas First Ward," 7.

88. Las Vegas Second Ward general minutes, vol. 1, 1940–45, June 18, 1941, 80.

89. Las Vegas Second Ward general minutes, vol. 1, 1940–45, June 12, 1941, 78. These minutes note that by August 3, 1942 (168), the names of eleven men from the North Las Vegas Ward who had entered the army were submitted to the Presiding Bishopric Office.

90. Las Vegas Second Ward general minutes, vol. 1, 1940–45, July 9, 1941, 87.

91. Las Vegas Second Ward general minutes, vol. 1, 1940–45, August 1, 1941, 93.

92. Las Vegas Second Ward general minutes, vol. 1, 1940–45, January 26, 1942, 127.

93. Las Vegas Second Ward general minutes, vol. 1, 1940–45, October 26, 1942, 186. The servicemen were continually on the mind of Bishop White and his counselors throughout the duration of the war. This is evidenced from church minutes from the North Las Vegas Ward. For example, the following year, it was again recorded in bishopric minutes dated August 8, 1943, "We discussed the men in the armed forces" (233). Further, in a sacrament meeting held December 19, 1943, "Bishop White presented two letters from soldiers Jack Schofield and Albert Tomack" (253). In another sacrament meeting held March 12, 1944, the minutes record, "Bishop White spoke briefly told [*sic*] of the experience of two soldiers holding Church services" (267). Again in a sacrament meeting dated July 2, 1944, minutes reveal, "Bishop White

spoke first & read a letter from one of our boys in the Armed Services of our country Bro. Lawrence Nelson. Jack Scofield one of our members home on a Furlough followed." Two weeks later, the minutes for July 16, 1944, note, "A letter was read written by Bishop White to be sent to the soldiers from our ward" (281). The war took its toll on many. On July 23, 1944, Bishop White announced, "Memorial services will be held for Brother Sheel…who was killed June 6 in action in France [probably Normandy]" (282). This same day in a bishopric meeting, "most of the time was taken up discussing members to head the organization to take care of the soldiers that attend & belong to the Church." Further, "a letter was presented by the Bishop from Mac Mattheson who is in the Armed Forces." Two weeks before the war ended, minutes dated August 19, 1945, state, "Bishop White…introduced Sargent Archie Wasden who has been overseas three years" (323).

94. Las Vegas Second Ward general minutes, vol. 1, 1940–45, October 26, 1941, 111.

95. Las Vegas Second Ward general minutes, vol. 1, 1940–45, November 20, 1941, 115. By June 18, 1942 (160), it was mentioned herein that there were 621 members in the North Las Vegas Ward.

96. Las Vegas Second Ward general minutes, vol. 1, 1940–45, December 13 and 14, 1941, 120. It was decided that the meeting times would remain as they were for both wards unless things became more serious with the war.

97. Las Vegas Second Ward general minutes, vol. 1, 1940–45, August 16, 1942, 171.

98. Elbert Edwards, "Military in Clark County," History of Clark County manuscript and correspondence, 1942–48, box 1, folder 7, Edwards Papers.

99. Moehring, *Resort City in the Sun Belt*, 32.

100. Moehring, *Resort City in the Sun Belt*, 39.

101. For example, Private First Class Albert Tomsik, a Las Vegas native and "a band leader at home," is mentioned as one of the Marines meeting in some unknown part of the Pacific. See article by Technical Sergeant Paul G. Long, "Mormon Marine Battle Veterans Meet," *Church News*, September 23, 1944. Captain Thomas L. Thomas of Las Vegas is also identified the following year overseas in the military. See "150 Servicemen at Conference in Paris," *Church News*, May 5, 1945, 8. Three days later, "L.D.S. Soldier Conference Held in Paris," *Church News*, August 11, 1945, 9, lists Captain Thomas as "the first assistant group leader" of the Latter-day Saint servicemen's group involved with planning the Paris conference. Less than a decade later, Thomas was serving in the first Las Vegas Stake as a counselor in the stake presidency. See Waite and Waite, "Reflections," 223.

102. "Fifteen from Vegas Enroll at B.Y.U.," *Las Vegas Age*, December 26, 1941.

103. See, for example, "LDS Baptismal," *Las Vegas Age*, January 28, 1945, 4.

104. "Latter [Day] Saints Organize at Basic," *Las Vegas Age*, October 23, 1942, 4. See also "LDS Branch for BMI Is Planned," *Las Vegas Evening Review-Journal*, October 16, 1942, 3.

105. Las Vegas Second Ward general minutes, vol. 2, 1954–59, July 12, 1959.

106. See, for example, the Las Vegas Second Ward general minutes, vol. 1, 1940–45, CHL, for the dates of May 29, June 15, June 27, July 13, August 30, and December 1, 1940. Monthly temple excursions to the St. George Temple continued into the following year. Herein, sacrament meeting minutes dated March 23, 1941, note

"temple excursion every third Saturday in each month." Later, there was also an annual Memorial Day bus excursion to the St. George Temple for church members. See "LDS Excursion to St. George Set," *Las Vegas Review-Journal,* May 29, 1953, 6, which notes that a group of thirty-eight would make the journey from Las Vegas to St. George and back in a day.

107. Mahlon Edwards, telephone conversation with the author, November 3, 2020. Edwards also remembered that while some made the trip, others paid seventy-five cents per name to seniors living in St. George to do the temple work for them. Las Vegas Second Ward general minutes, vol. 3, April 23, 1961, 17, notes that members who could not "go to the temple were encouraged to pay for names to be done for them."

108. Wendell Waite, telephone conversation with the author, November 3, 2020. Las Vegas Second Ward general minutes, vol. 2, 1954–59, September 15, 1957, notes, "Temple cottage in St. George available to people wishing to spend several days in St. George at the temple."

109. "Nevada Serenaders Give Fine Concert," *Las Vegas Age,* May 9, 1941, 5.

110. Las Vegas Second Ward general minutes, vol. 1, 1940–45, provides many examples of the Singing Mothers performing as well as other forms of music. Early evidence of the Singing Mothers singing during the administration of the sacrament is recorded herein for the dates of January 12 (58), March 2 (59), and November 2, 1941 (111). Herein, on April 6, 1941, it is also recorded that members of the Singing Mothers in both the Las Vegas Ward and the North Las Vegas Ward sang together while church members partook of the sacrament. Alice Hoffman recalled that in the late 1950s, the Singing Mothers would wear black and white when they performed at sacrament meetings. It is also apparent that these groups were organized in wards and later in local stakes. In fact, Hoffman accompanied the Las Vegas Ninth Ward Singing Mothers during the years 1958–59. During these years, she was teaching second grade and did not have a piano at home. During her lunch breaks, she would practice at the old Fifth Street elementary school. Joyce Haldeman, email to the author, November 8, 2020. Performing music during the sacrament service is no longer a practice in Latter-day Saint sacrament meetings, though a sacrament hymn is sung before the sacrament is blessed and passed.

111. "Church Official Calls for Loyalty to Government," *Las Vegas Evening Review-Journal,* January 6, 1941, 1.

112. "Dance Is Held at Church on Friday," *Las Vegas Review-Journal,* December 11, 1944, 9.

113. "Relief Society Honors Presidents," *Church News,* March 25, 1944, 7.

114. "Pioneer Daughters in Convention Here," *Las Vegas Age,* February 6, 1942, 5. A dozen years later, the Clark County chapter of the Daughters of the Utah Pioneers took on the "Pioneer Project" to preserve "the first permanent structure ever built" at the Old Las Vegas Mormon Fort. See "Daughters of Pioneer Project: 'Old Fort' in Nevada Will Be Preserved," *Church News,* April 16, 1955, 12. Preservation plans were in place the following year. See "Old Las Vegas Fort Will Be Preserved," *Church News,* March 3, 1956, 13. For a listing of stages of ownership, occupancy, and preservation of the fort, see "City of Las Vegas Bicentennial Heritage 76 Program,"

contents of binder 6, folder 1, "History of the Las Vegas Area Course Notes," MS-00311, Edwards Papers.

115. "Members of Latter Day Saints Church Take Care of Own in Extensive Relief Society Program," *Las Vegas Review-Journal*, August 15, 1948, 21. The Relief Society organization is still known locally and throughout the world for its members' charitable acts, not only to Latter-day Saints but to all people of varied cultures and faiths globally. The Relief Society is the largest women's organization in the world. See "Relief Society in Action Highlights," Church of Jesus Christ of Latter-day Saints Newsroom, https://newsroom.churchofjesuschrist.org/article/relief-society-in -action-highlights?lang=eng, accessed February 17, 2021.

116. "Church Meeting Is Largest Ever Held in Vegas," *Las Vegas Evening Review-Journal* and *Boulder City Journal*, October 11, 1943, 3.

117. "LDS Homecoming Planned Friday," *Las Vegas Age*, December 23, 1945, 5.

118. "L.D.S. Christmas Festival to Be Presented at Church Saturday," *Las Vegas Age*, December 22, 1946, 3.

119. "Holiday Fun Set for Men at Air Base," *Las Vegas Review-Journal*, December 19, 1948, 11.

120. "L.D.S. Church Holds Annual Spring Time Banquet Thursday Evening," *Las Vegas Age*, April 28, 1946, 5.

121. "10,000 Witness Pioneer Parade Ushering in Las Vegas' Fourth Annual Hell-dorado Celebration and Third Rodeo Competition," *Las Vegas Review-Journal*, April 29, 1938, 1.

122. "Pictures of Two Helldorado Parades During the Recent Celebration," *Las Vegas Age*, June 1, 1947, 13.

123. "Heldorado [*sic*] Is Under Way," *Las Vegas Review-Journal*, May 12, 1950, 1.

124. Chet Sobsey, "30,000 See Big Parade," *Las Vegas Review-Journal*, May 13, 1955, 3.

125. "Church Directory," under the category "Latter-day Saints," *Las Vegas Age*, January 26, 1947, 7, provides the weekly schedule for the North Las Vegas Ward; see also "Church Directory," under the category "Latter-day Saints," *Las Vegas Age*, November 24, 1946, 8, which provides the schedule for the Las Vegas First Ward. Further, under the same category, "Latter-day Saints," *Las Vegas Age*, October 27, 1946, the schedule for both wards is given.

126. "Church Directory," *Las Vegas Age*, April 6, 1947, 5, displayed meeting times for the Las Vegas, North Las Vegas, and Charleston Wards. "Las Vegas Now Has Three Wards," *Church News*, March 1, 1947, 8, also mentioned this additional ward.

127. The *Las Vegas Sun* estimated Las Vegas's population at 24,624 in 1950. See "Timeline," *Las Vegas Sun*, https://lasvegassun.com/history/timeline/#:~:text=1950 %3A%20Population%20of%20Las%20Vegas,Jan, accessed February 17, 2021.

128. "Las Vegas Has 33 Churches; One for Every 700 Residents," *Las Vegas Review-Journal*, January 19, 1949, 43.

129. Earl, "History of the Las Vegas First Ward," 8.

130. Maggie Lillis, "J. Harold Brinley Legacy Lives on Through School Family," https://www.reviewjournal.com/uncategorized/j-harold-brinley-legacy-lives-on -through-las-vegas-area-school-family/, accessed August 13, 2021.

131. "Pres. McKay Dedicates Las Vegas Second Chapel," *Church News*, November 27, 1949, 15C. Plans for this new chapel had been in the making as early as the first

meeting of the newly organized North Las Vegas Ward (a.k.a. the Las Vegas Second Ward) in 1940. Minutes note that in their first bishopric meeting, held March 5, 1940, choosing a site for a new chapel was discussed. This was needed as the Las Vegas Ward and the North Las Vegas Ward were sharing the same building and membership was growing. Las Vegas Second Ward general minutes, vol. 1, 1940–45, March 5, 1940, 3, CHL. Plans for funding and building a new meetinghouse were continually discussed by the bishoprics in the early 1940s, led by Bishop White of the North Las Vegas Ward and Bishop Reed Whipple of the Las Vegas Ward; the wards agreed to share the costs. See Las Vegas Second Ward general minutes, vol. 1, 1940–45, for the dates of July 11, 1941 (88); October 17, 1941 (109–10); and August 25, 1942 (173). During these years, these two wards shared the same building with great cooperation.

132. "LDS to Dedicate New Ward Church with Two Impressive Programs," *Las Vegas Review-Journal,* November 13, 1949, 12.

133. Florence Lee Jones, "New Church Is Testimonial to Faith of Mormon Flock in Future Expansions of Las Vegas, South Nevada," *Las Vegas Review-Journal,* November 13, 1949, 12.

134. Ray Rawson, interview by Fred E. Woods and Martin Andersen, June 24, 2020, Las Vegas, transcript in possession of the author. Events were also held to raise money for these early church buildings. For example, in an article titled "Carnival, Dance Set Saturday," the *Las Vegas Evening Review-Journal* and *Boulder City Journal,* October 8, 1948, advertised a community social with "proceeds from the dance and carnival to go to construction of the new church." At the time, the event was held at the church building located at Eighth and Linden Streets, which was in the final stages of construction.

135. Waite and Waite, "Reflections," 224.

136. "Pres. Myers of Moapa Envisions Rapid Growth of Church in Nevada," *Church News,* June 25, 1952, 7.

137. Earl, "History of the Las Vegas First Ward," 8–9. During this period, growing and storing extra food was an important element of the church welfare program and was encouraged throughout the church. The local Las Vegas press also took note of it. See, for example, "Mormons Stock Up in 7 Fat Years Against Lean Ones If They Come," *Las Vegas Age,* September 8, 1946, 4. Three years later, the *Church News* announced, "Moapa Stake Purchases Paradise Valley Ranch for a Welfare Project," *Church News,* June 19, 1949, 4. Two months later, the stake bishop's storehouse building, costing $30,000, was dedicated, as reported in "Storehouse Dedicated in Las Vegas," *Church News,* November 30, 1949, 4.

138. The news of the creation of the Moapa Stake even made the front page of the *Las Vegas Age:* "Moapa Valley Now a Stake," *Las Vegas Age,* June 15, 1912, 1.

139. Andrew Jenson, "Moapa Stake of Zion," 521. Arrington, *The Mormons in Nevada,* 26, notes that Panaca, established in 1864, is the oldest permanent Latter-day Saint settlement in the state of Nevada.

140. "To Televise L.D.S. Confab to Reach Overflow Crowd," *Las Vegas Review-Journal,* June 5, 1953, cited by Williams, "Historical Study," 67.

141. "New Taylorsville and Moapa Stakes Formed in Utah, Nevada," *Church News,* October 16, 1954, 3.

142. Williams, "Historical Study," 68.

143. The news reported that would result in the largest gathering of church members in the state of Nevada ever assembled. See "Largest Nevada LDS Gathering Seen for McKay," *Las Vegas Review-Journal,* November 11, 1954, 3.

144. "Full Text of President McKay's Address at Las Vegas," *Church News,* November 20, 1954, 2–3. Herein (2), President McKay also praised the Latter-day Saint women who provided inspirational hymns with their Singing Mothers organization and was mindful of their many hours of practice and training.

145. "Mormon Pioneers to Be Depicted in 'Vegas' Pageant," *Church News,* May 28, 1955, 4.

146. "Century of Vegas History Unfolds at Pageant Here," *Las Vegas Review-Journal,* June 8, 1955, 1.

147. "4,000 See Church Centennial Festival," *Church News,* June 25, 1955, 11. See also "Centennial Observance Concluded Last Night," *Las Vegas Review-Journal,* June 15, 1955, 2, which details the festival, including a "'Mardi Gras Samba' performed by 96 colorfully costumed girls,…a solo interpretive Indian dance,…[and] the Las Vegas Rythmettes."

148. Las Vegas Second Ward general minutes, vol. 2, 1954–59, January 8, 1956.

149. "Baccalaureate for 160 Slated," *Las Vegas Review-Journal,* May 20, 1951, 1; "Baccalaureate Services for Class of 1956 to Be Sunday," *Las Vegas Review-Journal,* May 26, 1956, 2.

150. For example, "LDS Missionary Speaks Sunday," *Las Vegas Review-Journal,* November 19, 1950, 12, announced the return of Kent Bunker, who had served a full-time mission in both Hawaii and Australia. Several years later, James T. Marshall, a graduate of Las Vegas High School (1953), accepted a mission call to serve two years in the Northern States Mission, headquartered in Chicago. See "Called to Mission," *Las Vegas Review-Journal,* December 26, 1955, 14. Internationally, the Las Vegas Second Ward general minutes, vol. 2, 1954–59, October 23, 1955, CHL, note that Sister Denza Aiken had just returned from her mission to Norway; the January 22, 1956, sacrament meeting minutes note that there was a "farewell testimonial in honor of Jan Stewart prior to his leaving for the Australian mission." On September 13, 1959, the *Las Vegas Review-Journal* announced, "Robert C. Bohn, will go to the West German Mission." "J. McCulloch to Fill LDS Church Mission," *Las Vegas Review-Journal,* December 13, 1956, 29, additionally notes that Jerry McCulloch, graduate of Las Vegas High School, was to serve a mission in New Zealand. This same year, "Mission," *Las Vegas Review-Journal,* June 3, 1956, 7, announced that Betty McDonald was called on a mission to Uruguay. The following year, "LDS Missionary Returns After Two-Year Mission," *Las Vegas Review-Journal,* December 8, 1957, 12, reported that Milton W. Hammond returned from serving a mission to the British Isles.

151. "Las Vegas Will Start Work on 4 New Chapels in 1956," *Church News,* December 31, 1955, 6.

152. "Area Church Membership Booms During 1955 to About 20,000; New Construction Planned to Meet Need," *Las Vegas Review-Journal,* January 1, 1956, 10.

153. "Lake Mead Stake: James I. Gibson Chosen President," *Church News,* August 25, 1956, 2. Gibson served as stake president for sixteen years, a lengthy time for that era. When he was released, the *Review-Journal* mistakenly printed the headline

"Gibson Loses Mormon Post," *Las Vegas Review-Journal,* March 15, 1973, 4, as if it were a political contest. In response to this folly, Las Vegas Latter-day Saint historian Elbert B. Edwards wrote a letter to the editor. In an article titled "Like R-J, However," *Las Vegas Review-Journal,* March 26, 1973, 15, Edwards explained that people are released from church positions to give others a chance to serve and suggested that a better headline would have been "Gibson Honored in Release from Mormon Post."

154. "Las Vegas Stake Reorganization: Elder Reed Whipple Sustained President," *Church News,* November 10, 1956, 2.

155. "Las Vegas Stake Farm Proves Most Productive," *Church News,* November 17, 1956, 10. Las Vegas Second Ward general minutes, vol. 2, 1954–59, March 27, 1957 notes, "A new box has been set up at the Welfare Farm near the gate so that those working there may record their name and hours worked. The church wants to know the total hours worked on the farm and to give receipts for the work done. It is thought this new system will be an improvement over the former way of asking workers to go sign their names in the time book in the tool shed." "LDS Runs Welfare Farm for Its Needy," *Las Vegas Review-Journal,* February 15, 1976, 52, reveals that two decades later, an additional 640-acre church welfare farm in Las Vegas was going strong, with two hundred cows and six hundred cattle.

156. "Table of Broadcasts for April Conference," *Church News,* March 26, 1955, 3. Herein is mentioned that station KLAS was going to broadcast the April general conference via both radio and television.

157. Williams, "Historical Study," 131–32. "New Stakes Formed in Nevada, California," *Church News,* November 12, 1960, 7, notes that the newly created North Las Vegas Stake had fifty-one hundred members.

158. Moises Denis, Zoom interview by the author, January 24, 2020, transcript in possession of the author.

159. Williams, "Historical Study," 147.

CHAPTER 3. IGNORANCE, EDUCATION, AND CULTURAL REFINEMENT

1. See Hal Rothman and Mike Davis, eds., *The Grit Beneath the Glitter: Tales from the Real Las Vegas,* for a credible treatment by many scholars on the diversity, character, and reality of Las Vegas. On the diversity of Las Vegas by way of chapter treatments of various ethnic groups, see Jerry L. Simich and Thomas L. Wright, eds., *The Peoples of Las Vegas: One City, Many Faces* and *More Peoples of Las Vegas.*

2. Land and Land, *Short History of Las Vegas,* xiv. Rocha's foreword provides a wonderful overview of Vegas, his hometown.

3. Elaine Kennedy, interview by Fred E. Woods and Martin Andersen, June 24, 2020, Las Vegas, transcript in possession of the author.

4. David Littlejohn, ed., *The Real Las Vegas: Life Beyond the Strip,* 26. Littlejohn observed what might be perceived as an element of defensiveness by Las Vegas locals: "There seems to be no question that living in Las Vegas generates a kind of prickly defensiveness against criticism from outside—even though…locals are quick to criticize the city themselves. Decades of movies, TV shows, and popular books and articles about mobsters, crime, gross taste, and sleazy sex have created an international image that even new residents of Las Vegas have to deal with."

5. Claytee D. White, interview by Fred E. Woods and Martin Andersen, March 7, 2020, Las Vegas, transcript in possession of the author. Herein, White also expressed her opinion that the Church of Jesus Christ of Latter-day Saints had a great influence in Las Vegas, not only in a religious/spiritual way but also in government and business. She remarked, "It spans the entire gamut." Claytee D. White is the inaugural director of the Oral History Research Center at the University of Nevada, Las Vegas, Libraries (hereafter cited as Oral History Research Center).

6. Stanley A. Steward, *Where Sin Abounds: A Religious History of Las Vegas*, 1. In fact, at one time it was reported that Las Vegas had "the highest number of churches per capita than any city in the country." See "Las Vegas Also Boasts High Number of Churches," *Las Vegas Review-Journal*, August 1, 1982, 198. A decade later, there were a total of 430 churches and synagogues in Las Vegas, "with 48 different faiths and services conducted in six languages." See "Las Vegas Hosts Variety of Religious Faiths and Services," *Las Vegas Sun*, July 19, 1992, 105. Two years beyond that, a telephone poll representing hundreds of Las Vegans' values reported that 93 percent of the respondents believed in God. See Jane Ann Morrison, "Las Vegans Claim High Moral Views," *Las Vegas Sun*, May 26, 1994, 1.

7. Steward, *Where Sin Abounds*, 139. Regarding Las Vegas's reputation and its influence, see Foster, *Stigma Cities*, 125–50; Larry Gragg, *Becoming America's Playground: Las Vegas in the 1950s* and *Bright Light City: Las Vegas in Popular Culture*; and Michael Green, "The Boundaries of Being a Nevadan: National Reputation and Exceptionalism."

8. Davis, "Saints in Sin City," iii.

9. Davis, "Saints in Sin City," 78.

10. Davis, "Saints in Sin City," 1.

11. Eugene P. Moehring, "Town Making on the Southern Nevada Frontier: Las Vegas, 1905–1925," 95. Herein, Moehring notes with references to the establishment of various religious denominations in early Las Vegas history, "Oddly enough, the Mormons, who had originally pioneered the area in 1855, were among the last groups to establish an official presence." He points out that the Methodists, Presbyterians, Catholics, and Episcopalians all set up places of worship before the Latter-day Saints.

12. Mayor Carolyn Goodman, interview by Fred E. Woods and Martin Andersen, June 24, 2020, Las Vegas, transcript in possession of the author.

13. Joan Burkhart, *Nevadan Today;* "Don Christensen Speaks for the Vegas Saints," *Las Vegas Sun*, September 20, 1987, 177. It should be mentioned that this comment is a bit dated as it was made several decades ago. (The *Nevadan* is a Sunday supplement to the *Las Vegas Review-Journal.*)

14. Mayor John Lee, interview by Fred E. Woods and Martin Andersen, June 23, 2020, North Las Vegas, transcript in possession of the author.

15. Littlejohn, *Real Las Vegas*, 31.

16. Mike Green, interview by Fred E. Woods and Martin Andersen, February 7, 2020, Las Vegas, transcript in possession of the author. Green is an accomplished professor of both Nevada and Las Vegas history.

17. On the community characteristics of Las Vegas in general, see Hal Rothman, *Neon Metropolis: How Las Vegas Started the Twenty-First Century*, 291–316.

18. Rex J. Rowley, "Faith Islands in Hedonopolis: Ambivalent Adaptation in Las Vegas," 2265. See also Rex J. Rowley, *Everyday Las Vegas: Local Life in a Tourist Town*, especially chapter 8, "Religion in Sin City," 188–208, for evidence of the active role religion plays as a whole in the Las Vegas metropolitan region.

19. Lori Leibovich, "House of the Holy," 169.

20. Barbara, Kevin, Michael, Jill Buckley, and Lindsay Stilwell, interview by Claytee D. White, January 28, 2017, Oral History Project of Ward 1, West Charleston Neighborhoods, Oral History Research Center (OH 02083).

21. Joseph Thiriot, interview by Claytee D. White, August 10, 2000, Las Vegas, Boyer Early Las Vegas Oral History Project, Oral History Research Center (OH 018130, transcript 8).

22. This is the first known attestation of anti-"Mormon" literature in a Las Vegas newspaper, the *Age*, during the first half of the twentieth century, when other newspapers in the United States and in Europe had an abundance of references against the Saints. The first attestation of anti-Latter-day Saint literature in the *Las Vegas Review-Journal* was not until 1976. (This is not to insinuate that either newspaper was against the Saints, but, rather, they were just reporting the current happenings of the times.) The first *Review-Journal* anti material occurs in an advertisement that notes that the Reverend Marvin Cowan, a former Latter-day Saint, would be lecturing at the Bethany Baptist Church in Boulder City on a number of doctrinal topics related to the Church of Jesus Christ of Latter-day Saints. See *Las Vegas Review-Journal*, August 7, 1976, 4. Two years later, the press reported that evangelist Bob West from Alabama was in Las Vegas to teach against the Latter-day Saint faith via lectures held at the Las Vegas Convention Center. See "Crusading Evangelist against Mormonism," *Las Vegas Review-Journal*, June 19, 1978, 13. In 1984 an ad surfaced regarding the anti-Latter-day Saint film *The God Makers*. See "Does the Average Mormon Really Know What Their Church Believes? Come and Find Out...," *Las Vegas Review-Journal*, February 22, 1984, 13.

23. Frank Cope, interview by Marianne Johnson, March 15, 1978, Ralph Roske Oral History Project on Early Las Vegas, Special Collections and Archives, Oral History Research Center (OH 426).

24. Chet Carrigan, interview by Robert Kahre, February 17, 1981, Roske Oral History Project (OH 00345).

25. Mary Hausch, interview by Claytee D. White, April 7, 2002, Las Vegas, Voices of the Historic John S. Park Neighborhood, Oral History Research Center (OH 00808, transcript 48).

26. Barbara G. Brents, interview by Claytee D. White, January 12, 2010, Voices of the Historic John S. Park Neighborhood, Oral History Research Center (OH 00124).

27. Earl and Gloria Alger, interview by Claytee D. White, October 29, 2009, in the Alger home in Las Vegas, Boyer Early Las Vegas Oral History Project, Oral History Research Center (OH 00086).

28. See Appendix A for a listing of Nevada mothers of the year from 1945 to the present, including an asterisk next to each one who was also a Latter-day Saint.

29. Jana Dixon, interview by Fred E. Woods and Martin Andersen, March 4, 2020, Las Vegas, transcript in possession of the author.

30. David Clayton, "Will Sexy Salon Make the Cut?," *Las Vegas Sun*, July 18, 1993, 41, 44; "Woman Battles Lingerie Hair Salon," *Las Vegas Sun*, July 17, 1993, 18. For the owner's (Davey-O's) opposing point of view, see his arguments in "Moral Senate Panel Rejects Topless Cuts," *Las Vegas Review-Journal*, July 1, 1993, 50.

31. Michael Bailey Wixom and Heidi Gresham Wixom, interview by the author, February 18, 2021, transcript in possession of the author. Mike Wixom, a member of the Nevada higher education board of regents, email to the author, February 19, 2021, provides the statute: "NRS 643.203 Unlawful to engage in practice of barbering unless wearing suitable clean outer garments; regulations. 1. It is unlawful for a person to engage in the practice of barbering unless he or she is wearing clean outer garments which are suitable to allow the safe and hygienic practice of barbering. 2. The Board shall adopt regulations which prescribe standards for the garments required by subsection 1 (Added to NRS by 1993, 2646)." Yet it appears the statute came in a little late, as the Wixoms recounted with a smile that they had learned from local police officers that the nearby erotic car wash had already caused ten car wrecks.

32. Brian Wargo, "Sign of the Times, Billboards Under Fire," *Las Vegas Sun*, May 18, 2006, 2.

33. https://www.power2parent.org/whatwedo.html, accessed February 22, 2021.

34. Linda Chapman, "Sobering Award," *Beehive Sentinel*, May 14, 1986, 5.

35. Michael Welssenstein, "Casino's Foes Use Different Strategies," *Las Vegas Sun*, January 16, 2000, 23, 28. See also "Churches Set to Block Wide-Open Henderson," *Las Vegas Review-Journal*, June 7, 1955, 1, wherein several local Latter-day Saint bishops "moved to block…gambling and liquor interests" in Henderson. Others would oppose such measures, feeling their rights of expansion had not been met.

36. Joyce Haldeman, interview by Fred E. Woods and Martin Andersen, March 5, 2020, Las Vegas, transcript in possession of the author.

37. Janet Brigham, "Beyond the Glitter," *Ensign*, February 1979, 38. Family Home Evening is a Latter-day Saint church event that occurs weekly in the homes of church members, usually on Monday nights, launched in 1915. See "2015 Marks Two Milestones for Family Home Evening," *Church News*, https://www.churchofjesus christ.org, accessed February 16, 2021. This weekly activity continues to be mentioned in the local Vegas news a century later. See, for example, Ginger Meurer, "Home Sweet Home," *Las Vegas Review-Journal*, January 9, 2016, 10. There was also a concerted effort by women for the ERA and various meetings held in support of this view. See, for example, "Women Plan State Conference," *Las Vegas Review-Journal*, January 13, 1977, 44

38. Lisa Mayo-DeRiso, email to the author, February 22, 2021.

39. Judie Brailsford-Marcucci, interview by the author, February 22, 2021, Las Vegas, transcript in possession of the author.

40. Williams, "Historical Study," 66. Wendell Waite and Bonita "Bonnie" Waite, "Reflections: History of the North Las Vegas Stake," unpublished manuscript, 2000, 139, note that the seminary program "had been started in 1948 with J. Harold Brinley as the first teacher. As the program grew, he became the supervisor of all the seminaries in Southern Nevada and Kingman, Arizona. He stepped down in 1965,

and Theron Swainston became the seminary supervisor for Las Vegas and North Las Vegas. Marlon Walker was assigned to supervise the seminaries in Henderson, Boulder City, and Kingman."

41. "Seminary Class First in Las Vegas," *Church News,* March 9, 1949, 22. In addition to a vibrant seminary class, several years later, a Junior Genealogical Society was also formed in Las Vegas, the first of its kind in the Moapa Stake. It was organized in January 1953, and members made trips to the St. George, Manti, Salt Lake, and Logan Temples in Utah, as well as to the Idaho Falls, Idaho, and Mesa, Arizona, Temples. Their adult sponsors were Mr. and Mrs. Earl J. Bohne. See "Moapa Stake Group Makes Temple Visits," *Church News,* October 17, 1953, 12.

42. Williams, "Historical Study," 66.

43. Ruth Johnson, Zoom interview by the author, May 18, 2020, transcript in possession of the author.

44. Ray Rawson, interview by Fred E. Woods and Martin Andersen, June 24, 2020, Las Vegas, transcript in possession of the author.

45. Tami Hulse, interview by Fred E. Woods and Martin Andersen, July 6, 2020, Provo, UT, transcript in possession of the author.

46. Mary Beth Scow, interview by Fred E. Woods and Martin Andersen, March 6, 2020, Henderson, transcript in possession of the author.

47. Tammy Stout, interview by Fred E. Woods and Martin Andersen, March 6, 2020, North Las Vegas, transcript in possession of the author.

48. Mark Albright, interview by Fred E. Woods and Martin Andersen, June 24, 2020, Las Vegas, transcript in possession of the author.

49. Sheila Moulton, interview by Fred E. Woods and Martin Andersen, June 23, 2020, Las Vegas, transcript in possession of the author.

50. Jana Dixon, email to the author, March 1, 2021. Dixon said that this experience took place in 2017, her last year of teaching seminary.

51. Lee, interview. Lee later joined the Church of Jesus Christ of Latter-day Saints as a young adult.

52. Senator Richard Bryan, interview by Fred E. Woods and Martin Andersen, June 23, 2020, Las Vegas, typescript in possession of the author.

53. Joshua Popp, interview by Fred E. Woods and Martin Andersen, July 15, 2020, North Las Vegas, transcript in possession of the author. At the time of the interview, Popp was soon to leave on a mission to the Dominican Republic.

54. For example, "LDS Students Win High School Offices," *Church News,* May 11, 1963, 12, which notes that four Latter-day Saint seminary students had been elected as student body officers "and are carrying out duties of their offices with enthusiasm.... All four students are outstanding in school, Church, and community activities."

55. Popp, interview.

56. Paige Smith, interview by Fred E. Woods and Martin Andersen, June 24, 2020, transcript in possession of the author. Yet Smith thought perhaps the Latter-day Saint youth could be more inclusive. She stated, "The one thing that I do kind of notice sometimes is they're a little bit exclusive. And I'm not sure if that's because they feel comfortable with their friends.... I'm not sure if it's maybe because others

don't have the same high moral standards, because I know for myself I don't want to associate myself with people maybe who don't hold themselves to a certain standard. So, sometimes people say that they may be a little bit exclusive, and that's kind of a teenager's life anyway in general." Ruth Johnson also recalled that when she interviewed a former principal of Legacy High School in Las Vegas, the one thing that was mentioned that the Latter-day Saint youth could have improved upon in her school was to be more inclusive and minister more to those outside their circle of church friends. Though admiring of their example in general, this administrator stated, "I really wish that they would just be willing to step out sometimes and befriend other people and really help those kids that are really struggling." Ruth Johnson, interview by the author, May 27, 2020, Las Vegas, transcript in possession of the author. On the other hand, former seminary teacher Tami Hulse felt that the camaraderie formed in seminary gave the Latter-day Saint youth the strength and courage to stand up for their high standards in the face of strong teen peer pressure when challenges arose at school. Hulse, interview.

57. Davis, "Saints in Sin City," 69–70.

58. Tom Tyler, Zoom interview by the author, November 11, 2020, Provo, UT, transcript in possession of the author. Tyler served in this position from 1982 to 1983 and 1986 to 1990. From 1983 to 1986, he served as a mission president for the Church of Jesus Christ of Latter-day Saints in San Antonio, Texas. One of those local church leaders, Mark Albright, also acknowledged the effort church leaders made to build church buildings "close to the high schools so that kids in the morning can get out of their seminary and just walk a block or two to their high schools." Albright, interview.

59. Stout, interview.

60. Robin Dixon, interview by Fred E. Woods and Martin Andersen, February 8, 2020, North Las Vegas, transcript in possession of the author.

61. Cristi Bulloch, interview by Fred E. Woods and Martin Andersen, March 5, 2020, Las Vegas, transcript in possession of the author.

62. Bulloch, interview.

63. David Dixon, interview by Fred E. Woods and Martin Andersen, March 4, 2020, Las Vegas, transcript in possession of the author.

64. Johnson, interview.

65. Johnson, Zoom interview. Herein, Johnson said that the three principals she interviewed in her district were at Shadow Ridge, Mojave, and Legacy High Schools. It is noteworthy that in his review of a draft of my manuscript, Las Vegas Latter-day Saint resident David Dixon mentioned, "Shadow Ridge is a marvelous example of the seminary program and its affiliation with the high school, but you need to mention that Shadow Ridge's experience is a representation of all high schools in Las Vegas. Every high school would have similar experiences."

66. Waite and Waite, "Reflections," 140.

67. Mark Hutchison, interview by Fred E. Woods and Martin Andersen, March 5, 2020, Las Vegas, transcript in possession of the author.

68. Kyle Stevens, interview by Fred E. Woods and Martin Andersen, March 6, 2020, Las Vegas, transcript in possession of the author.

69. William H. Stoddard, interview by Fred E. Woods and Martin Andersen, June

24, 2020, Las Vegas, transcript in possession of the author. Stoddard formerly presided in an ecclesiastical assignment over the Las Vegas region as an Area Authority Seventy and was recently appointed the Las Vegas Nevada Temple president in 2021. Church of Jesus Christ Temples, "Las Vegas Nevada Temple," https://churchofjesus christtemples.org/las-vegas-nevada-temple/presidents/, accessed February 20, 2021. He will serve alongside his wife, Carol, who will serve as temple matron. "Read About These 6 New Temple Presidents and Martrons," *Church News*, https://www .thechurchnews.com/callings/2021-01-29/new-temple-presidents-payson-utah-boston -massachusetts-denver-colorado-202599, accessed February 20, 2021.

70. Cited by Jerry Earl Johnston, "Bryce Harper Is Breaking Down Mormon Stereotypes," *Deseret News*, May 14, 2015, https://www.deseret.com/2015/5/14/20564683 /bryce-harper-is-breaking-down-mormon-stereotypes, accessed April 24, 2020.

71. Steve Fotheringham, interview by the author, February 11, 2021, Las Vegas Institute of Religion, transcript in possession of the author. See also John Przybys, "As If on a Dare He Catches Air," *Las Vegas Review-Journal*, May 13, 2012, 95; Lauren Noorda, "Hot Wheels," *Las Vegas Review-Journal*, September 19, 2006, 59; "A Busy Weekend of Back Flips, Beer, Burlesque," *Las Vegas Review-Journal*, June 3, 2011, 124.

72. Williams, "Historical Study," 134. The author thanks Bruce W. Hansen, Las Vegas institute director, for reviewing a draft of the entire manuscript and for bringing to his attention that the original location of the institute has been moved as well, and pointing him to the article noted below. The current location of the Las Vegas institute is 1095 University Road. The building was expanded four decades after its construction. See Kareen Hale, "Expanded Institute of Religion Prepares for Dedication," *Beehive*, February 18–25, 1997, 3–4, 6–7, 10–11.

73. David Rowberry, interview by Fred E. Woods and Martin Andersen, February 8, 2020, Henderson, transcript in possession of the author.

74. Kenny Guinn was interim UNLV president (1994–95) during the search for a permanent president. Prior to this time, Guinn was also appointed superintendent of the Clark County School District (1969–78). In 1998 he was elected governor of Nevada and served in this office from 1999 to 2007. Guinn passed away in 2010. See Office of the President, University of Nevada, Las Vegas, "About Kenny C. Guinn," https://www.unlv.edu/president/past/guinn, accessed May 20, 2020.

75. Rowberry, interview. Herein, Rowberry further stated that he was involved with the campus interfaith community, serving as president of the interfaith council for a number of years. General involvement with the campus stretched back well before Rowberry's time. For example, in early 1974, the LDSSA staged a twenty-four-hour basketball marathon at the UNLV basketball court to raise money for a charity, "Project Share," which assists "under-privileged children in South America and the Philippines." Well-known comedian Jerry Van Dyke, the "Vegas Vampire," and others were also scheduled to participate. See "LDS Cage Marathon," *Las Vegas Review-Journal*, January 31, 1974, 27.

76. Rowberry, interview.

77. Bruce W. Hansen, interview by Fred E. Woods and Martin Andersen, February 8, 2020, UNLV Institute of Religion, Las Vegas, transcript in possession of the author.

78. Hansen, interview.

79. Ingrid Zarate, interview by Fred E. Woods and Martin Andersen, February 6, 2020, UNLV Institute of Religion, Las Vegas, transcript in possession of the author.

80. Zarate, interview.

81. Nathan Norr, interview by Fred E. Woods and Martin Andersen, February 6, 2020, UNLV Institute of Religion, Las Vegas, transcript in possession of the author.

82. Charlie Zobell, Zoom interview by the author, June 11, 2020, transcript in possession of the author.

83. Charlotte Conti, interview by Charles Conti, March 20, 1978, Roske Oral History Project (OH 00415). Yet the tide may be changing, as there are currently no Latter-day Saints serving on the Las Vegas City Council. A list of the current mayor and council members can be viewed at https://www.lasvegasnevada.gov/Government/Mayor-City-Council, accessed May 20, 2020.

84. Kenric F. Ward, *Saints in Babylon: Mormons and Las Vegas*, 47.

85. The term *Jack Mormon* is used here in reference to a Latter-day Saint who is not true to their religion. However, in the nineteenth century, it was used to refer to someone who was a friend to the Saints, although they were not a member of the Church of Jesus Christ of Latter-day Saints.

86. Kennedy, interview.

87. Davis, "Saints in Sin City," 72–73.

88. Bulloch, interview.

89. Haldeman, interview.

90. Gary Thompson, "Honor Means Scow to Return as Mentor to Other Parents," *Las Vegas Review-Journal,* May 10, 2009, 99.

91. Scow, interview. Ruth Johnson also recalled, "We were roundly criticized for being a bunch of housewives that didn't know anything. We were just a bunch of 'Mormon Moms,' and we couldn't possibly know what it would take to make the best decisions in that kind of a huge administrative environment.… We kind of decided to take that on and wear it…because we knew that the things that we wanted as Mormon moms was clear communication, transparency in the district, policies that were family friendly, opportunities to engage at the levels where parents could be heard and understood and responded to. And so, we worked towards those things." Johnson, Zoom interview.

92. Johnson, Zoom interview.

93. Johnson, interview.

94. Senator Harry Reid, interview by Fred E. Woods and Martin Andersen, June 23, 2020, Las Vegas, transcript in possession of the author.

95. Bryan, interview. Yet Bryan mentioned that during the era of Superintendent J. Harold Brinley, "a very prominent figure in the educational history of southern Nevada,…from time to time there were people that were concerned that maybe he [Brinley] would hire only members of the church." Gordon Kent, "Brinley Invites Probe," *Las Vegas Review-Journal,* August 19, 1961, 15, confirmed there was speculation that Clark County teachers were partially hired based on their religion, but school administrator Brinley boldly denied it. He stated, "I invite anyone to come in and see for himself what the ratio of religious affiliation is in our school district of members of one religion as opposed to another." See also "No Handcuffs, Please," *Las Vegas Review-Journal,* August 20, 1961, 18, on this topic. This issue also surfaced

a decade later. See Mary Hausch, "Guinn Denies Hiring for Religion," *Las Vegas Review-Journal,* December 9, 1972, 15, wherein Clark County School District superintendent Dr. Kenny C. Guinn denied that district teacher-hiring practices had anything to do with a person's choice of religion.

96. See Appendix B for a list of the thirty-five Latter-day Saint educators who have had buildings named after them in the Clark County School District.

97. Wendell Waite, interview by the author, January 19, 2020, St. George, UT, transcript in possession of the author. When asked what brings and keeps Latter-day Saints in the Las Vegas region, Senator Harry Reid said, "We have tremendous influx of people from Southern California.... We have no income tax, business is easier to conduct here than in California.... People are coming here also from Phoenix. Just a better place to live, and of course we have a tremendous influx from places other than Arizona and California. One thing that we're trying to improve is our schools because they are growing so rapidly. We have had to on two separate occasions dedicate eighteen schools in one year.... We have now, I think, the fifth- to sixth-largest school district in the country. We have pushing 400,000 students, so we're working to improve our K–12 education. Our university programs, I think, are quite good. We have an excellent community college system.... I think we have about 50,000 students in our community colleges." Reid, interview.

98. Jeanette Clark, Zoom interview by the author, August 28, 2020, transcript in possession of the author.

99. Terilyn Taylor, interview by Fred E. Woods and Martin Andersen, March 5, 2020, Las Vegas, transcript in possession of the author.

100. As of 2020, Jeffrey Skouson is no longer in this position.

101. Jenny Jackson, interview by Fred E. Woods and Martin Andersen, March 5, 2020, Las Vegas, transcript in possession of the author.

102. Jackson, interview.

103. Wendy Randall, interview by Fred E. Woods and Martin Andersen, March 8, 2020, Las Vegas, transcript in possession of the author.

104. David Skouson, interview by Fred E. Woods and Martin Andersen, March 8, 2020, Las Vegas, transcript in possession of the author.

105. Jeffrey Skouson, interview by Fred E. Woods and Martin Andersen, March 8, 2020, Las Vegas, transcript in possession of the author.

106. Elise Noorda, interview by Fred E. Woods and Martin Andersen, June 22, 2020, Las Vegas, transcript in possession of the author. For more information on this inspiring youth organization, see https://www.zionsyouth.org/, accessed February 20, 2021.

Chapter 4. Business and Entertainment

1. The name change was controversial, and some Las Vegas locals still refer to this monumental structure as the Boulder Dam.

2. Gene A. Sessions and Sterling D. Sessions, *Utah International: A Biography of Business,* 5.

3. Sessions and Sessions, *Utah International,* 42. On this page there is an image from the Church History Library of W. H. Wattis playing golf with these church authorities.

4. Sessions and Sessions, *Utah International,* xvii, 58. Herein (55), note that the six companies were made up of Utah Construction, Bechtel-Kaiser-Warren, M-K, Shea, Pacific Bridge, and MacDonald & Kahn.

5. Sessions and Sessions, *Utah International.* The authors further note (66) that Eccles, son of David Eccles, the successful Utah business mining entrepreneur, was later appointed by President Franklin D. Roosevelt to lead the Federal Reserve System while also serving as the president of the Utah Construction company.

6. Sessions and Sessions, *Utah International,* xviii.

7. Sessions and Sessions, *Utah International,* 60.

8. Ward, *Saints in Babylon,* 32.

9. "Boulder City Churches," under the subheading "Latter Day Saints," *Las Vegas Age,* June 26, 1932, 2. Three months earlier, "Boulder Briefs," *Las Vegas Age,* March 16, 1932, 3, announced, "The Latter Day Saints will hold Sunday school at 631 California Street next Sunday." Just over two weeks later, "Boulder City Churches," under the subheading "L.D.S. School," *Las Vegas Age,* April 3, 1932, revealed that this address was the home of Mrs. W. Pierce, where it was announced Sunday school would be held at 10:00 A.M.

10. "L.D.S. Relief Meets," *Las Vegas Age,* "Boulder Section," June 9, 1932, 3.

11. Wendell Waite and Bonita "Bonnie" Waite, "Reflections: History of the North Las Vegas Stake," unpublished manuscript, 2000, 11, 15. Wendell Waite also recalled, "They cut this chapel in half and moved it in pieces to Boulder City where it was reconstituted and served for many years until they grew and had a chapel, a modern-day chapel of their own." Wendell Waite, interview by the author, January 19, 2020, St. George, transcript in possession of the author.

12. In an email from Mark Dixon to the author, May 5, 2020, Dixon noted that his grandfather Stapley "came by himself, then after a period of time sent for his family then living in Payson. They did live in a tent city for a time, but my recollection is it was in Pittman, or now Henderson. There was a train that ran from LV to the Dam that carried the workers."

13. Mark Dixon, interview by Fred E. Woods and Martin Andersen, February 8, 2020, North Las Vegas, transcript in possession of the author.

14. Wendell Waite, conversation with the author at his home in St. George, January 19, 2020. These comments were made informally outside of the taped interview the author conducted the same day with Waite.

15. "Glenn Waite Autobiography," unpublished manuscript in possession of the author, courtesy of Wendell Waite.

16. Chauncey C. Riddle, telephone interview by the author, February 21, 2020, transcript in possession of the author.

17. Eric Christensen, interview by the author, March 6, 2020, Las Vegas, transcript in possession of the author. Herein, Christensen wrote that the business was launched on Fremont Street in 1939 and lasted more than fifty years. See also https://www.mjchristensen.com/company/about-us/, accessed August 13, 2021.

18. Christensen, interview. For an excellent overview of the historical development of Las Vegas from 1930 to the end of the twentieth century, see Moehring, *Resort City in the Sun Belt.*

19. Steward, *Where Sin Abounds,* 11–12.

20. Jerry Cohen, "The Mormon Connection," *Las Vegas Review-Journal*, May 9, 1976, 5.

21. "Howard Hughes Picks Mormons for Efficiency," *Church News*, January 30, 1954, 4.

22. Ed Koch and Mary Manning, "He Reached, Howard Hughes Pulled Back His Empire," *Las Vegas Sun*, June 29, 2007, 29, recalled, "Gay also was noted for hiring five of the six executive aides who tended to Hughes' needs when he lived at the Desert Inn. Five of them, like Gay, were members of the Church of Jesus Christ of Latter-day Saints. They were often called 'The Mormon Mafia.'"

23. Paul Winn, a former employee of Hughes, felt it was not the fact that Bill Gay was a Latter-day Saint that won him a job but rather a connection he made through Hughes's secretary, Nadine Henley. Winn, an active, practicing church member who worked under both Hughes and Gay, recollected that after Henley worked around Gay for a while, she thought "Bill was one of the brightest guys she had met, and so she recommended him to Hughes that Bill head up the staff,…so, that's the…Mormon connection with Howard Hughes." Paul Winn, interview by Fred E. Woods and Martin Andersen, February 6, 2020, Mob Museum, Las Vegas, transcript in possession of the author. Although Winn is in a position to know, what is not stated is that it is quite possible that it was a combination of Gay's brains, ethics, and church standards that impressed Nadine Henley to recommend him to Hughes. It appears he stood head and shoulders above his peers in both his work ethic and his personal life. Gay in turn hired Latter-day Saint men he could trust, and Hughes came to trust these Latter-day Saint assistants.

24. Donald L. Barlett and James B. Steele, *Howard Hughes: His Life & Madness*, 161–62. Herein, the authors further note, "The nondrinking, nonsmoking Mormons had become so intertwined with Romaine Street [the Hughes business office] that when a job opening occurred notices went up in Mormon church bulletin boards all over Los Angeles" (212).

25. "Obituary: Frank William Gay," *Deseret News*, May 28, 2007, https://www.deseret.com/2007/5/28/19757717/obituary-frank-william-gay, accessed April 16, 2020.

26. Hughes bought the Desert Inn, Frontier, Sands, Castaways, and Landmark hotels and casinos and the Silver Slipper Casino in Las Vegas, as well as Harold's Club in Reno. See http://www.lvstriphistory.com/ie/hughes.htm, accessed April 17, 2020. Hughes passed away in 1976. Shortly thereafter, a 1968 will surfaced, mailed to the Church of Jesus Christ of Latter-day Saints, purporting to give the church, as well as Melvin Dummar and other church members, a portion of the inheritance. Known as the "Mormon will," the handwritten will later proved to be a forgery. See "Hughes Mormon Will Is Forgery," *Las Vegas Review-Journal*, June 9, 1978, 1. The local district judge who oversaw the extended trial, lasting seven months, was Keith Hayes, also a Latter-day Saint who was praised for his evenhandedness. At Hayes's funeral, one speaker humorously told an audience of about one thousand that the two people Hayes wanted to visit with most in the next life were his mother and then Hughes, of whom he had a question to ask, which brought a roar of laughter. See Gary Ebbels, "Vegans Bid Farewell to Judge Keith Hayes," *Las Vegas Review-Journal*, November 30, 1979, 5. For an overview of the life of Hughes, see Geoff Schumacher, *Howard Hughes: Power, Paranoia, and Palace Intrigue.*

27. Sheila Caudle, "E. Parry Thomas Seen as 'Mr. Las Vegas,'" *Las Vegas Review-Journal,* June 28, 1977, 100.

28. Jack Sheehan, *Quiet Kingmaker of Las Vegas: E. Parry Thomas,* 47, 143.

29. Sheehan, *Quiet Kingmaker,* 15.

30. Senator Harry Reid, interview by Fred E. Woods and Martin Andersen, June 23, 2020, Las Vegas, transcript in possession of the author.

31. Sheehan, *Quiet Kingmaker,* 57–58.

32. Sheehan, *Quiet Kingmaker,* 61–62.

33. Reid, interview.

34. Mike Green, interview by Fred E. Woods and Martin Andersen, February 7, 2020, Las Vegas, transcript in possession of the author. Green is a gifted and experienced UNLV history professor who is an expert on both Las Vegas and Nevada history in general. He is the author of several publications, including *Nevada: A History of the Silver State* and coauthor (with Eugene P. Moehring) of *Las Vegas: A Centennial History.*

35. Bob Gottlieb and Peter Wiley, "Don't Touch the Dice: The Las Vegas/Utah Connection," 27.

36. Davis, "Saints in Sin City, 9. Lamar Noorda, a local Saint, also recalled another connection with Jewish friends in Las Vegas. Noorda remembered a Rabbi Dan from one of the local synagogues who needed a place to use temporarily for their religious meetings. He offered to rent the local church meetinghouse where Noorda attended. Noorda explained that the Saints could not rent the building but were glad to let them use it on Saturdays for free. They took him up on the offer, and for about a year and a half, they used the Latter-day Saint meetinghouse. Noorda added that Rabbi Dan returned the favor in part by teaching Hebrew-language lessons to the Noorda family and other Saints in the local stake who were planning trips to Israel. Lamar Noorda, interview by Fred E. Woods and Martin Andersen, June 22, 2020, Las Vegas, transcript in possession of the author.

37. E. Parry Thomas, quoted in Sheehan, *Quiet Kingmaker,* 14.

38. Thomas, quoted in Sheehan, *Quiet Kingmaker,* 314.

39. Thomas, quoted in Sheehan, *Quiet Kingmaker,* 308.

40. Thomas, quoted in Sheehan, *Quiet Kingmaker,* 70.

41. Thomas, quoted in Sheehan, *Quiet Kingmaker,* 71.

42. Nikki Troxclair, "UNLV Advocate E. Parry Thomas Remembered for Lasting Impact," August 29, 2016, https://www.unlv.edu/news/article/unlv-advocate-e-parry -thomas-remembered-lasting-impact, accessed April 18, 2020. See also https://www .thomasandmack.com/history/, accessed August 13, 2021, which notes the Thomas & Mack Center was finished in 1983 at a cost of almost $30 million.

43. Sheehan, *Quiet Kingmaker,* 13.

44. Sheehan, *Quiet Kingmaker,* 13.

45. Sheehan, *Quiet Kingmaker,* 18.

46. Sheehan, *Quiet Kingmaker,* 270.

47. Tom Thomas, interview by the author, February 6, 2020, Las Vegas, transcription in possession of the author.

48. Sheehan, *Quiet Kingmaker,* 271–72.

49. Sheehan, *Quiet Kingmaker,* 246. Parry also has two other sons who have

NOTES

contributed to the Las Vegas community. Although not closely aligned with the church, Peter, an attorney, and Roger, an interior designer, have both been successful in the marketplace.

50. Sheehan, *Quiet Kingmaker*, 284.

51. Leibovich, "Houses of the Holy," 172.

52. Gottlieb and Wiley, "Don't Touch the Dice," 31–32.

53. Ward, *Saints in Babylon*, 62. On the other hand, when a $5,000 donation from the Hotel Association of Las Vegas was offered to the building fund of the Las Vegas Fifth and Sixth Wards in 1953, the First Presidency weighed in on the offer, and the message sent back to Moapa Stake president Thomas Myers was "that no money should be accepted from gambling interests for any purpose." President J. Reuben Clark told President Myers, "We cannot match the tithes of the people with that kind of money." See Williams, "Historical Study," 108.

54. On the struggle of religious people in general with the gaming environment, see John Przybys, "Dilemma for the Faithful," *Las Vegas Sun*, October 22, 1995, 1A, 14A.

55. "Dr. David Speaks Out on Gambling," *Las Vegas Review-Journal*, September 17, 1966, 10.

56. McClain Bybee, Zoom interview by the author, May 18, 2020, transcript in possession of the author; McClain Bybee, interview by Fred E. Woods and Martin Andersen, May 27, 2020, Orem, UT, transcript of interview in possession of the author.

57. Bybee, Zoom interview; Bybee, interview.

58. Latter-day Saints believe the Melchizedek priesthood was functioning in the primitive Christian Church and that Peter, the chief apostle, received the keys (directive power) of this higher priesthood to direct the affairs of the early church (Matt. 16:18–19). The Melchizedek priesthood is also named and alluded to in several places in the New Testament, especially in the book of Hebrews: 2:17–18; 5:6, 10; 6:20; 7:11, 15, 17, 21. Latter-day Saints believe this priesthood was restored to the earth in 1829 and currently directs the affairs of the Church of Jesus Christ of Latter-day Saints. It is considered by church members as the authority and power to act in the name of God.

59. Gottlieb and Wiley, "Don't Touch the Dice," 32.

60. LeGrand Richards to President Rulon A. Earl, November 23, 1965, copy in possession of the author.

61. First Presidency (David O. McKay, Hugh B. Brown, N. Eldon Tanner, and Joseph Fielding Smith) to stake presidents in Las Vegas and Reno and the presidents of the California Missions, August 1966, copy in possession of the author.

62. First Presidency (Spencer W. Kimball, N. Eldon Tanner, and Marion G. Romney) to stake presidents in Las Vegas and Reno and the president of the Las Vegas Mission, May 18, 1977, copy in possession of the author.

63. James Kastelic, "Crane Committed to Mormon Community," *Las Vegas Review-Journal*, October 19, 1980, 179.

64. Ward, *Saints of Babylon*, 63. However, the issue was raised five years earlier when McClain Bybee, then a member of the Las Vegas Mission presidency, was asked by the regional representatives in the Las Vegas region to draft on their behalf a recommendation on this sensitive issue for the general church leaders to review.

Bybee felt that the Lord had guided him on how to deal with this complex situation by focusing on church members' worthiness to receive a temple recommendation and the priesthood, rather than on job description. His draft letter received universal approval and was sent by Bybee to Elder Vaughn J. Featherstone via Elder James K. Seastrand, one of the regional representatives. M. McClain Bybee to Elder Vaughn J. Featherstone, August 31, 1981, copy in possession of the author. Ultimately, it reached the desk of the First Presidency, who directed there be a change in policy. Bybee, interview. Though the standard for temple recommends was focused on the worthiness of individuals and not on positions of employment in the gaming industry, the First Presidency (Ezra Taft Benson, Gordon B. Hinckley, and Thomas S. Monson) continued to take a firm stand against gambling. In a letter issued to general authorities and other church leaders worldwide on September 26, 1986, they stated, "There can be no question about the moral ramifications of gambling. As it has in the past, The Church of Jesus Christ of Latter-day Saints stands opposed to gambling, including the government-sponsored lotteries" (copy of letter in possession of the author).

65. Jay Bingham, interview by the author, February 6, 2020, at his home in Las Vegas, transcript in possession of the author.

66. Janet Brigham, "Beyond the Glitter," *Ensign,* February 1979, 37. In the twenty-first century, the position of the church on gambling has not changed. For example, in the spring of 2005, church president Gordon B. Hinckley clearly reiterated the position of the church on the gaming industry. See Gordon B. Hinckley, "Gambling," April 2005 General Conference, https://www.churchofjesuschrist.org/study /general-conference/2005/04/gambling?lang=eng, accessed on May 28, 2020. In the church general guidelines, item 21.1.19, "Gambling and Lotteries," in *Handbook 2: Administering the Church, 2010* (Salt Lake City: Church of Jesus Christ of Latter-day Saints, 2010), the current policy states, "The Church opposes gambling in any form, including government-sponsored lotteries" (184).

67. David Dixon, telephone conversation with the author, August 14, 2021. For good information on the topic of labor unions, see James P. Kraft, *Vegas at Odds: Labor Conflict in a Leisure Economy, 1960–1985;* Courtney Alexander, "Rise to Power: The Recent History of the Culinary Union in Las Vegas," in *Grit Beneath the Glitter,* ed. Rothman and Davis, 145–75.

68. Gottlieb and Wiley, "Don't Touch the Dice," 22, 26. Evidence that there was a connection between Vegas Village and local church members is illustrated in the Las Vegas Second Ward general minutes, vol. 2, 1954–59, June 24, 1959, which note that in a ward executive meeting the Latter-day Saint youth were planning to hold a bake sale at Vegas Village. Further, Las Vegas Second Ward general minutes, vol. 3, 1960–65, January 25, 1961, 29, sacrament meeting notations, state, "Those helping to take inventory at Vegas Village are to meet in the relief society room following sacrament meeting."

69. "Ground Is Broken for New Supermart on North Main," *Las Vegas Review-Journal,* March 3, 1955, 1, notes, "Ralph J. Harman is president of the operating company with Jack Wollenzein as vice president and Al Wendelboe secretary."

70. Dave and Gayle Harman, interview by the author, June 11, 2020, Dave Harman Real Estate Academy, Orem, UT, transcript in possession of the author.

71. Dave and Gayle Harman, interview.

72. Steward, *Where Sin Abounds*, 11.

73. Davis, "Saints in Sin City," 74–75.

74. Ed Kanet, email to the author, February 28, 2021. The author thanks Kanet for going the extra mile to gather images of local Latter-day Saint periodicals as well as images of the Las Vegas Temple. This included a scanned copy of the entire 2008 *Guide*.

75. "Who Gets the Bee Hive Newspaper and How It Is Distributed," *Bee Hive* 5, no. 10 (1980): 2, Lied Library Special Collections, University of Nevada, Las Vegas, hereafter cited as Lied Library Special Collections. Herein, it was further noted that the *Beehive Standard Weekly* was the only periodical of its kind in southern Nevada. In addition, it was selected for inclusion in various archives, including the Church History Library (Salt Lake City), UNLV, and Brigham Young University. For a treatment on the genesis and development of the *Beehive*, see also https://arizonabeehive.com/about-us/, accessed March 1, 2021. This website explains that the *Arizona Beehive* was also launched in October 1993 and continues to the present.

76. "Flick Flak: A Guide to Family Viewing," *Beehive Sentinel*, April 30, 1986, 20, Lied Library Special Collections.

77. See, for example, miscellaneous announcements of this sort in *Beehive Sentinel*, April 16, 1986, 21; April 30, 1986, 21, Lied Library Special Collections.

78. "Hire a Non-Smoker," *Beehive*, 6, no. 13 (1981): 11.

79. Nadeoul Eden, "Harry Reid," *Beehive Sentinel*, March 5, 1986, 16–17, Lied Library Special Collections.

80. Gottlieb and Wiley, "Don't Touch the Dice," 25.

81. Charles W. Zobell, "150 Years of Faith: Church Celebrates Anniversary," *Las Vegas Review-Journal*, October 1, 1980, 29. On this same page are official congratulations from several businesses to the church in its sesquicentennial year.

82. "Church 'for All Ages' Not Just an Activity for Sunday," *Las Vegas Review-Journal*, October 1, 1980, 8B.

83. S. Mahlon Edwards, email to the author, April 27, 2020.

84. David Dixon, interview by Fred E. Woods and Martin Andersen, March 4, 2020, Las Vegas, transcription in possession of the author.

85. Bingham served on the Clark County Commission for three terms. After he retired from public office, Bingham continued to work with construction and development.

86. Bingham, interview.

87. Bingham, interview. Bingham, a trusted Latter-day Saint, also later served as a local stake president and member of the Las Vegas Temple presidency.

88. Chris Broderick, "LV Lawyer Named to Supreme Court," *Las Vegas Review-Journal*, March 17, 1982, 1. Herein, Broderick noted that in 1965 Steffen began practicing law. "The Honorable Thomas L. Steffen Passes Away at Age 90" stated that Steffen served on the Nevada Supreme Court from 1982 to 1997 and died September 1, 2020. https://nvcourts.gov/Supreme/News/Passing_of_Former_Justice_Thomas_L__Steffen/, accessed August 14, 2021. For more information on Judge Steffen, see "State Supreme Court Justice Is Judge and an LDS Missionary," *Beehive Sentinel*, May 14, 1989, 19.

89. S. Mahlon Edwards, email to the author, April 27, 2020.

90. Elise Noorda, interview by Fred E. Woods and Martin Andersen, June 22, 2020, Las Vegas, transcript in possession of the author.

91. "'I Really Believe It!': Mormon Rock Star Brandon Flowers Shares His Faith on CBS News," https://www.ldsliving.com/-I-Really-Believe-It-Mormon-Rock-Star -Brandon-Flowers-Shares-His-Faith-on-CBS-News/s/88913, accessed August 12, 2021.

92. "Knight in Vegas," *Las Vegas Sun,* November 28, 2003, citing Knight, notes that she first performed in Vegas in 1967, entertained for years at the Flamingo, and owned a home first in Las Vegas and then later in Henderson. https://lasvegassun .com/news/2003/nov/28/knight-in-vegas/, accessed May 11, 2020.

93. Jamie Armstrong, "How Gladys Knight Became a Latter-day Saint," LDS *Living,* June 4, 2016, https://www.ldsliving.com/How-Gladys-Knight-Became-a -Mormon/s/76709, accessed May 11, 2020.

94. Armstrong, "How Gladys Knight Became a Latter-day Saint."

95. "Knight Choir Wins," *Las Vegas Review-Journal,* February 9, 2006, 5.

96. Armstrong, "How Gladys Knight Became a Latter-day Saint."

97. Stacy Johnson, "Donny and Marie Announce the End of Their Las Vegas Show," *Provo Daily Herald,* March 21, 2019, https://www.heraldextra.com/news/local /donny-and-marie-announce-the-end-of-their-las-vegas/article_69002cb6-b8bc-5d2c -aba3-417dc119b125.html.

98. Charles Trepany, "'Goodnight, Everybody': Marie and Donny Close Las Vegas Live Show After 11 Years," *USA Today,* November 18, 2019, https://www.usatoday.com /story/entertainment/music/2019/11/18/marie-donny-osmond-fight-tears-during-last -las-vegas-show/4233723002/, accessed April 21, 2020.

99. "Donny and Marie End Their Long-Running Vegas Residency with Emotional Show," *Good Morning America,* November 18, 2019, https://www.goodmorning america.com/culture/story/donny-marie-osmond-end-long-running-vegas-residency -67104017, accessed April 21, 2020. The stellar musical duo received a standing ovation at their final performance. See John Katsilometes, "Donny & Marie Bring Down the Curtain," *Las Vegas Review-Journal,* November 17, 2019, 3.

100. Donny Osmond, interview by Fred E. Woods and Martin Andersen, March 18, 2019, Vineyard, UT, transcript in possession of the author.

101. Marie Osmond, interview by Fred E. Woods and Martin Andersen, February 23, 2019, Las Vegas, transcription in possession of the author.

102. Marie Osmond, interview.

103. Donny Osmond, interview.

104. Donny Osmond, interview.

105. The last Osmond family performance in Las Vegas was in 2007 for their fiftieth-anniversary show. The news reported that back in the 1970s, Elvis Presley had given them the idea to wear jumpsuits for performances as he did, and they took Presley's advice. See "Elvis Gave Fashion Advice to Osmonds," *Las Vegas Review-Journal,* August 16, 2007, 3. Alan Osmond recalled that after they wore their new jumpsuits to perform, Elvis came backstage to meet with the Osmond brothers. Elvis said, "Hey, man, I love the jumpsuits." Alan Osmond, interview by Fred E. Woods and Martin Andersen, September 28, 2018, Orem, UT, transcript in possession of the author. Ron Clark, the Osmonds' publicist and road manager for

fourteen years, remembered that Elvis was impressed by the Osmond family and drew spiritually close to Olive, the Osmond mother. One year Elvis even let the family use his Las Vegas suite while he was out of town for several weeks. During this time, Clark remembered, "We had sacrament…in shot glasses behind his bar. Every Sunday we had our own sacrament services with shot glasses and bread…. It was quite an experience seeing how they [the Osmonds] related with these superstars. And in two record years, back to back, the Osmonds outsold both Elvis and the Jackson 5." Ron Clark, interview by Fred E. Woods and Martin Andersen, July 20, 2018, Orem, UT, transcript in possession of the author. Donny Osmond remembered that Elvis's suite was in the Hilton, which is now known as the Westgate. Osmond added, "My mom had a great relationship with Elvis Presley because Elvis wanted to be a preacher, and he would call my Mom every once in a while and talk about the gospel because he loved gospel music." Donny Osmond, interview.

106. "Show Stealing Osmonds with Andy Williams," *Las Vegas Review-Journal,* May 25, 1967, 21.

107. Sandra Widener, "Osmond Family to Bring 'America Fest' to Silver Bowl," *Las Vegas Review-Journal,* May 9, 1984, 52.

108. Waite and Waite, "Reflections," 25–26.

109. Waite and Waite, "Reflections," 26.

110. Waite and Waite, "Reflections," 30. One prominent example that the Singing Mothers had not only existed but had been influential is evidenced in "Full Text of President McKay's Address at Las Vegas," *Church News,* November 20, 1954, 2, noting that President McKay had praised the Singing Mothers organization for their performance as well as their hard work in preparation for events.

111. Waite and Waite, "Reflections," 31.

112. Waite and Waite, "Reflections," 34–36.

113. Waite and Waite, "Reflections," 38–40.

114. "92 Units to Participate in Big Mormon Parade," *Las Vegas Review-Journal,* July 19, 1963, 2.

115. Waite and Waite, "Reflections," 26. The authors further note, "Shortly after the Center was sold in 1970, the Stake acquired land south of the Walnut and Carey Chapel and built a sports complex with four lighted ball fields" (28). In the spring of 2020, the press announced that the Neon Museum is expanding and has plans to renovate the Reed Whipple Cultural Center. https://lasvegassun.com/news/2019/may/15/neon-2020-is-coming-to-the-iconic-neon-museum-in-l/, accessed August 13, 2021.

116. Christensen, interview.

117. Waite and Waite, "Reflections," 245.

Chapter 5. Latter-day Saints in Elected Office and Community Service

1. "Mr. and Mrs. Charles C. Ronnow Celebrate Fiftieth Anniversary," *Las Vegas Age,* June 20, 1941, 2.

2. http://www.clarkcountynv.gov/parks/Documents/centennial/commissioners/commissioner-i-earl.pdf, accessed April 21, 2020.

3. Ward, *Saints in Babylon,* 29.

4. Ward, *Saints in Babylon*, 26.

5. Ward, *Saints in Babylon*, 27. Arrington, *The Mormons in Nevada*, 62, adds that Whipple "was a member of the Las Vegas City Commission for 20 years, president of the Area Council of the Boy Scouts of America, and president of the Las Vegas Lions Club. For many years he was chairman of the Fair and Recreation Board of Las Vegas, and a principal figure in the development of Las Vegas as a major force in the nation's convention industry." Additional contributions included "Red Cross committees,...past director of the Las Vegas Community Chest,...treasurer of a local tuberculosis association, [and]...Chamber of Commerce member. Whipple also served on the Governor's Traffic Safety Council." See "Commission Struggle: Veteran Reed Whipple in Clash with Buck," *Las Vegas Review-Journal*, May 5, 1963, 4. A good treatment of his life is K. J. Evans, "Reed Whipple...Quiet Man of God," *Las Vegas Review-Journal*, September 12, 1999, 208. See also "Funeral Services Set for Pioneer Vegan Whipple," *Las Vegas Review-Journal*, May 19, 1986, 1; and Christopher Beall, "Las Vegas Pioneer Dies," *Las Vegas Review-Journal*, May 18, 1986, 1.

6. "Berkeley Bunker Appointed to Fill Vacancy in Senate," *Las Vegas Age*, November 29, 1940, 1. Less than two years later, Senator Bunker was elected as the only representative in the House. "Berkeley L. Bunker," *Las Vegas Age*, August 30, 1940, 1, noted, "As a Las Vegas businessman he has won a reputation for dependability and fair dealing. Perhaps the greatest honor that could be done [for] a young man was his election by the people of the LDS Church to the important position of Bishop of the Las Vegas Stake." Although it was the ecclesiastical calling to lead his ward, not his stake, and the fact that he was not "elected" by the people, but rather sustained, the message that he was a respected citizen and church member no doubt reached the ears of the public. For more information on Bunker's life and contributions, see "Berkeley Bunker (1906–1999) Politician, Patriarch and Preacher," *Las Vegas Sun*, May 2, 1999, 183–84.

7. "Senator Bunker Given Farewell," *Las Vegas Age*, December 6, 1940, 1.

8. "President Bunker in Series of Broadcasts," *Las Vegas Age*, February 28, 1941, 1. Wendell Waite and Bonita "Bonnie" Waite, "Reflections: History of the North Las Vegas Stake," unpublished manuscript, 2000, 10, note that Bryan L. Bunker was appointed as the stake president of the Moapa Stake in 1939. During his years in Las Vegas, Bunker served his local community by establishing the Las Vegas United Fund; was an active Scout, achieving the prestigious Silver Beaver Award; and was a leader in the Chamber of Commerce. He was the founder of the Bunker Brothers Mortuary, and after his release as stake president, he continued his impressive church service, which included presiding over the California Mission from 1952 to 1955. Then from 1956 to 1960, Bunker served as the president of the Las Vegas Stake Mission. He then returned to preside over the California Mission from 1960 to 1962. From 1964 to 1966 and from 1968 to 1971, he was a counselor in the Salt Lake Temple presidency. Bunker passed away on April 6, 1971, following a lifetime of church service. See http://www.bunker.org/obituaries/bryanlamondbunker.html, accessed April 21, 2020. See also "Bunker Services Set for Saturday," *Las Vegas Review-Journal*, April 8, 1971, 3.

9. "Church Leader Implores America, 'Put on the Whole Armor of God,'" *Las Vegas Age*, March 7, 1941, 4.

10. "Bryan Bunker Plans Series of Broadcasts," *Las Vegas Age,* February 21, 1941, 1.

11. The Bunker Brothers Mortuary was launched in 1942 and is still a successful business. See https://www.bunkersmortuary.com/our-history, accessed May 20, 2020.

12. Joyce Haldeman, interview by Fred E. Woods and Martin Andersen, March 5, 2020, Las Vegas, transcript in possession of the author.

13. Ray Rawson, interview by Fred E. Woods and Martin Andersen, June 24, 2020, Las Vegas, transcript in possession of the author.

14. Bruce Woodbury, interview by Fred E. Woods and Martin Andersen, February 7, 2020, Henderson, Nevada, transcript in possession of the author.

15. Woodbury, interview.

16. Jay Bingham, interview by Fred E. Woods and Martin Andersen, February 6, 2020, Las Vegas, transcript in possession of the author. For a select list of elected or appointed officials in the Las Vegas metropolitan area, including Bingham, see Appendix C.

17. Senator Harry Reid, interview by Fred E. Woods and Martin Andersen, June 23, 2020, Las Vegas, transcript in possession of the author.

18. John L. Smith, Zoom interview by the author, May 19, 2020, Springville, UT, transcript in possession of the author.

19. Helen Foley, interview by Fred E. Woods and Martin Andersen, June 27, 2020, Las Vegas, typescript in possession of the author.

20. Fred Kennedy, interview by Fred E. Woods and Martin Andersen, June 24, 2020, Las Vegas, transcript in possession of the author.

21. Senator Richard Bryan, Zoom interview by the author, May 26, 2020, Springville, UT, transcript in possession of the author.

22. Charlie Zobell, Zoom interview by the author, June 11, 2020, transcript in possession of the author.

23. Jackie Valley and John Katsilometes, "Longtime 'Cowboy Sheriff' Ralph Lamb Dies at 88," *Las Vegas Sun,* https://lasvegassun.com/news/2015/jul/03/longtime -cowboy-sheriff-ralph-lamb-dies-88/, accessed May 20, 2020; *Vegas,* https://www.imdb .com/title/tt2262383/, accessed August 16, 2021.

24. McClain Bybee, interview by Fred E. Woods and Martin Andersen, May 27, 2020, Orem, UT, transcript in possession of the author.

25. Marsha Leason, interview by Fred E. Woods and Martin Andersen, March 5, 2020, Las Vegas, transcript in possession of the author.

26. Leason, interview. Jay Bingham also remembered Sheriff Lamb's encounter with the famed motorcycle gang: "When the Hells Angels were coming to town…he went out with a couple of his officers, blocked the road, and stopped them and told them you're not coming to my town, and they had to turn around and leave." Bingham, interview.

27. Kyle Stevens made this remark about the size of the audience as an eyewitness inasmuch as he attended Lamb's funeral. Further, Stevens mentioned, "Gaming mogul Steve Wynn assisted, preached, he was involved specifically in a very, very interesting tribute to the sheriff." Kyle Stevens, interview by Fred E. Woods and Martin Andersen, March 6, 2020, Las Vegas, transcript in possession of the author.

28. Leason, interview.

29. Leason, interview.

30. Ashley Hall, interview by Fred E. Woods and Martin Andersen, February 26, 2020, Las Vegas, transcript in possession of the author. Marsha Leason remembered that her uncle Ralph "hit Frank Sinatra in the jaw and put him through a plate glass window at the Sands Hotel." Leason, interview.

31. A. D. Hopkins, "Ralph Lamb...Mr. Metro," *Las Vegas Sun,* September 12, 1999, 201. The Las Vegas Metropolitan Police Department is a combined law-enforcement agency for the city of Las Vegas and Clark County. Eric Kerns, who retired from the Metro force after a twenty-five-year career (1992–2017), spoke of Lamb's legacy as a "tough sheriff" who was "very powerful politically." Kerns estimated that about 10 percent of the officers in the Metro department were Latter-day Saints who have contributed much good in this region for decades since Lamb's retirement. He said, "I prayed every day in my police work." Kerns also recalled feeling guided by divine assistance on many occasions and related specific examples of counseling a suicidal woman and miraculously finding a nine-year-old boy named Jeremy who had been lost in the desert, beyond the assigned search area Kerns felt impressed to go. He also felt guided in his leadership as a sergeant teaching various principles and values to other officers in his department. Eric Kerns, Zoom interview by the author, February 12, 2020, transcript in possession of the author.

32. Hall, interview.

33. "At the Top in City Hall," *Beehive Sentinel,* April 30, 1986, 11, Lied Library Special Collections, University of Nevada, Las Vegas, hereafter cited as Lied Library Special Collections.

34. Former state senator Helen Foley recalled that Broadbent "was one of the greatest members of the LDS community here in Southern Nevada." She added that Broadbent did "a tremendous job" working for the Bureau of Reclamation and later as the director of the McCarran Airport. Foley, interview. Mahlon Edwards remembered that Broadbent was a man who was known for his honesty by all who knew him. Mahlon Edwards, Zoom interview by the author, December 1, 2020, notes in possession of the author. At the time of his passing, *Sun* reporter Will Oremus also referred to Broadbent simply as "an honest man." See Will Oremus, "Longtime Public Servant Broadbent Dies," *Las Vegas Sun,* https://lasvegassun.com/news/2003/aug/11/longtime-public-servant-broadbent-dies/, accessed December 1, 2020.

35. Judie Brailsford-Marcucci, interview by the author, February 22, 2021, Las Vegas; Judie Brailsford-Marcucci interview by Fred E. Woods and Martin Andersen, June 24, 2020, Las Vegas, transcript in possession of the author.

36. Bingham, interview. Floyd Lamb's reputation was tarnished when he was convicted of attempted extortion in 1983. Like his brother Sheriff Ralph Lamb, Floyd was "a rough-and-tumble rancher...and one of the most influential politicians in Nevada before his downfall." See Ed Koch, "Lamb, Longtime Nevada Politician, Rancher, Dies," *Las Vegas Sun,* https://lasvegassun.com/news/2002/jun/03/lamb-longtime-nevada-politician-rancher-dies/, accessed November 26, 2020. Fifteen years before Bingham even began serving on the county commission, Gibson was already a powerful force in the state legislature. See "Gibson Said 'Undisputed Ruler of Legislature,'" *Las Vegas Review-Journal,* April 18, 1969, 10.

37. The four were Jay Bingham, Paul Christensen, Karen Hayes, and Bruce

Woodbury. The author thanks Joyce Haldeman for bringing this information to his attention.

38. Bingham, interview.

39. Mark Hutchison, interview by Fred E. Woods and Martin Andersen, March 5, 2020, Las Vegas, transcript in possession of the author.

40. https://www.reviewjournal.com/local/local-las-vegas/aaron-williams-who -broke-racial-barriers-in-nevada-dies-at-90/, accessed August 13, 2021.

41. Aaron Williams, interview by Claytee D. White, August 16, 2005, Las Vegas, African Americans in Las Vegas: A Collaborative Oral History Project, Oral History Research Center, University Libraries, University of Nevada, Las Vegas, 19–21.

42. Howard Bulloch, interview by Fred E. Woods and Martin Andersen, February 6, 2020, Las Vegas, transcript in possession of the author.

43. Woodbury, interview.

44. Michael Scott Davidson, "Clark County Commissioner Scow Surprises with Resignation Announcement," *Las Vegas Review-Journal,* June 20, 2017, announced that Scow "abruptly announced that she will resign her seat this month." See https:// www.reviewjournal.com/news/politics-and-government/clark-county/clark-county -commissioner-scow-surprises-with-resignation-announcement/, accessed April 28, 2020. Clark explained in a conversation prior to her March 6, 2020, interview with the author that she resigned due to family health reasons.

45. Mary Beth Scow, interview by Fred E. Woods and Martin Anderson, March 6, 2020, Henderson, NV, transcript in possession of the author.

46. Scow, interview.

47. Hutchison, interview.

48. Smith, Zoom interview.

49. Jon Ralston, Zoom interview by the author, June 3, 2020, Springville, UT, transcript in possession of the author. In another interview Ralston observed that when he moved to Vegas in 1984, the community was much smaller than it is now. He added that the Latter-day Saints in the 1980s "had a disproportionate influence in especially low turnout primaries." Further, "they were known,…they vote.… So, there was a significant percentage of Mormons in office and who formed groups here, political influential groups. Citizens for Responsible Government was one, which was known as the Mormon group. It wasn't all Mormons, but you had to kiss their ring to be elected to anything in Nevada at that time.… They were generally thought of as men or women of moral rectitude." Jon Ralston, interview by Fred E. Woods and Martin Andersen, June 22, 2020, Las Vegas, transcript in possession of the author.

50. Ned Day, "Abortion Issue Fragments Mormon 'Voting Bloc,'" *Las Vegas Review-Journal,* October 29, 1986, 23.

51. Jon Ralston, "County Democrats Indulge in Some Public Pandering," *Las Vegas Review-Journal,* September 4, 1988, 30.

52. Hayes, who served both in the Nevada Assembly and on the Clark County Commission, was very influential on a number of important issues, such as the Equal Rights Amendment and sensitive matters like abortion. Hayes felt that serving in an elected office did not require her to talk about her religion but noted that

how she lived her life is what really mattered. She remarked, "Everyone knew I was LDS; I didn't have to tell them." Karen Hayes King, Zoom interview by the author, February 14, 2021, Las Vegas, transcript in possession of the author. Karen was married to Judge Keith Hayes, and together they left a legacy of service to the Las Vegas community.

53. Brailsford-Marcucci, interview. In a later interview the following year, she adjusted the percentages to 32 percent elected officers, with a Latter-day Saint community at that time of about 12 percent. See Judie Brailsford-Marcucci and Heidi Gresham Wixom, interview by the author, February 22, 2021, transcript in possession of the author.

54. Stevens, interview. Like a Latter-day Saint bishop or stake president, a regional representative had ecclesiastical responsibility for a given region. This particular title is no longer used.

55. S. Mahlon Edwards, email to the author, April 27, 2020. In this correspondence, Edwards also referred to Jace Radke, "Commission Chairwoman, Former Officials Indicted," *Las Vegas Sun*, November 7, 2003, https://lasvegassun.com/news/2003/nov/07/commission-chairwoman-former-officials-indicted/, accessed April 27, 2020.

56. Shari Buck, telephone interview by the author, February 13, 2020, transcription in possession of the author.

57. Reid, interview.

58. Arrington, *The Mormons in Nevada,* 63. See also Senator Harry Reid with Mark Warren, *The Good Fight: Hard Lessons from Searchlight to Washington* (New York: G. P. Putnam's Sons, 2008). In Nevada's gaming regulatory system, the Gaming Commission is a level above the Nevada Gaming Control Board.

59. Reid, interview.

60. https://www.britannica.com/biography/Harry-Reid, accessed August 16, 2021.

61. Smith, Zoom interview.

62. Ralston, Zoom interview.

63. Former state senator Helen Foley, commenting about the diverse political opinions of Latter-day Saints, stated, "I find it inspiring that people don't need to walk lock-step and that they can have their own strong opinions and still be very, very confident leaders." Foley, interview.

64. Haldeman, interview. This church program was switched to what is referred to simply as "ministering" in April 2018, which includes service by and to both men and women. This new approach is similar to home teaching but allows more flexibility in meeting the needs of others. Reid said he had served in several church leadership callings over the years and remarked, "I've been active in the church my whole life.... Membership in the church has been good for me and my family." When working in the Senate, Reid was also involved with assisting general church leaders in various issues involving missionary work in foreign countries. His relationship with Senator Mike Enzi also helped the church overcome opposition to and advance the development of Martin's Cove, a church historic site about an hour's drive southwest of Casper, Wyoming. Reid, interview. For more information on Martin's Cove, see https://history.churchofjesuschrist.org/subsection/historic-sites/wyoming/martins-cove?lang=eng, accessed November 17, 2020.

65. Bryan, Zoom interview.

66. Reid, interview. Senator Reid passed away December 28, 2021.

67. "Judge Lloyd D. George," US District Court, District of Nevada, https://www
.nvd.uscourts.gov/court-information/judges/judge-lloyd-d-george/, accessed April
29, 2020.

68. Ed Koch and Mary Manning, "Federal Building To Be Named After George,"
https://lasvegassun.com/news/1999/oct/27/federal-building-to-be-named-after
-george/, accessed August 16, 2021.

69. George was also instrumental in establishing a byu Management Society for
Las Vegas in 1984. See "byu Society Starts Chapter in Vegas," *Las Vegas Review-Journal*,
March 1, 1984, 61. See also an interview with Judge George in Olivia Hurst, "lds
Keeping Order in the (Federal) Court," *New Beehive* in association with the *Latter-
day Sentinel* newspaper, May 14, 1986, 1, 18–19, Lied Library Special Collections.

70. Hutchison, interview.

71. William H. Stoddard, interview by Fred E. Woods and Martin Andersen,
June 24, 2020, Las Vegas, transcript in possession of the author. The Church of Jesus
Christ of Latter-day Saints announced that commencing January 1, 2020, a new
church program for children and youth would be instituted, which would replace
Scouting, "intended to reduce burdens on families, with greater flexibility to adapt
to the needs of individuals and families around the world in many different circumstances." "Church to End Relationship with Scouting; Announces New Activity Program for Children and Youth," https://www.churchofjesuschrist.org/church/news
/church-to-end-relationship-with-scouting-announces-new-activity-program-for
-children-and-youth?lang=eng, accessed November 27, 2020.

72. Senator Richard Bryan, interview by Fred E. Woods and Martin Andersen,
June 23, 2020, Las Vegas, typescript in possession of the author.

73. Eric Christensen, interview by the author, March 6, 2020, Las Vegas, transcript
in possession of the author.

74. "Training to Be Given Boy Scout Workers in Vegas," *Las Vegas Age*, February 22, 1930, 2, notes, "Troop committee of Troop 63, l.d.s. church sponsor: Bryan
Bunker, chairman, Ira Earl, C. C. Ronnow, Fred Alward, acting; Leslie Edwards,
scoutmaster."

75. Chauncey C. Riddle, telephone interview by the author, February 21, 2020,
transcript in possession of the author.

76. Earl, "History of the Las Vegas First Ward," 13–14. "Board Awards Seven Scout
Merit Badges," *Las Vegas Age*, July 19, 1930, 1, indicates that two of the three Scouts
who earned a combined seven merit badges were from Troop 63. "Report of Boy
Scout Activities," *Las Vegas Age*, February 24, 1931, 1, listed twenty-two Tenderfoot
Scouts and one Second-Class Scout in Troop 63 that year. Two months later, "Scouts
Given Awards at Court of Honor," *Las Vegas Age*, April 28, 1931, 1, announced that
Troop 63 won a trophy for best attendance. "Earl Is First Eagle Scout," *Las Vegas Age*,
January 12, 1932, 1, states that Don Earl, son of Ira Earl, Troop 63, was to be the first
Scout awarded the rank of Eagle in southern Nevada. Several boys from this troop
were also to receive merit badges at the court of honor. "Mormon Bishop Is Escort
for Scouts," *Las Vegas Age*, August 7, 1930, 1, reveals that the Church of Jesus Christ of
Latter-day Saints was closely involved with Scouting in southern Nevada in general

during this era. Decades later, Latter-day Saint young men earned the rank of Eagle Scout at a steady pace. See, for example, "Five Las Vegas 6th Ward Scouts Win Eagle Badges," *Church News*, February 23, 1957, 13.

77. "Camp Rally Day for Boy Scouts," *Las Vegas Age*, June 14, 1930, 3, lists Leslie Edwards as the Scoutmaster of Troop 63.

78. See "Wiley Is Named Scout Executive," *Las Vegas Age*, February 1, 1930, 1. An endnote in a previous chapter, "Scout Board Is Appointed," *Las Vegas Age*, October 9, 1931, 2, referenced Ira J. Earl's appointment as chairman of the local Scouting organization the following year.

79. Jane Ann Morrison, *Nevadan*, "No More Peach Pits," *Las Vegas Review-Journal*, June 26, 1977, 156.

80. "Scout Board Is Appointed," *Las Vegas Age*, October 9, 1931, 2, notes that Ira J. Earl was appointed as chairman of the local Scouting organization.

81. Ward, *Saints in Babylon*, 62, here confuses Joseph Ira Earl (1852–1934) of Bunkerville with his son Ira Joseph Earl (1884–1957). Ira moved to Las Vegas in 1920 and lived there until his death, while his father, Joseph, never lived in Las Vegas. Either way, a digital search reveals that this quote is not found in the *Las Vegas Age*. Therefore, it is assumed this statement must have been from another local newspaper.

82. "Scouts Offer Ball Tonight," *Las Vegas Age*, April 23, 1932, 1. In this article, Earl announced that Troop 63 would be sponsoring a dance to raise annual operational funds for the Scouting program. During this era, the Latter-day Saint church buildings also served as a place for members of the community to congregate for other types of meetings. For example, a mother-daughter banquet was held in one church building by the local Camp Fire Girls. See "Mother and Daughter Banquet," *Las Vegas Age*, March 30, 1940, 2.

83. Waite and Waite, "Reflections," 43.

84. Jason Swensen, "Church to End Relationship with Scouting; Announces New Activity Program for Children and Youth," *Church News*, May 8, 2018, https://www.churchofjesuschrist.org/church/news/church-to-end-relationship-with-scouting-announces-new-activity-program-for-children-and-youth?lang=eng, accessed April 29, 2020.

85. "How Much Power for Mormons? Church Impact on Las Vegas," *Las Vegas Review-Journal*, May 29, 1975, 17.

86. "Mission Presidents Counseled to Love," *Church News*, June 28, 1975, 13. See also "Las Vegas Mormons Get Mission," *Las Vegas Review-Journal*, March 10, 1975, 3.

87. For example, a decade earlier, an unknown entity ran ads offering free copies of the Book of Mormon. See advertisement titled "BOOK OF MORMON: Get Your Free Copy," *Las Vegas Review-Journal*, April 14 and 15, 1964, 34. This same year, an advertisement announced, "Book of Mormon Archaeology 'Cinema' Slides" to Be Shown at the Las Vegas Stake Center." It beckoned, "Bring your non-LDS friends," *Las Vegas Review-Journal*, January 30, 1964, 12. Missionaries also continued to be sent from Las Vegas to share the gospel.

This period of full-time missionary service often leaves an indelible impression on those who choose to serve and forms positive character traits. For example, Mike Henle, "LDS Missionaries Traveling on Faith," *Las Vegas Review-Journal*, June

6, 2015, 9, reported on the persistence paid by former Nevada lieutenant governor Mark Hutchison as a young missionary. An observant insurance agent observed Hutchison going door-to-door with his companion, carrying their religious message, and actually offered them employment. The agent said, "Anyone who could knock on doors all day long and talk to complete strangers could certainly sell insurance!" The missionaries declined the offer, but did end up teaching the agent and his family about the Latter-day Saint message.

Unfortunately, on the local front, about the same time Hutchison's inspiring story was published, the missionaries' clean-cut appearance and door-knocking was imitated by two burglars in Las Vegas who wore "white shirts, black pants, black ties, black shoes, and black backpacks" and entered the home of a helpless victim, whom they held "at gunpoint before fleeing the scene, police said." See Steven Slivka, "Police Seek Two Men Who Posed as Mormon Missionaries in Robbery," *Las Vegas Review-Journal,* August 21, 2013, 13.

88. McClain Bybee, Zoom interview by the author, May 18, 2020, transcript in possession of the author.

89. "Discussion," *Las Vegas Review-Journal,* April 12, 1986, 22.

90. "Holiday Program Planned by Mormon Organizations," *Las Vegas Review-Journal,* December 11, 1976, 4.

91. "Don't You Wish Families Could Stay Together Forever?," *Las Vegas Review-Journal,* April 8, 1988, 50.

92. Mike Neider, Las Vegas Mission president from 2011 to 2014, indicated that the Las Vegas Mission averaged about one thousand baptisms during his era and was one of the top three missions in the United States. Neider also recalled that the number of baptisms had a lot to do with the supportive church members. Mike Neider, Zoom interview by the author, May 20, 2020, transcript in possession of the author.

93. Latter-day Saint attorney and experienced local church leader Mark Albright identified the boundaries of the Las Vegas Missions and added, "There's lots of missionary work going on, lots of baptisms happening on the edges of Las Vegas as you get away from Las Vegas Boulevard." Albright also observed, "A lot of [church] members have told me they don't even go to Las Vegas Boulevard unless there's a visitor from out of town that wants to see it." Mark Albright, interview by Fred E. Woods and Martin Andersen, June 24, 2020, Las Vegas, transcript in possession of the author.

94. Curtis D. Reese, email to the author, February 13, 2021.

95. Mo Denis, email to the author, February 11, 2021.

96. Mo Denis, interview by the author, January 24, 2021. Herein, Denis further mentioned that there were about four thousand Hispanic Latter-day Saints in the Las Vegas metro region and estimated that the Hispanic population in this area and in the state as a whole is about 25–28 percent. Denis pointed out the reason for the initiative was that the Latter-day Saint population should be higher among Hispanics.

97. Tom Thomas, email to the author, February 16, 2021.

98. "Nevada Historian Writing *R-J* Bicentennial Series," *Las Vegas Review-Journal,* June 3, 1975, 12.

99. Daryl Gibson, "Clark County Readies Bicentennial Fete," *Las Vegas Review-Journal*, June 27, 1976, 17. Ashley Hall, former Las Vegas city manager, related to the author that Zona had told him "several times that the LDS Bicentennial Activities made the celebration one of the top in the nation" (Ashley Hall, email to the author, February 1, 2020). A rich collection of the bicentennial is located at the UNLV Lied Library Special Collections and Archives, Clark County Bicentennial Collections T103, MS-00183. Box 1, in an unnumbered folder labeled "Fourth of July, 1976," contains a letter to Lila Zona from Latter-day Saint apostle Elder L. Tom Perry, expressing his appreciation for her leadership and the local Latter-day Saint contribution to the centennial commemoration (L. Tom Perry to Lila P. Zona, Chairman Clark County Bicentennial, August 17, 1976).

100. "Independence Day a Day to Remember," *Las Vegas Review-Journal*, July 7, 1976, 38.

101. Tiffany Ashton Zweifel, "Members Plunge in to Help Each Other, Community," *Church News*, July 17, 1999, 3, 11.

102. The annual nativity was hosted by the Las Vegas Stake (1990–2008) under George's direction. After a two-year hiatus, due to outgrowing its water district location, the nativity began to be hosted again by the Red Rock Stake in Summerlin. See "It's Looking a Lot Like Bethlehem," *Las Vegas Review-Journal*, December 10, 2010, 136.

103. "Church to Host Holiday Pageant," *Las Vegas Review-Journal*, December 12, 1994, 27.

104. "Church Presenting Nativity Pageant," *Las Vegas Review-Journal*, December 13, 1995, 25.

105. Cheryl Stewart Osborn, "The Cornwall Family Building the Christmas Spirit," *Deseret Saints Magazine*, December 2002, 9.

106. Osborn, "Cornwall Family," 8.

107. Jean Cornwall, interview by Fred E. Woods and Martin Andersen, July 15, 2020, Las Vegas, transcript in possession of the author. Herein, Cornwall notes that after twenty years of success, another stake took over the annual nativity event when LaPrele George was no longer able to do it. The event lasted for only about another two years, due to concerns with time and material costs as well as security issues. Vegas Latter-day Saint David Dixon further noted, "The live nativity is no longer done in Las Vegas. It got to be a big deal and very popular, which committed many people in the valley across multiple Stakes, and I think the resources required to put it on became prohibitive. The local [church] authorities stopped it. It was a great event and very well done and very professional. People from all faiths attended. It was a great community event. It was also a great missionary tool." David Dixon, email to the author, November 21, 2020.

108. LaPrele George, Zoom interview by the author, February 11, 2020, transcript in possession of the author. Before George began directing the nativity, the press reported that she had been involved in a variety of associations. For example, in 1985 she was elected to the BYU Alumni Association board of directors. She also directed the church video production for the Latter-day Saint temple committee. In addition, George was also serving as a stake cultural director and on the Foundation for Ancient Research and Mormon Studies board at BYU. George also earned a degree

in music from BYU, was involved with the local Desert Chorale, and volunteered at Opportunity Village. See "Newsmakers," under the subtitle "Awarded," *Las Vegas Review-Journal,* May 16, 1985, 48.

109. Cristi Bulloch, interview.

110. Cristi Bulloch, email to the author, February 9, 2021.

111. Bulloch, email to the author.

112. Bryan, interview.

113. Renee Summerour, "Donny Osmond Unveils Giving Machine in Downtown Summerlin," *Las Vegas Review-Journal,* November 14, 2019, https://www.review journal.com/life/donny-osmond-unveils-giving-machine-in-downtown-summerlin -1892942/, accessed April 29, 2020.

114. Haldeman, interview. Haldeman also later noted that Donny Osmond had taken time out of his busy schedule to successfully promote the Giving Machines, just two days before his last Las Vegas Donny and Marie show. Joyce Haldeman, email to the author, May 19, 2020.

115. Jana Dixon, email to the author, February 26, 2021. Herein, Dixon further noted that her liaison with the USVETS organization was Chuck Woodruff, a member of the Highland Hills Stake High Council who was also a military veteran. (A high council is a group of twelve men selected to help administer Latter-day Saint church business under the direction of a stake presidency.)

116. Jana Dixon, interview by Fred E. Woods and Martin Andersen, March 4, 2020, Las Vegas, transcript in possession of the author. Carolyn Goodman began serving as mayor of Las Vegas in 2011.

117. Bob Brown, interview by Fred E. Woods and Martin Andersen, June 27, 2020, Opportunity Village, Oakey Campus, transcript in possession of the author. Opportunity Village was established in 1954. See https://www.opportunityvillage.org, accessed February 16, 2021. In 1979, the Latter-day Saint organization Deseret Industries was formed, which also seeks to assist people with special needs. See "A Labor of Love: Deseret Industries," *Las Vegas Review-Journal,* October 1, 1980, 27. Linda Chapin, "D.I.: It's More than Just a Thrift Store," *Beehive Sentinel,* March 19, 1986, 8, commented, "The real value at Deseret Industries is not the price tag. It's what it does for people."

118. Hutchison, interview. One of those special-needs adults is the son of the late judge Lloyd D. George and his wife, LaPrele. Albright, interview.

119. Hutchison, interview.

120. Hutchison, interview.

121. "Crocheted Comforts," *Las Vegas Review-Journal,* May 29, 2014, 138.

122. Keith Thomas, email to the author, February 5, 2021. Thomas also described an interfaith project wherein Latter-day Saints joined hands with other denominations to assist the Zion United Methodist Church in Las Vegas, whose church building in the historic Westside neighborhood burned down June 6, 2017. Though ZUMC's fire insurance covered reconstruction, it did not take care of costs related to "hymnals, choir robes, electronics (computers), etc." Therefore, the Church of Jesus Christ of Latter-day Saints presented a check for $10,000 to ZUMC via local church leadership. Keith Thomas, email to the author, February 3, 2021. Interviews by the

author with Shamsuddin Waheed, imam for the Las Vegas Muslim community (on March 3, 2021), and with Gard Jameson, president of the Interfaith Council of Southern Nevada for the past three decades (on March 5, 2021), reveal that Latter-day Saints such as Thomas have worked well with the Las Vegas interfaith community for many years on a variety of projects.

123. Church of Jesus Christ of Latter-day Saints Newsroom, "Facts and Statistics," https://newsroom.churchofjesuschrist.org/facts-and-statistics/state/nevada, accessed May 1, 2020.

124. For more information about the Helping Hands program, see "Helping Hands," https://www.churchofjesuschrist.org/topics/humanitarian-service/helping -hands?lang=eng, accessed May 1, 2020.

125. For more information on the Just Serve program, see "Just Serve," https:// www.justserve.org/, accessed May 1, 2020.

126. "High Praise," *Las Vegas Sun,* July 30, 1991, 14.

127. Ruth Johnson, interview by Fred E. Woods and Martin Andersen, May 27, 2020, transcript in possession of the author.

CHAPTER 6. ECCLESIASTICAL COMMUNITY SERVICE
TO A LOCAL CONGREGATION IN NEED

1. "Teen-Ager Arrested for Blaze at Church," *Las Vegas Review-Journal,* April 14, 1983, P.M., 4A.

2. The obituary for Charles Johnson notes that he was born in Provo, Utah, in 1931 and married Eleanor "Ellie" Law in 1955 and that they moved to Las Vegas shortly after he earned a law degree, where he opened a law office in 1963. Johnson had a lifetime of significant service within the Church of Jesus Christ of Latter-day Saints and in the Las Vegas community. Noteworthy is the fact that in 2008, he received the "Peacemaker of the Year Award from the Mediators of Southern Nevada," Charles Johnson obituary, *Las Vegas Review-Journal,* https://obits.review journal.com/obituaries/lvrj/obituary.aspx?n=charles-johnson&pid=152672616&fhid =13804, accessed July 8, 2020.

3. Image shown in "Teen Held in Church Fire," *Las Vegas-Review-Journal,* April 14, 1983, 4A.

4. Eleanor "Ellie" Johnson, interview by Fred E. Woods and Martin Andersen, July 13, 2020, Las Vegas, transcript in possession of the author.

5. Eleanor "Ellie" Johnson, telephone conversation with the author, June 29, 2020. A stake is a unit of the Church of Jesus Christ of Latter-day Saints and is generally made up of several thousand church members. It would be similar to a diocese in the Roman Catholic Church. By this time, the Church of Jesus Christ of Latter-day Saints had blossomed to about one hundred thousand members in the Clark County region. For a history of the early beginnings of Latter-day Saints in the Las Vegas region, see Woods, *Gamble in the Desert.*

6. For an excellent treatment on this topic, see Church of Jesus Christ of Latter-day Saints, "Race and the Priesthood," https://www.churchofjesuschrist.org/study /manual/gospel-topics-essays/race-and-the-priesthood?lang=eng, accessed February 17, 2021.

7. Nefretiti Makenta, "A View from West Las Vegas," in *Real Las Vegas,* ed.

Littlejohn, 109–10. Herein, the author further notes, "Though open-housing laws have helped disperse black families to other regions of Clark County, West Las Vegas remained (as of the 1990 census) home to 41 percent African Americans in the city of Las Vegas itself, and 17 percent of those in the county." For an excellent general treatment on the history of Blacks in Las Vegas from 1905 to 2000, see Eugene P. Moehring's chapter "Civil Rights in a Resort City," in *Resort City in the Sun Belt*, 173–202. See also http://www.onlinenevada.org/articles/african-americans-las-vegas, accessed September 10, 2020, and the best online source, http://digital.library.unlv .edu/aae/research, accessed September 10, 2020. This digital source is the home of "Documenting the African American Experience in Las Vegas, a project of the UNLV University libraries," of which Claytee D. White serves as director. For a more extensive discussion of Las Vegas's historical race relations and civil rights, see also Jon L. Smith, *The Westside Slugger: Joe Neal's Lifelong Fight for Social Justice*.

8. Makenta, "View from West Las Vegas," in *Real Las Vegas*, ed. Littlejohn, 113.

9. Makenta, "View from West Las Vegas," in *Real Las Vegas*, ed. Littlejohn, 111–12.

10. Gragg, *Becoming America's Playground*, 109.

11. Gragg, *Becoming America's Playground*, 114.

12. According to Ada Glover, her grandparents, along with the Reverend D. W. Smith, Lily Smith, Hazel Smith, and Judd Smith, established the Evergreen Baptist Church in 1946 on the corner of E Street and Van Buren. At the time, the church had a congregation of about sixty-five members. Glover added that the church later moved to 1100 North Eighth Street. Ada Glover, interview by Fred E. Woods and Martin Andersen, July 14, 2020, Greater Evergreen Missionary Baptist Church, Las Vegas, transcript in possession of the author.

13. "Teen Held in Church Fire," 4A.

14. "Teen Held in Church Fire," 4A.

15. Bernard Hawkins III, interview by Fred E. Woods and Martin Andersen, July 14, 2020, Greater Evergreen Missionary Baptist Church, Las Vegas, transcript in possession of the author.

16. President Charles Johnson also called upon other stake presidents in the Las Vegas region to assist and received additional aid. He spoke of this in a speech delivered on February 9, 1986, which was recorded on VHS. Johnson's wife, Ellie, had a DVD copy of the two-hour festivities the day the new church building was dedicated, a copy of which is in the possession of the author. The author expresses thanks to Ellie Johnson for this kind gesture. Ellie Johnson also confirmed that her husband, Charles, met with his counselors and the leaders of the Greater Evergreen Missionary Baptist Church each Sunday. See Johnson, interview.

17. After serving as a marine in the Korean War, Halverson opened Southwest Air Conditioning, which still operates as a family business. He had a lifetime of church service, which included serving in bishoprics and the Scouting program. He was survived by five children, twenty-five grandchildren, and forty-six great-grandchildren. Gary Halverson obituary, *Las Vegas Review-Journal*, https://obits .reviewjournal.com/obituaries/lvrj/obituary.aspx?n=gary-halverson&pid=190403156 &fhid=12179, accessed July 8, 2020.

18. The local Latter-day Saint newspaper, the *Beehive*, reported that Cornwall had spent three years in the US Air Force and was the father of six children. He

enjoyed singing, and his wife believed he could have been a professional singer. Cornwall was serving as Scoutmaster and had served as Elder's Quorum president before his call to serve as second counselor in the Las Vegas Ward bishopric in 1979. Cited in https://www.familysearch.org/tree/person/memories/KWHS-ZFY, accessed July 8, 2020.

19. Justin Roberts, a teenager who worked for Cornwall and was under his direction as a church youth leader, described his boss and leader as a "hard worker" with a "tender soul." Roberts added, "He was one of those that would always work behind the scenes and do things because it was right to do, and he instilled in us as a young men leader that same work ethic, that same 'do things because it's right, not because you need to get the attention.'" Justin Roberts, interview by Fred E. Woods and Martin Andersen, July 13, 2020, Las Vegas, transcript in possession of the author.

20. Jean Cornwall, interview by Fred E. Woods and Martin Andersen, July 15, 2020, Las Vegas, transcript in possession of the author. Jean Cornwall is the spouse of Douglas Cornwall, who has died. Regarding charitable donations collected from the Saints for the Greater Evergreen Missionary Baptist Church, and their subsequent gratitude for their kindness, Linda Givens stated, "I remember when the LDS church people started raising money for the Evergreen Baptist church.... In sacrament meeting every Sunday, they collected money from us to contribute to the church, and it was every ward in Las Vegas, as far as I remember.... And before they ever opened their church to their congregation, they invited all of the LDS community to come tour their church, and they had a reception for us, and it was quite nice. And they were so appreciative, so, so appreciative of what we had done to help them. And I think it made all of us feel really great that we had had a part in helping to raise money to rebuild their church, which they did." Linda Givens, interview by Fred E. Woods and Martin Andersen, July 14, 2020, Las Vegas, transcript in possession of the author.

21. Frank Bingham, telephone interview by the author, July 1, 2020, transcript in possession of the author.

22. Charlie Zobell, Zoom interview by the author, June 11, 2020, transcript in possession of the author.

23. Johnson, interview.

24. The first Black man to receive the priesthood in Nevada was Robert Lindsey, of Henderson. See Sherman R. Frederick, "Nevada Gets Its First Black Mormon Priest," *Las Vegas Review-Journal*, June 19, 1978, 1.

25. Dwayne Ence, telephone interview by the author, July 1, 2020, transcript in possession of the author.

26. Hawkins, interview.

27. Loretta Whitney, telephone interview by the author, July 7, 2020, transcript in possession of the author.

28. Loretta Whitney, interview by Fred E. Woods and Martin Andersen, July 14, 2020, Greater Evergreen Missionary Baptist Church, Las Vegas, transcript in possession of the author.

29. Pastor Welton T. Smith III, interview by Fred E. Woods and Martin Andersen, June 25, 2020, Las Vegas, transcript in possession of the author.

30. Patricia Morgan, "Fire Delays but Doesn't Stop Building of Baptist Church," *Las Vegas Review-Journal,* February 8, 1986, 15.

31. Johnson, interview.

32. Eleanor Johnson Journal, February 8, 1986, copy of entry sent to author July 1, 2020, transcript in possession of the author. The event actually took place on Sunday, February 9, 1986. Ada Glover recalled that "those that could walk" from the congregation marched, while "the older people didn't march,…they drove their cars." Glover, interview.

33. Whitney, telephone interview, July 7, 2020.

34. Whitney, telephone interview, July 7, 2020.

35. Morgan, "Fire Delays," 15.

36. Morgan, "Fire Delays," 15. The author thanks Stacey Fott, library technician II, Public Services, Special Collections and Archives, University of Nevada, Las Vegas, for her help in finding and sending the articles in the *Las Vegas Review-Journal* that covered the story of the burning of the Baptist church and its completion three years later.

37. Ada Glover remembered, "Everybody was just happy and joyful in the spirit of the Lord." Glover, interview.

38. Eleanor Johnson Journal, February 8, 1986. In this entry, Johnson further recorded that she and her children sat next to Governor Bryan and his wife. At this time, Harry Reid was a member of the House of Representatives (he was elected to the US Senate that fall), and James Seastrand was serving as mayor of North Las Vegas. Reid was a member of the church, as was the late Seastrand. The Baptist church was located close to the boundary between Las Vegas and North Las Vegas; while it is in the city of Las Vegas, some of its members obviously live in North Las Vegas.

39. Dwayne Ence, interview by Fred E. Woods and Martin Andersen, July 6, 2020, Park City, UT, transcript in possession of the author.

40. Johnson, telephone conversation.

41. Roberts, interview.

42. Roberts, interview.

43. Lynn Hughes, interview by Fred E. Woods and Martin Andersen, July 14, 2020, Las Vegas, transcript in possession of the author.

44. Derek Ence, interview.

45. David Ence, telephone conversation with the author, July 2, 2020. David's friend and fellow Scout Lynn Hughes, who participated in the project, remembered it turned out to be a project that was "highly unusual," as "[they] normally didn't do Eagle Scout projects on that large of a scale." Hughes added, "I enjoyed meeting with the individuals from the…Evergreen Baptist Church. They were there working with us. I believe they had a youth ministry there who were assisting.… I do think that has affected my life in…having respect for people of other cultures;…they were all wonderful." Hughes, interview.

46. David Ence, interview by Fred E. Woods and Martin Andersen, July 15, 2020, home of David Ence, Tucson, transcript in possession of the author.

47. Bonnie Ence, telephone interview by the author, July 1, 2020, transcript in possession of the author.

48. Cornwall, interview.

49. Ned Day, "How About a Nuke Dump in Tijuana or Medicine Hat?," *Las Vegas Review-Journal*, June 22, 1986, 25.

50. Lamar Noorda, interview by Fred E. Woods and Martin Andersen, June 22, 2020, Las Vegas, transcript in possession of the author.

51. Lamar Noorda, interview.

52. Elise Noorda, interview by Fred E. Woods and Martin Andersen, June 22, 2020, Las Vegas, transcript in possession of the author.

53. Debra Smith, wife of Pastor Smith, was responsible for gathering the images in the Hall of History. She said, "The LDS family was a part of the retelling and the rebuilding of the Evergreen.… We give glory and honor to God for what he has done." Debra Smith, interview by Fred E. Woods and Martin Andersen, July 14, 2020, Greater Evergreen Missionary Baptist Church, Las Vegas, transcript in possession of the author.

54. Pastor Welton T. Smith III asked the author and Martin Andersen to take a walk with him to see this photograph, which is dear to his heart and his congregation, before we commenced an interview with him on June 25, 2020. There are three men pictured standing in the photo: Johnson, on the left; Whitney, center; and stake president Terry D. Rogers on the right, who also provided assistance along with some members of the Las Vegas West Stake he presided over.

55. Pastor Smith, interview.

56. Deacon Adolph Huddleston, interview by Fred E. Woods and Martin Andersen, June 25, 2020, transcript in possession of the author.

57. Whitney, interview, July 14, 2020.

58. Along with his temple spokesperson assignment, Johnson also later served as a counselor in the Las Vegas Temple presidency. Charles Johnson obituary, *Las Vegas Review-Journal*, https://obits.reviewjournal.com/obituaries/lvrj/obituary.aspx?n=charles-johnson&pid=152672616&fhid=13804, accessed July 8, 2020.

59. The meeting was held December 28, 1984, at the Las Vegas City Hall.

60. Whitney, interview, July 14, 2020.

61. Bonnie Ence, telephone interview.

CHAPTER 7. THE STORY OF THE LAS VEGAS TEMPLE

1. According to S. Mahlon Edwards, this statement was posted on the bulletin board in the Las Vegas Temple men's locker room in May 1997. The author thanks Edwards for sharing this information with him.

2. Donald David Atkin, "He Restoreth My Soul," Psalms 23:3, in "My Life's History," unpublished family manuscript, quotation segment courtesy of S. Mahlon Edwards, whom the author thanks for his assistance. "Ward Teaching Leaders November, 1954," *Church News*, January 15, 1955, 9, indicates that the Las Vegas Stake was among the top twenty-five stakes in their ward teaching visits, with just over 90 percent of the families in this region being taught. A year later, statistics for this same program had reached nearly 94 percent. See "Ward Teaching Leaders, October 1955," *Church News*, December 17, 1955, 9. In 1959, 98 percent of the families were taught from the Las Vegas Fourth Ward. See "Las Vegas Wards Average High Teaching Records," *Church News*, August 29, 1959, 18. Ward teaching was also known as home teaching and visiting teaching, which were church programs for ministering

to men, women, and families up until 2018, when the program was changed to
create greater flexibility and renamed the "ministering" program. See Camille West,
"Ministering to Replace Home and Visiting Teaching," https://www.churchofjesus
christ.org/church/news/ministering-to-replace-home-and-visiting-teaching?lang=eng,
accessed May 9, 2020. Their ward and branch sacrament meetings were also exemplary and were published among others who had an attendance record of 50 percent or better in March 1955. See "Ward and Branch Sacrament Meeting," *Church
News,* May 28, 1955, 9.

    3. "Life and Mission of Robert Orson Gibson," 297–99, unpublished manuscript
in possession of the author. The author thanks Terilyn Taylor for obtaining a copy
of this manuscript for him.

    4. Scott Seastrand, interview by Fred E. Woods and Martin Andersen, February
7, 2020, Seastrand home, Las Vegas, transcript in possession of the author.

    5. Elbert B. Edwards, "The Las Vegas Nevada Temple," 17–18, unpublished and
undated manuscript in possession of the author, who thanks Elbert's son Mahlon
for providing him with a copy of this temple history. Elbert Edwards was the
temple-committee historian at the time he wrote and compiled the information
in this sixty-seven-page document. He passed away on October 7, 1989, just over
two months before the temple was dedicated, on December 16, 1989. S. Mahlon
Edwards, email to the author, February 23, 2021. This manuscript is similar and
often identical to "A Brief History of Southern Nevada and of the Las Vegas
Temple Committee," unpublished document, comp. Ashley J. Hall. The author
thanks Hall for providing him with a copy of this document. The author chose to
primarily use the Elbert B. Edwards manuscript inasmuch as he was designated
as the official temple-committee historian. In his temple history (19), Edwards
mentions the inconvenience of traveling from the Las Vegas region to the nearest temple in St. George, which required a two-hour drive each way. Further,
there was greater concern for temple marriages, as families and friends were often
required to leave Vegas at 3:00 A.M. for the temple ceremony. They often arrived
home weary after four hours of travel and then needed to make "feverish preparations" for open houses and receptions and, for the couples, honeymoon travel.
Local Las Vegas Saint Mark Dixon stated, "We wanted a temple.... You either got
in the car and drove to Saint George, or usually every week there would be buses
that went from Las Vegas from the various building sites at three o'clock in the
morning to Saint George. They would do two [temple] sessions and be home
by three o'clock in the afternoon." Mark Dixon, interview by Fred E. Woods and
Martin Andersen, February 8, 2020, North Las Vegas, transcript in possession of
the author.

    6. Edwards, "Las Vegas Nevada Temple," 19. At age sixty-three, Gibson was
called to be a regional representative in 1973 and served for seven years. He died on
August 13, 1988, from cancer. See "First Presidency Calls 14 Regional Representatives," *Church News,* June 23, 1973, 4–5; "Death," *Church News,* August 20, 1988, 13. The
author expresses appreciation to Church History Library archivist Jeff Thompson
for finding this ecclesiastical and biographical information.

    7. James K. Seastrand oral history interview, August 16, September 12, 1983;
June 4, October 15, 1984, January 11, 1985, interview by Laurence A. Owen, Oral

History Program of the North Las Vegas Nevada Stake, MS 2735 519, Church History Library, the Church of Jesus Christ of Latter-day Saints, Salt Lake City.

8. Seastrand oral history interview, 20. Elder John H. Groberg, emeritus general authority, recalled that he thought he told the local Vegas church leaders that he "had been in discussion with the Brethren [Salt Lake general church leaders] and that Las Vegas was in the mix, on the horizon." However, he did not remember stating that he had seen a list of the first one hundred temples, though he added, he may have done so. John H. Groberg, telephone conversation with the author, late April 2020.

9. Seastrand oral history interview.

10. Seastrand oral history interview.

11. Less than a decade later, Las Vegas could claim a church general authority of its own when local businessman David E. Sorenson was called to be a member of the Second Quorum of the Seventy in 1992, at the age of fifty-nine. A seasoned church leader who was serving as the president of the Las Vegas Stake at the time of his appointment, Sorenson had been prepared for general leadership. See "Las Vegan Named to Quorum of Seventy," *Las Vegas Review-Journal,* June 20, 1992, 16. Two years later, local Vegas attorney Dennis E. Simmons was also appointed a General Authority Seventy. See John Przybys, "Las Vegas Lawyer Named to High Mormon Post," *Las Vegas Review-Journal,* April 30, 1996, 61.

12. The president of the Central Stake to whom Earl was a counselor was Frank Dixon. Dixon and his wife, Nancy Stapley, moved to Las Vegas shortly after Dixon graduated from Idaho State University. He was given an offer to stay in Idaho and teach school, but the salary in Las Vegas was a third higher, so they moved to southern Nevada. During the time Seastrand was involved in various church meetings with leaders in the region, Dixon and Earl had similar experiences. On several occasions while driving visiting general authorities to the airport following a stake conference, they had conversations about the temple. On one visit, Elder Bruce R. McConkie told them, "You write the brethren, tell them what you think you can do and what you need." He added, "I have seen the list of the first one hundred temples, and Las Vegas is on it." Mark Dixon, interview.

13. Seastrand oral history interview.

14. Seastrand oral history interview.

15. "LDS Leader Announces Plan to Build LV Temple," *Las Vegas Review-Journal,* April 8, 1984, 19.

16. "Churches Are Strong and Growing," *Las Vegas Review-Journal,* February 16, 1984, 112, notes that these statistics came from church spokesman Charles Johnson, who became a key member of the temple committee just a few months later.

17. Elaine Kennedy, interview by Fred E. Woods and Martin Andersen, June 24, 2020, Las Vegas, transcript in possession of the author.

18. Charlie Zobell, Zoom interview by the author, June 11, 2020, transcript in possession of the author.

19. Robin Dixon, interview by Fred E. Woods and Martin Andersen, February 8, 2020, Dixon home, North Las Vegas, transcript in possession of the author.

20. "LDS Leader Announces Plan," 19.

21. Tom Thomas, interview by Fred E. Woods and Martin Andersen, February 6, 2020, Las Vegas, transcript in possession of the author.

22. First Presidency (Spencer W. Kimball, Marion D. Romney, and Gordon B. Hinckley) to Elder James K. Seastrand, May 21, 1984, copy of letter in possession of the author. The author thanks Judie Brailsford-Marcucci for making him aware of this letter she also has a copy of.

23. Edwards, "Las Vegas Nevada Temple," 27. The following year, three days before the groundbreaking, "Behind It All," *Beehive Sentinel,* November 27, 1985, 11, published the names of the executive temple-committee members and their responsibilities: Elder James K. Seastrand, chairman of the temple committee; President Grant Bowler, vice chairman of the temple committee and groundbreaking-assembly chairman; Reed Whipple, finance chairman; Lloyd C. Doull, executive secretary to Elder Harvey Dahl, regional representative for southern Nevada; Boyd C. Bulloch, communications and coordination director; Helene Amos, administrative aide; Kent W. Davis, business manager; Lloyd M. Taggart, media liaison; and Elder B. Edwards, temple historian.

24. Judie Brailsford-Marcucci, interview by the author, February 22, 2021, Las Vegas, transcript in possession of the author.

25. Edwards, "Las Vegas Nevada Temple," 27–28.

26. James K. Seastrand to unknown, miscellaneous document dated January 28, 1985. Original in possession of his son Scott Seastrand.

27. At the time of Seastrand's death in November 1997, the *Las Vegas Sun* printed an article headlined "Former NLV Mayor Seastrand Dies" and acknowledged, "The community has lost a soft-spoken man of vision who never deviated from what he thought was the right thing to do." https://lasvegassun.com/news/1997/nov/03/former-nlv-mayor-seastrand-dies/, accessed March 26, 2020.

28. Seastrand, interview.

29. Zobell, Zoom interview.

30. Boyd Bulloch, interview by Fred E. Woods and Martin Andersen, February 6, 2020, Las Vegas, typescript in possession of the author.

31. Report from Gwen Ferrell to James K. Seastrand, miscellaneous document in possession of Scott Seastrand.

32. Report from Maxine Taylor to James K. Seastrand, miscellaneous document in possession of Scott Seastrand.

33. Report from C. [Charles] L. Brailsford to James K. Seastrand, January 23, 1985, miscellaneous document in possession of Scott Seastrand. For examples of newspaper opposition against the temple, see "No Different," *Las Vegas Review-Journal,* December 4, 1984; Dorothy Jones and Paul Jones, "The Temple on the Mount," *Las Vegas Sun,* December 6, 1984.

34. Ed Decker has traveled extensively to try to curtail the growth of the church in the late twentieth century since leaving the church. He coauthored a book with Dave Hunt as a companion to his 1982 film *The God Makers,* titled *The God Makers: A Shocking Expose of What the Mormon Church REALLY Believes* (1984). An academic rebuttal to this work was addressed by scholar Gilbert W. Scharffs, in his book *The Truth About "The God Makers"* (1986), which lists and addresses more than

six hundred errors or falsehoods. See https://www.fairlatterdaysaints.org/archive
/publications/the-truth-about-the-god-makers, accessed August 14, 2021.

35. In addition, Brailsford-Marcucci recalled that before the temple was dedicated, President Hinckley spoke to a large audience of Latter-day Saints at the
Thomas & Mack Convention Center. There on the steps she witnessed Ed Decker
passing out anti-Mormon literature, and suddenly Decker's son, who was serving
a full-time mission for the church in the Vegas region, appeared. After greeting his
father, he said, "We're on opposite sides." She found it fascinating "to see the bright-
faced beautiful young man who was there also passing out Church pamphlets, and
yet they had a cordial meeting." Brailsford-Marcucci, interview.

36. Cheryl Hymer, "A Bad Pitch," *Las Vegas Review-Journal,* May 28, 1984, 16.

37. Charles William Johnson letter, January 24, 1985, miscellaneous papers of
James K. Seastrand, in possession of his son Scott Seastrand.

38. Charles William Johnson letter, January 24, 1985.

39. See, for example, the ads listed in these real-estate categories: "402-Acreage"
under the caption "Near New Proposed Mormon Temple," *Las Vegas Review-Journal,*
May 13, 1984, 91; and "468—Real Estate Exchanged," noting, "Sunrise Mountain,
unobstructed view…2 blocks from Mormon temples," *Las Vegas Review-Journal,*
May 4, 1984, 100. Five years later, when the temple was finally completed and dedicated, the ads continued as evidenced in the caption "Mormon Temple, ½ acre
custom home lots near Temple on Sunrise Mtn.," under the category in the real-
estate section "416 Lots," *Las Vegas Review-Journal,* March 26, 1989, 70.

40. "Dedicatory Prayer," https://www.churchofjesuschrist.org/temples/details/las
-vegas-nevada-temple/prayer/1989-12-16?lang=eng, accessed March 26, 2020.

41. George G. Tate, "The Family and Personal History of George Gerald Tate,"
unpublished, December 2008, rev. December 2009 for third printing, 161.

42. Tate, "Family and Personal History," 161.

43. Tate, "Family and Personal History," 161. Tate later explained to the author that
Evan Nelson was an architect with the division of temples and special projects. He
also indicated that about the same time he received the phone call, church leaders
had been examining various temple plans then under review and realized that some
of them did not function as well as they wanted and needed to be enlarged. This
situation, coupled with Clark County zoning conditions, allowed the Las Vegas
Temple to be larger than the standard plan that was first discussed. George Tate,
telephone conversation with the author, May 4, 2020.

44. Tate, "Family and Personal History," 161.

45. Tate, "Family and Personal History," 162.

46. George Tate, interview by Fred E. Woods and Martin Andersen, February 8,
2020, Tate home, St. George, UT, transcript in possession of the author. The author
also thanks Tate for reviewing a draft of this chapter on the Las Vegas Temple.

47. Tate, "Family and Personal History," 162.

48. Hall was remembered for getting things done in his role as Las Vegas city
manager. See Larry Werner, "City Manager Gets Good Marks on Recent Actions,"
Las Vegas Review-Journal, April 8, 1984, 17. Hall served as the city manager from 1983
to 1991, which encompassed the years from the announcement of the Las Vegas

Temple to its dedication. Hall also served as the director of the Southern Nevada Latter-day Saint Public Affairs Council from 1988 to 2010. Ashley Hall, email to the author, February 10, 2021. In addition, Hall served for thirty-five years in the Nevada Army National Guard and earned the rank of brigadier general. Upon retirement in 2000, he became an ambassador for the Guard. See Marian Green, "Retired Guard General Steps Back into Service as Reserve Ambassador," *Las Vegas Review-Journal,* June 27, 2012, 59.

49. Ashley Hall, interview by Fred E. Woods and Martin Andersen, February 20, 2020, Las Vegas, transcript in possession of the author.

50. Tate, "Family and Personal History," 162. Jim Seastrand mentioned that it was seven voting members of the county commission, two of whom were Latter-day Saints, and two additional church members who had been elected in November 1984. Thus, a majority would have occurred with a four-to-three vote. Seastrand explained, "The opposition planned to file suit to stop the temple if it were approved…on religious entanglement grounds." See James K. Seastrand to unknown, dated January 28, 1985.

51. In a private interview decades later, Brailsford-Marcucci remembered that her friend had overheard the conversation in a local bar. See Brailsford-Marcucci, interview. In a later interview, Brailsford-Marcucci pointed out the importance of staying connected with every strata of society and observed that sometimes Latter-day Saints in other areas stay too insulated within their own social circles; she felt that being connected with the community at large was important for all parties concerned. See Judie Brailsford-Marcucci and Heidi Gresham Wixom, interview by the author, February 22, 2021, transcript in possession of the author.

52. Report by "Judie Brailsford Member of Las Vegas Committee Secretary to Public Communications Committee," to James K. Seastrand, etc., miscellaneous document in possession of Scott Seastrand. Brailsford-Marcucci mentioned in her interview that Kent Oram, a political adviser to the Clark County Commission, was helpful in making arrangements to solve this problem. See Brailsford-Marcucci, interview.

53. S. Mahlon Edwards, interview by the author, January 19, 2020, Edwards home, Washington, UT, transcript in possession of the author.

54. Jody Walker, interview by the author, February 22, 2021, transcript in possession of the author.

55. Dale Pugh, "Mormon Temple Site OK'd," *Las Vegas Review-Journal,* December 29, 1984, 1, 4A.

56. Wendell Waite, interview by the author, January 19, 2020, St. George, UT, transcript in possession of the author.

57. Edwards, interview. At the time that the decision whether to build a temple in Las Vegas was being made, Manny Cortez (1939–2006) was a county commissioner as well as the chairman of the Board of Directors of the Las Vegas Convention and Visitors Authority (1983–90). Pugh, "Mormon Temple Site OK'd," 1.

58. Ward, *Saints in Babylon,* 50.

59. Report from Gwen Ferrell to James K. Seastrand, miscellaneous document in possession of Scott Seastrand.

60. "The Right Decision on Mormon Temple," *Las Vegas Review-Journal,* December 31, 1984, 17.

61. Tate, interview.

62. Tate, interview.

63. Bruce Woodbury, interview by Fred E. Woods and Martin Andersen, February 7, 2020, Boulder City, transcript in possession of the author.

64. Seastrand, interview.

65. "Right Decision," 6B.

66. Tate, interview.

67. James K. Seastrand miscellaneous document titled "Brother Reed Whipple." It appears that Seastrand was collecting various documents from various people who were involved with the temple committees to create a history based on the fact that other manuscripts that immediately follow bear the names of people who were involved with the temple and their personal experiences related to the temple. The original document is in the possession of Scott Seastrand, son of James K. Seastrand.

68. Woodbury, interview.

69. Shari Buck, telephone interview by the author, February 13, 2020, transcript in possession of the author.

70. Ed Smith, interview by Fred E. Woods and Martin Andersen, February 8, 2020, Las Vegas, transcript in possession of the author.

71. Molly New, "'It Was an Amazing, Inspirational Thing,'" *Beehive Sentinel,* November 25, 1985, 9.

72. "Cubs Turn Fun into Temple $$," *Beehive Sentinel,* December 11, 1985, 11.

73. "How LDS Are Raising Funds for the Temple," *Beehive Sentinel,* November 27, 1985, 12.

74. Edwards, interview. About one year before the temple dedication, the Vegas Saints in the metro area had already raised nearly $10 million. This is evidenced by a letter sent to the temple committee by Berkeley Bunker, who was the chairman of the temple finance committee and a member of the general temple committee. See Berkeley L. Bunker to temple committee, January 24, 1989, copy in possession of the author, courtesy of Judie Brailsford-Marcucci.

75. Edwards, "Las Vegas Nevada Temple," 46–48. Herein, Edwards mentioned that James Seastrand made a list of the people who would constitute the "official groundbreaking party." Along with the visiting general authorities, Edwards noted the others invited to attend were "the two local regional representatives, 14 local stake presidents, the groundbreaking chairman, the seven Clark County Commissioners, Governor Bryan, the spouses of the above, and those persons assigned special duties."

76. Molly New, "Is It Secret? What Goes On in LDS Temples," *Beehive Sentinel,* November 27, 1985, 16.

77. Ray Fries, "Another Emblem of Las Vegas," *Beehive Sentinel,* November 27, 1985, 8.

78. Ned Day, "Las Vegans Should Welcome Mormon Temple," *Las Vegas Review-Journal,* October 16, 1985, 20.

79. "Bryan, Richard H.," https://bioguideretro.congress.gov/Home/MemberDetails?memIndex=B000993, accessed August 16, 2021.

80. Senator Richard Bryan, interview by Fred E. Woods and Martin Andersen, June 23, 2020, Las Vegas, typescript in possession of the author. Bryan also attended the temple open house when it was completed.

81. "Ground Broken for LV Temple," *Las Vegas Review-Journal,* December 1, 1985, 1. See also "Groundbreaking Ceremonies Slated for Mormon Temple," *Las Vegas Review-Journal,* November 29, 1985, 23, wherein church spokesman Don Christensen, speaking of the coming Las Vegas Temple, said, "Interest level among church members and others is very high."

82. Robert C. Maxson, "More than a Top Mormon," *Las Vegas Sun,* October 11, 1987, 182. Maxson's editorial was generated by a previous excellent article about Christensen, by Joan Burkhart in the *Nevadan Today,* "Don Christensen Speaks for the Vegas Saints," *Las Vegas Sun,* September 20, 1987, 177–78, previously cited.

83. Crismon S. Lewis, "The Prayer You Missed," *Beehive Sentinel,* December 11, 1985, 2.

84. "Ground Broken for Temple in Las Vegas," *Ensign,* February 1986, 75. See also Charlie Zobell, "Las Vegas Temple Benefits Praised," *Las Vegas Review-Journal,* December 1, 1985, 1.

85. "Ground Broken," 75.

86. Olivia Hurst, "Largest Temple Groundbreaking Ever," *Beehive Sentinel,* December 11, 1985, 12.

87. Charlie Zobell, "Las Vegas Temple," 3.

88. Seastrand oral history interview.

89. "Why Are LDS So Happy to Have a Temple Here?," *Beehive Sentinel,* December 11, 1985, 16–17.

90. "Groundbreaking Allows LDS to 'Drive' Home a Message on Families," *Beehive Sentinel,* December 11, 1985, 13.

91. Edwards, "Las Vegas Nevada Temple," 49.

92. Edwards, "Las Vegas Nevada Temple," 51.

93. "James Kent Seastrand Remembrances," 7, courtesy of Scott Seastrand, whom the author thanks for providing him with a copy of this document as well as many others. Seastrand, born in 1929, died eight years after the Las Vegas Temple dedication. His wife, Rosel, wrote on the final page of his "Remembrances," 8, that Jim passed on November 2, 1997, as he was "delivering a talk on the subject of the Millennium to an Inter-faith group of about six religions." Seastrand was not only the man to watch over the building of the Las Vegas Temple, but his influence reached beyond church boundaries. Lisa Kim Bach, "Seastrand's Life Celebrated," *Las Vegas Sun,* November 8, 1997, 1, noted, "The hundreds of people who came to bury Seastrand…celebrated his life with tears and fond smiles, taking comfort in his enduring legacy of community and religious service." Not long thereafter, an organization named in his behalf was also established, titled the James Seastrand Helping Hands of North Las Vegas. This volunteer program "helps to improve the quality of life for frail elderly and people with disabling disorders. It also provides services to help them maintain their independence." In 2000, Helping Hands received the "Outstanding Community Service" award for a nonprofit organization. See "James Seastrand Helping Hands of North Las Vegas," *Las Vegas Sun,* November 12, 2000, 141.

94. Newspaper clipping from "Big Asset," *Las Vegas Sun,* October 20, 1984, in James K. Seastrand collection in possession of his son Scott Seastrand. The good publicity about the Saints was supported by an Irish Catholic named Mike O'Callaghan, former governor of Nevada and executive editor of the *Sun.* According to Boyd Bulloch, about this same time, Bulloch visited the *Sun* newspaper office at O'Callaghan's request. Bulloch recalled, "[O'Callaghan] took me down the hall, and he said to one of his staff members, 'Now you write articles about our Las Vegas Temple,' and he…says, 'You make sure there's absolutely nothing negative about the Las Vegas Temple.'" Boyd Bulloch, interview. Even after the death of O'Callaghan in 2004, the *Sun* continued to print positive material about the temple. See, for example, https://www.ldsliving.com/LDS-Temple-Featured-on-the-Cover-of-the-Las-Vegas-Sun/s/81828.

95. Cristi Bulloch, interview by Fred E. Woods and Martin Andersen, March 5, 2020, Las Vegas, transcript in possession of the author.

96. Jana Dixon, interview by Fred E. Woods and Martin Andersen, March 4, 2020, Las Vegas, transcript in possession of the author.

97. Smith, interview. The meticulous preparation for the open-house tours is illustrated by maps, charts, and lists that included supervision of various areas such as parking, lost and found, training, first aid, rest areas, shoe coverings, special needs, language coordinators, media, community relations, exhibits, wheelchairs, daily hosting, bus drivers, security, VIP tours, and more. This is augmented by a sixteen-page instructional manual for leaders titled "Open House and Dedication, 1989." Letters were also sent to professionals, inviting them to the open house dressed in appropriate attire. Copies of these documents are in the possession of the author, courtesy of temple-committee member Judie Brailsford-Marcucci.

98. "Temple Open House," *Las Vegas Sun,* November 17, 1989, 36.

99. "Nearly 300,000 Tour New Temple," *Church News,* December 16, 1989, 3.

100. Buck, interview. The meticulous preparations for these tours are illustrated by a seven-page, single-spaced suggested tour guide that was prepared for guides who took the blind on tours. "Tour for Blind," document in possession of the author, courtesy of Judie Brailsford-Marcucci.

101. Walker, interview.

102. Hall, interview. A baptismal font is found in every Latter-day Saint temple to perform proxy work for the ancestors of church members who have died. The practice of baptisms for the dead is referred to in this biblical passage: "Else what shall they do which are baptized for the dead, if the dead rise not at all? Why are they then baptized for the dead?" (1 Cor. 15:29).

103. Hall, interview.

104. Bruce W. Hansen, interview by Fred E. Woods and Martin Andersen, February 8, 2020, UNLV Institute of Religion, Las Vegas, transcript in possession of the author.

105. Thomas, interview.

106. Robert "Hal" Parker to "Open House Committee Member," undated, in James K. Seastrand miscellaneous collection, in possession of his son Scott Seastrand.

107. All of the quotations and content regarding comments expressed by visitors after the temple open-house tour were taken from a seventeen-page manuscript titled "Church of Jesus Christ of Latter-day Saints Las Vegas, Nevada, Temple Open House, November 15–December 9, 1989." On the cover page is written "The following pages contain a summary of the comment cards during the Open House. They represent a random sampling of the common responses on the comment cards." Papers of James K. Seastrand, courtesy of Scott Seastrand. The author counted 210 samples, of which only a few examples are referred to here.

108. Ranae Kanet, "Temple Generates Missionary Effort," *Latter-day Family Journal,* December 1989, 16. Of the nearly three hundred thousand who toured the temple, about one-third of them (ninety-nine thousand) also visited the missionary pavilion following their tour. The temple open house resulted in the missionaries tripling their teaching appointments. "Las Vegas Nevada Temple," 3D Temple Models, http://3dtemples.photogent.com/3d-lds-temples/las-vegas-nevada-temple/, accessed February 24, 2021.

109. "A Look Back at the Year's News," *Las Vegas Review-Journal,* December 31, 1989, 15.

110. Rothman, *Neon Metropolis,* 3.

111. Ward, *Saints in Babylon,* 49.

112. Cristi Bulloch, interview.

113. John Ryan, "Las Vegas Nevada Temple Adds Graceful Beauty to Area," *Las Vegas Sun,* December 11, 1989, 2B.

114. Lisa DeRiso, interview by the author, February 12, 2021, transcript in possession of the author.

115. Brailsford-Marcucci, interview.

116. David Finnigan, "Las Vegas Businessman Named Temple President," *Las Vegas Sun,* May 13, 1989, 17. Herein, it is noted that Tanner's wife, Bette, would assist him as temple matron.

117. Items deposited in the cornerstone included the Latter-day Saint scriptures, hymn book, various local church histories, temple-committee minutes, *Church News* articles about the temple development, the temple history by Elbert B. Edwards, images of the Mormon Fort and Las Vegas Temple committee and the temple, and so on. "Las Vegas Nevada Temple Cornerstone Items," James K. Seastrand private collection, courtesy of his son Scott Seastrand. Frank Dixon, president of the Central Stake, was responsible for gathering the items deposited in the cornerstone. In January 1990, just weeks after the temple dedication, Grant Bowler, assistant temple-committee chairman, wrote this note of thanks to Dixon for his contribution: "President Dixon, you played a most important role in gathering, selecting, and preparing important and sacred memorabilia to be placed in the Cornerstone Vault of the Lord's House. This was a special assignment for a Special Man, you. When the names are placed on the scroll above,…your name will be among the *best.*" Grant M. Bowler to Frank Dixon, January 1990, courtesy of Mark Dixon, copy in possession of the author.

118. John L. Hart, "Las Vegas Temple, 'a Crowning Jewel,'" *Church News,* December 23, 1989, 3.

119. Hart, "Las Vegas Temple," 3.

120. "Lord's Work Moved Forward During '80s," *Church News*, December 30, 1989, 12.

121. "Dedicatory Prayer," Las Vegas Nevada Temple, December 16, 1989, Church of Jesus Christ of Latter-day Saints, https://www.churchofjesuschrist.org/temples/details/las-vegas-nevada-temple/prayer/1989-12-16?lang=eng, accessed March 26, 2020. See Appendix D for the entire dedicatory prayer.

122. "Las Vegas Plaque Honors Pioneers," *Church News*, June 28, 1997, 5. See also Lisa Kim Bach, "The Pioneer Spirit: 150 Years of Mormon History," *Las Vegas Review-Journal*, June 22, 1997, 1A.

123. "Southern Nevada Home to over 48 Different Religious Faiths," *Las Vegas Sun*, July 18, 1991, 119.

124. "LV Architectural Firms Honored," *Las Vegas Sun*, December 9, 1990, 185, notes that the architectural firm Tate & Snyder was presented merit awards for the design of the temple by the Las Vegas chapter of the American Institute of Architects.

125. Tate, "Family and Personal History," 164. Since Tate initially wrote this manuscript in 2008, he is no longer working as a volunteer in the Las Vegas Temple but is retired and living in St. George, UT, which also has a temple.

126. Robin Dixon, interview.

127. Buck, telephone interview. Buck served on the North Las Vegas City Council from 1999 to 2009 and as mayor of North Las Vegas from 2009 to 2013.

128. Hall, interview.

129. Cristi Bulloch, interview.

130. Church of Jesus Christ of Latter-day Saints, "Facts and Statistics," https://newsroom.churchofjesuschrist.org/facts-and-statistics/state/nevada, accessed May 1, 2020.

131. Oscar Goodman, Zoom interview by the author, February 8, 2021, transcript in possession of the author.

132. Brian Greenspun, Zoom interview by the author, February 11, 2021, transcript in possession of the author.

133. Jon Ralston, interview by Fred E. Woods and Martin Andersen, June 22, 2020, Las Vegas, transcript in possession of the author.

134. John L. Smith, Zoom interview by the author, May 19, 2020, Springville, UT, transcript in possession of the author.

135. Bryan, interview.

136. Jim Gibson, Zoom interview by the author, February 10, 2021, transcript in possession of the author.

Bibliography

Arrington, Leonard J. "The Harvest of '49." In *Great Basin Kingdom: An Economic History of the Latter-day Saints, 1830–1900*, 64–93. Lincoln: University of Nebraska Press, 1958.

———. *The Mormons in Nevada.* Las Vegas: Las Vegas Sun, 1979.

Barlett, Donald L., and James B. Steele. *Howard Hughes: His Life & Madness.* New York and London: W. W. Norton, 1979.

Bean, George Washington. *The Journal of George Washington Bean, Las Vegas Springs, New Mexico Territory, 1856–1857.* Edited by Harry C. Dees. Reno: Nevada Historical Quarterly, 1972.

Black, Susan Easton, comp. *Membership of the Church of Jesus Christ of Latter-day Saints, 1830–1848.* 50 vols. Provo: Religious Studies Center, Brigham Young University, 1984–88.

Bowler, Lynn G. *Zion on the Muddy: The Latter-day Saints Settle the Muddy, and Organize Nevada's Oldest Stake.* 2nd ed. Logandale, NV: Logandale Stake, 2004.

Brooks, Juanita. "The Mormons in Carson County, Utah Territory." *Nevada Historical Society Quarterly* 8, no. 1 (1965): 3–23.

Carter, Kate B. "The Las Vegas Fort." *Our Pioneer Heritage* 18 (1975): 97–136. Salt Lake City: International Society Daughters of the Utah Pioneers, 1994.

Davis, Mark R. "Saints in Sin City: Religion and Community Building in Twentieth Century Las Vegas." Master's thesis, Brigham Young University, 2010.

Dunbar, Andrew J., and Dennis McBride. *Building Hoover Dam: An Oral History of the Great Depression.* New York: Twayne, 1993.

Edwards, Elbert. "Early Mormon Settlements in Southern Nevada." *Nevada Historical Society Quarterly* 8, no. 1 (1965): 25–43.

———. *200 Years in Nevada: A Story of People Who Opened, Explored and Developed the Land.* Bicentennial History. Salt Lake City: Publishers Press, 1978.

Esshom, Frank. *Pioneers and Prominent Men of Utah.* Salt Lake City: Utah Pioneers, 1913.

Findlay, John M. *People of Chance: Gambling in American Society from Jamestown to Las Vegas.* New York: Oxford University Press, 1986.

Fleek, Sherman L. *History May Be Searched in Vain: A Military History of the Mormon Battalion.* Spokane, WA: Arthur H. Clark, 2006.

Foster, Jonathan. *Stigma Cities: The Reputation and History of Birmingham, San Francisco, and Las Vegas.* Norman: University of Oklahoma Press, 2018.

Fremont, John Charles. *Narratives of Exploration and Adventure.* New York: Longmans, Green, 1956.

Goldstein, Warren. *Playing for Keeps: A History of Early Baseball.* New York: Oxford University Press, 1960.

Gottlieb, Bob, and Peter Wiley. "Don't Touch the Dice: The Las Vegas/Utah Connection." *Utah Holiday,* September 1980.

Gragg, Larry. *Becoming America's Playground: Las Vegas in the 1950s.* Norman: University of Oklahoma Press, 2019.

———. *Bright Light City: Las Vegas in Popular Culture.* Lawrence: University Press of Kansas, 2013.

Green, Michael. "The Boundaries of Being a Nevadan: National Reputation and Exceptionalism." *Nevada Historical Society Quarterly* 60 (2017): 137–47.

———. *Nevada: A History of the Silver State.* Reno: University of Nevada Press, 2015.

Horne, Flora Diana Bean, comp. *Autobiography of George W. Bean: A Utah Pioneer of 1847, and His Family Records.* Salt Lake City: Utah Printing, 1945.

Hulse, James W. "W. A. Clark and the Las Vegas Connection." *Montana: The Magazine of Western History* 37, no. 1 (1987): 48–55.

Hunter, Milton R. *Brigham Young the Colonizer.* Salt Lake City: Deseret News Press, 1940.

———. "The Mormon Corridor." *Pacific Historical Review* 8, no. 2 (1939): 179–200.

Jenson, Andrew, comp. "History of the Las Vegas Mission." *Nevada State Historical Society Papers* 5 (1925–26): 119–284.

———. "Las Vegas Ward." In *Encyclopedic History of the Church of Jesus Christ of Latter-day Saints.* Salt Lake City: Deseret News, 1941.

———. *Latter-day Saint Biographical Encyclopedia.* Vol. 4. Salt Lake City: Publishers Press, 1971.

———. "Moapa Stake of Zion." In *Encyclopedic History of the Church of Jesus Christ of Latter-day Saints.* Salt Lake City: Deseret News, 1941.

Jones, Rebecca M. "Extracts from the Life Sketch of Nathaniel V. Jones." *Utah Historical Quarterly* 4, no. 1 (1931): 1–23.

Kenderdine, T. S. *A California Tramp and Later Footprints; or, Life on the Plains in the Golden State Thirty Years Ago, with Miscellaneous Sketches in Prose and Verse.* Newton, PA: n.p., 1888.

Kimball, Monique E. "A Matter of Faith: A Study of the Muddy Mission." *Nevada Historical Society Quarterly* 30, no. 4 (1987): 291–303.

Kowalewski, Jane Percy. "Strange Bedfellows: Mormons and Miners in Southern Nevada." Master's thesis, University of Nevada, Las Vegas, 1984.

Kraft, James P. *Vegas at Odds: Labor Conflict in a Leisure Economy, 1960–1985.* Baltimore: Johns Hopkins University Press, 2010.

Land, Barbara, and Myrick Land. *A Short History of Las Vegas.* Reno: University of Nevada Press, 1999.

Law, Wesley R. "Mormon Indian Mission, 1855." Master's thesis, 1959, Brigham Young University.

Leavitt, Francis H. "The Influence of Mormon People in the Settlement of Clark County." Master's thesis, University of Nevada, 1934.

Leibovich, Lori. "House of the Holy." In *The Real Life Vegas: Life Beyond the Strip,* edited by David Littlejohn, 167–80. New York: Oxford University Press, 1999.

Littlejohn, David, ed. *The Real Las Vegas: Life Beyond the Strip.* New York: Oxford University Press, 1999.

Lyman, Amasa, and Charles C. Rich. "Letter from Elders A. Lyman and C. C. Rich." *Latter-day Saints' Millennial Star* 14, no. 5 (1852): 75–76.

Lyman, Edward Leo. *The Overland Journey from Utah to California: Wagon Travel from the City of the Saints to the City of Angels.* Reno: University of Nevada Press, 2004.

———. *San Bernardino: The Rise and Fall of a California Community.* Salt Lake City: Signature Books, 1996.

Moehring, Eugene. *Resort City in the Sun Belt, 1930–2000.* 2nd ed. Reno: University of Nevada Press, 2000.

———. *Town Making on the Southern Nevada Frontier: Las Vegas, 1905–1925.* Reno: University of Nevada Press, 1989.

———. "Town Making on the Southern Nevada Frontier: Las Vegas, 1905–1925." In *History and Humanities: Essays in Honor of Wilbur Shepperson,* edited by Francis X. Hartigan. Reno: University of Nevada Press, 1989.

Moehring, Eugene P., and Michael S. Green. *Las Vegas: A Centennial History.* Reno: University of Nevada Press, 2005.

Newton, Marjorie. *Southern Cross Saints: The Mormons in Australia.* Laie, HI: Institute of Polynesian Studies, 1991.

Paher, Stanley W. *Las Vegas as It Began—as It Grew.* Las Vegas: Nevada Publications, 1971.

———. *Nevada: An Annotated Bibliography.* Las Vegas: Nevada Publications, 1980.

Reeder, Ray M. "The Mormon Trail: A History of the Salt Lake to Los Angeles Route to 1869." PhD diss., Brigham Young University, 1966.

Roske, Ralph J. *Las Vegas: A Desert Paradise.* Tulsa: Continental Heritage Press, 1986.

Rothman, Hal. *Neon Metropolis: How Las Vegas Started the Twenty-First Century.* Lawrence: University Press of Kansas, 2002.

Rothman, Hal, and Mike Davis, eds. *The Grit Beneath the Glitter: Tales from the Real Las Vegas.* Berkeley: University of California Press, 2002.

Rowberry, David R. "Nevada." In *Encyclopedia of Latter-day Saint History.* Salt Lake City: Deseret Book, 2000.

Rowley, Rex J. *Everyday Las Vegas: Local Life in a Tourist Town.* Reno: University of Nevada Press, 2013.

———. "Faith Islands in Hedonopolis: Ambivalent Adaptation in Las Vegas." In *The Changing World Religion Map: Sacred Places, Identities, Practices and Politics,* edited by Stanley D. Brunn, 4:2265–84. Dordrecht: Springer, 2015.

———. "Religion in Sin City." In *Everyday Las Vegas: Local Life in a Tourist Town,* 188–208. Reno: University of Nevada Press, 2013.

Schoenwetter, James, and John W. Hohmann. "Land Use Reconstruction at the Founding Settlement of Las Vegas, Nevada." *Historical Archaeology* 31, no. 4 (1997): 41–58.

Schumacher, Geoff. *Howard Hughes: Power, Paranoia, and Palace Intrigue.* Rev. ed. Reno: University of Nevada Press, 2020.

Sessions, Gene A., and Sterling D. Sessions. *Utah International: A Biography of Business.* Commemorative ed. Ogden: Weber State University and the Stewart Library, 2002.

Seymour, Harold. *Baseball: The Early Years.* New York: Oxford University Press, 1960.

Sheehan, Jack. *Quiet Kingmaker of Las Vegas: E. Parry Thomas.* Las Vegas: Stephens Press, 2009.

Sheridan, John Harris. *Howard Hughes, the Las Vegas Years: The Women, the Mormons, the Mafia.* Bloomington, IN: AuthorHouse, 2011.

Simich, Jerry L., and Thomas L. Wright, eds. *More Peoples of Las Vegas: One City, Many Faces.* Reno: University of Nevada Press, 2010.

———, eds. *The Peoples of Las Vegas: One City, Many Faces.* Reno: University of Nevada Press, 2005.

Smith, Jon L. *The Westside Slugger: Joe Neal's Lifelong Fight for Social Justice.* Reno: University of Nevada Press, 2019.

Stevens, Joseph E. *Hoover Dam: An American Adventure.* Norman: University of Oklahoma Press, 1988.

Steward, Stanley A. *Where Sin Abounds: A Religious History of Las Vegas.* Eugene, OR: Wipf & Stock, 2012.

Stout, Daniel A. (Winter 2004). "Secularization and the Religious Audience: A Study of Mormons and Las Vegas Media." *Mass Communication & Society* 7, no. 1 (2004): 61–75.

Walker, Josephine B., ed. *Bunker Family History.* Vol. 1. Delta, UT: Edward Bunker Family Association, 1957.

Ward, Kenric F. *Saints in Babylon: Mormons and Las Vegas.* Bloomington, IN: 1st Books Library. 2002.

Warner, Ted J. "Nevada, Pioneer Settlements In." In *Encyclopedia of Mormonism,* edited by Daniel H. Ludlow. New York: Macmillan, 1992.

Williams, Sharrell D. "A Historical Study of the Growth of the L.D.S. Church in Clark County, Nevada." Master's thesis, Brigham Young University, 1963.

Woodhouse, John. *John Woodhouse: His Pioneer Journal, 1830–1916.* Salt Lake City: James Mercer and Kate Woodhouse Mercer and Family, 1952. L. Tom Perry Special Collections Library.

Woods, Fred E. *A Gamble in the Desert: The Mormon Mission in Las Vegas (1855–1857).* Salt Lake City: Mormon Historic Sites Foundation, 2005.

Wyler, Wanda Ricks. *Thomas E. Ricks, Colonizer and Founder.* 2nd ed. Provo: M. C. Printing, 1989.

Young, Brigham. "Fifth General Epistle." *Latter-day Saints' Millennial Star* 13, no. 14 (1851): 213.

———. "Sixth General Epistle." *Latter-day Saints' Millennial Star* 14, no. 2 (1852): 24.

Index

Page numbers in *italics* indicate illustrations.

About the Author

Fred E. Woods is a native of Southern California and earned his PhD in Middle East studies from the University of Utah in 1991. Woods has been employed at Brigham Young University as a professor of religious education since 1998. Dr. Woods has been a visiting teaching and research professor at several universities and has received a number of fellowships and awards for his academic work, including the prestigious Richard L. Evans Chair of Religious Understanding (2005–10). During the time he wrote his book about the Latter-day Saints of Las Vegas, he held a professorship of moral education from byu, was awarded an Eadington Visiting Research Fellowship from unlv and a byu Faculty Award from the Charles Redd Center for Western Studies, and was appointed a Senior Research Fellow at Pembroke College, Oxford. In 2022, Dr. Woods was also awarded by the city of Las Vegas an excellence in historic preservation award for his contribution to a better understanding of Las Vegas Latter-day Saint history.

Professor Woods has also lectured extensively at universities at home and abroad and is a prolific author of many books and more than 150 articles. In addition, he has produced numerous documentaries, several of which are award-winning films. His research has taken him to dozens of countries, which has provided a breadth of experience and understanding of various faiths, cultures, and peoples. He has been a bridge builder in helping scholars and people of various faiths to better understand the Latter-day Saint teachings and culture, having spent decades both as a member of the lds faith as well as a person not raised in this faith tradition.